POLITICAL UNDESIRABLES

POLITICAL UNDESIRABLES

Citizenship, Denaturalization, and Reclamation in Iraq

ZAINAB SALEH

STANFORD UNIVERSITY PRESS
Stanford, California

Stanford University Press
Stanford, California

© 2026 by Zainab Saleh. All rights reserved.

No part of this book may be reproduced or transmitted in any form or by any means, electronic or mechanical, including photocopying and recording, or in any information storage or retrieval system, without the prior written permission of Stanford University Press.

Library of Congress Cataloging-in-Publication Data
Names: Saleh, Zainab, author.
Title: Political undesirables : citizenship, denaturalization, and reclamation in Iraq / Zainab Saleh.
Description: Stanford, California : Stanford University Press, 2026. | Includes bibliographical references and index.
Identifiers: LCCN 2025008018 (print) | LCCN 2025008019 (ebook) | ISBN 9781503643833 cloth | ISBN 9781503644649 paperback | ISBN 9781503644656 ebook
Subjects: LCSH: Citizenship—Iraq—History—20th century | Citizenship, Loss of—Iraq—History—20th century | Deportation—Iraq—History—20th century | Political persecution—Iraq—History—20th century | Minorities—Civil rights—Iraq—History—20th century | Iraq—Politics and government—20th century
Classification: LCC JQ1849.A92 S25 2025 (print) | LCC JQ1849.A92 (ebook) | DDC 323.60955/0904—dc23/eng/20250326

LC record available at https://lccn.loc.gov/2025008018
LC ebook record available at https://lccn.loc.gov/2025008019

Cover design: Lindy Kasler
Cover art: Mohammad Alshammarey, *Frozen Passport*, 2015.

The authorized representative in the EU for product safety and compliance is: Mare Nostrum Group B.V. | Mauritskade 21D | 1091 GC Amsterdam | The Netherlands | Email address: gpsr@mare-nostrum.co.uk | KVK chamber of commerce number: 96249943

To my maternal grandparents,
Zahra El-Zein and Muhammad Sharara

CONTENTS

	Preface: A Personal Haunting	ix
	Acknowledgments	xv
	INTRODUCTION **Between Uprootedness and Reclamation**	1
1	The Denationalization of Iraqi Jews	20
2	Homeland Eulogies	39
3	The Legal Construction of *Taba'iyya*	64
4	Haunted Homes	84
5	Gender Ruptures	104
	CONCLUSION **The Ghosts of Iraq**	125
	Notes	137
	Bibliography	153
	Index	177
	Index of Legislation	179

PREFACE: A PERSONAL HAUNTING

Questions of citizenship and belonging first caught my attention when I was around eight years old, living in Iraq. One day in the early 1980s, our neighbors' daughters, who went to school with me and my sister, disappeared. They did not show up in the morning to take the bus with us to school, and they were not there in the afternoon to play with us in the street. The younger daughter was in the same grade as my sister, and they were close friends. My mother told us that the two daughters and their mother had been deported to Iran by Saddam Hussein's regime because they were *taba'iyya*, Iraqis of Iranian origin.[1] Yet she explained that our neighbors were Iraqis, not Iranians, and that their expulsion was part of Saddam Hussein's campaign of terror. Though I was only eight at the time, I understood what my mother meant. After all, my father had been detained twice in the previous two years because he was a communist, and my aunt's husband had been sentenced to twenty years in prison on the flimsy pretext that he had contacts with foreign companies. My father's best friend, who was a communist and an opponent of Saddam Hussein's regime, had disappeared in prison. A neighbor's brother had disappeared in prison for his political activism. The elimination and imprisonment of opposition parties and figures were a public secret. The outbreak of the Iran-Iraq War in 1980, when the Iraqi army invaded parts of border cities with Iran, exacerbated the sense of anxiety, uncertainty, and fear among Iraqis. The denaturalization and deportation of *taba'iyya* was the latest episode in Hussein's reign of terror. Iraqis who were stripped of their citizenship at the time were subject to different forms of violence, including the confiscation of assets, property, and documents; the loss of careers and social networks; family separation; sexual violence against women; and the detainment and disappearance of young men.

During this time, every Iraqi citizen held a Certificate of Citizenship that documented the citizenship category their ancestors had held before the establishment of the Iraqi state in 1921. While the majority of the inhabitants of Ottoman Iraq had held Ottoman nationality, some opted to acquire Persian nationality in order to avoid paying taxes to the Sublime Porte and serving in the Ottoman army. Under the modern state of Iraq, British officials and the new Iraqi ruling elites drafted a nationality law that split Iraqi citizenship into two categories: Ottoman and *taba'iyya*. This classification was passed down through generations, as a person inherited their father's type of citizenship. During the Ba'th reign (1968–2003), the Ottoman nationality indicated an "authentic citizenship," and Iraqis whose ancestors held this nationality were defined as "authentic Iraqis." By contrast, Iraqis whose ancestors held the Persian nationality came to be known as *taba'iyya*. In 1980, the Ba'th regime employed this distinction to question the Iraqiness of *taba'iyya* and strip people of their nationality and deport them to the border with Iran. The vast majority of deportees were Shi'i Arabs or Shi'i Kurds, who came to be perceived by the regime as the enemy within, intent on destroying Iraq by allegedly showing loyalty to Iran. Saddam Hussein's regime denaturalized and deported between 40,000 and 400,000 Iraqis in the early 1980s.[2]

Our neighbor and her daughters were among these deportees. However, the regime gave some families who were awaiting deportation in camps the option to go back to their home if they agreed to cooperate with it. And this was what our neighbor decided to do. After three weeks, the mother and daughters returned home. My mother asked my sister and me to never speak of the deportation in front of the daughters, to pretend nothing had happened, and to understand that we had to exercise caution when talking with them so that they did not relate anything to their mother. We all pretended everything had gone back to normal. Our friends were back; we went to school with them and played together after school. The only difference was this open secret in the neighborhood: their mother had become an informant for the regime. But having a neighbor who was an informant wasn't unusual, as there were always rumors about people who had made such a bargain with the regime to stay alive or avoid retribution. Indeed, our schoolteachers were required to be Ba'th Party members, and we had to be careful around them. My sister and I embraced this reality—a reality for all kids our age at the time—and maintained a façade of normality while making sure not to share anything about our parents' anti-regime views.

The plight of *taba'iyya* was not the only story about citizenship I knew about as a child. When I was growing up, my mother also talked about Iraqi Jews who were denaturalized and deported in 1950–1951 after the ruling elites under the monarchy designated them as Zionists and loyalists of the newly established state of Israel. The accounts about Iraqi Jews from my mother echoed the narratives about *taba'iyya*; here was another instance when Iraqi authorities demonized and expelled Iraqis for political reasons. My parents (who were born in the early and mid-1930s) were the last generation of Iraqis to have Iraqi Jewish neighbors, teachers, and friends. Iraqi Jews had lived in Iraq for millennia, and many of them believed that they had been inhabitants of Iraq since the Babylonian captivity. After the British established the modern state of Iraq in 1921, Iraqi Jews came to play an important role in Iraq's intellectual, social, political, and commercial landscapes. They joined non-Jewish Iraqis in debating the nature of the Iraqi state, took part in the anticolonial struggle against the British, embraced leftist ideologies and modernity, and critiqued the traditional Jewish establishment.[3] In addition, some of them assumed prominent political positions as ministers and members of parliament in Iraq.[4] When the Iraqi Communist Party emerged as a political force in the 1940s, young Iraqi Jews—along with Iraqis from all different religious, ethnic, class, and gender backgrounds—joined in order to advocate for political independence and social justice and fight against fascism and conservative Arab nationalism. While the majority of Iraqi Jews perceived themselves as Iraqis and/or Arabs, a small number of them endorsed Zionism and aspired to migrate to Israel during the first half of the twentieth century.

The establishment of the state of Israel in 1948 and the onset of the Arab-Israeli conflict jeopardized the position of Iraqi Jews within Iraq. In March 1950, the Iraqi government passed a law giving Iraqi Jews the option to emigrate to Israel on the condition that they renounce their Iraqi citizenship. Following the bombing of Jewish institutions in Baghdad in 1950–1951, the majority of Iraqi Jews registered to emigrate. Shortly afterwards, the Iraqi government enacted a decree that granted it the right to confiscate the property of Iraqi Jews who signed up to leave the country. My mother's memories underscored that Iraqi Jews were Iraqi citizens who were uprooted from their country for political reasons.

Witnessing one's friends and neighbors deported and co-opted by the regime and listening to the stories about instances of expulsion in the past left an indelible impression on me. But these experiences of displacement also resonated with me—and my family—personally. My maternal grandfather was born and raised in Bint Jbeil, in south Lebanon. He came to Iraq in the early 1920s to study Islamic theology in the holy city of Najaf. He met the two requirements to gain Iraqi citizenship (being an Ottoman subject and a resident of Iraq on August 23, 1921), so he acquired Iraqi nationality, and his Iraqi Certificate of Citizenship was marked as Ottoman. However, my grandfather grew disenchanted with the Shiʻi religious establishment and decided to renounce his religious vocation. He was also inspired by leftist trends in Iraq that advocated for political independence, gender equality, and social justice. Since he had three daughters born in Iraq in the early 1930s, and since education for girls was becoming the norm among the educated classes in the country, he decided to stay in Iraq. By the late 1930s and early 1940s, my grandfather became a communist sympathizer and wrote articles in newspapers that critiqued the ruling elites who upheld the British colonial rule of Iraq and failed to do anything for the poor in the country. My grandfather was imprisoned a few times and fired from his teaching job many times under the monarchy. But he always ended up teaching Arabic in Jewish schools in Baghdad and formed strong intellectual and political ties with Iraqi Jewish students who were interested in Arabic literature or leftist ideologies.

After his release from another stint in prison in 1954, my grandfather decided to go back to his homeland in Lebanon to avoid further political persecution, leaving his family behind in Iraq, but after the fall of the monarchy in 1958, he returned to Iraq. During the Baʻth coup of 1963, my grandfather escaped imprisonment and death because he was abroad. However, he lost his Iraqi citizenship due to his political views and activism, though he managed to regain it in 1968. When my mother narrated her father's political activism and trouble with the government, she was quick to comment that only he—and not his family—was targeted by authorities. Though his family faced tremendous financial hardships during his imprisonment and exile because he had been the sole breadwinner, they were not targeted. Unlike the massive punishment meted out to Iraqi Jews in 1950–1951 and to *tabaʻiyya* in the 1980s, my grandfather was the only one who lost his citizenship. His family stayed in the country and went on with their daily lives. In addition, the fact that my grandfather hailed from Lebanon spared him from becoming stateless.

These instances of denaturalization and deportation made me cognizant of the precarity of citizenship as a right. More importantly, they made me curious about citizenship laws. When our neighbors were expelled in the early 1980s, my mother tried to reassure me that our family would not face the same fate because our Iraqi citizenship was "Ottoman." However, her reminiscences about the expulsion of Iraqi Jews and my grandfather did not square with her explanation about the expulsion of *taba'iyya*. If *taba'iyya* lost their Iraqi citizenship because their ancestors held Persian citizenship under the Ottomans, and if the citizenship of Iraqis whose ancestors had Ottoman nationality was authentic and inviolable, then how did ruling elites in the past justify the expulsion of Iraqi Jews and Iraqi communists—including my grandfather—since their Iraqi citizenship was marked as Ottoman?

This book is informed by questions dating back to these childhood experiences. Despite my young age, the disappearance of our neighbors has always haunted me. It made me realize that citizenship can serve as a mechanism for discipline and retribution and that the loss of citizenship entails a precious existence at the political, legal, cultural, and economic levels. As I conducted archival, ethnographic, and literary research for this book, I came to recognize that denaturalization and deportation have been integral to colonial and national rule in Iraq during the twentieth and twenty-first centuries. While certain Iraqi Shi'i scholars, Iraqi Assyrians, and Iraqi communists were stripped of their Iraqi citizenship on the ground that they posed a threat to national security, Iraqi Jews and *taba'iyya* faced collective punishment when a large segments of their communities were denaturalized and uprooted. The year 2025 marks the seventy-fifth anniversary of the expulsion of Iraqi Jews and the forty-fifth anniversary of the displacement of *taba'iyya*. On the one hand, this book is a scholarly work that examines how citizenship rights in Iraq have been contingent upon political docility and how Iraqi Jews and *taba'iyya* affirmed belonging to Iraq in order to challenge Othering discourses by ruling elites. On the other hand, it is a tribute to expelled Iraqis whose political aspirations, hybrid identities, and regional networks combined with geopolitical developments rendered them political undesirables to Iraqi authorities.

ACKNOWLEDGMENTS

This book has been in the making for more than twenty years, and I owe thanks to many people whose feedback and suggestions, kindness and patience, and generosity have helped me immeasurably. I'd like to thank Rima Semaan for hosting me in Atlanta for almost a year when my plans to do research in Iran collapsed in 2005 (following the election of Mahmoud Ahmadinejad as president of Iran), and I had to figure out another site for my fieldwork. I genuinely can't imagine how I could have survived that uncertain time without Rima's sense of humor, kindness, hospitality, and unwavering support. Rima made sure to introduce me to her colleagues at Emory University and friends in Atlanta and to alleviate my anxiety about my graduate degree by insisting on having fun. I also would like to thank Emory University's Middle East and South Asian Studies, where Rima taught, for giving me an office and including me in all their events and gatherings—particularly Robert W. Greeley, Nick Fabian, Roxani Margariti, Gordon D. Newby, Rakesh Ranjan, Ofra Yeglin, and Shalom Goldman. The Arab community to which Rima introduced me was welcoming and generous as well. In retrospect, I think of my time in Atlanta fondly. Atlanta has a special place in my heart because of all the warmth and support from everyone I met.

Though I already did so in my first book, I would like to reiterate my gratitude to the Iraqi community in London, whose support, trust, and investment in my work never waned over the years. It is quite astounding that it has been almost two decades since I first started my fieldwork in London and that some Iraqis have been long-term interlocutors who never tired of talking to me, sharing new updates, and introducing me to other Iraqis. Regrettably, due to the need to protect their privacy, I cannot thank them by name.

The librarians at the British Library and the National Archives in London, the Library of Congress in Washington, D.C., and the Hoover Institution at Stanford University were unfailingly helpful, patient, and generous. I am also indebted to the Provost's Office at Haverford College for funding research trips since I began working there in 2011. These grants were especially invaluable when I was stuck in the United States between 2008 and 2016, when getting a US visa as an Iraqi became extremely difficulty following the US invasion of Iraq in 2003. These funds enabled me to go to the Library of Congress during the summers to do extensive archival research about the Iraqi citizenship laws in the twentieth century.

I also would like to thank many friends and colleagues who provided insightful and thoughtful feedback on different parts of the book. The Iraq Studies reading group—consisting of Bridget Guarasci, Mona Damluji, Sara Farhan, Kali Rubaii, Kerem Uşşakli, Omar Sirri, Nida Alahmad, and Huma Gupta—provided a much-needed intellectual community during COVID-19. My conversations with scholars at the Center for Ethics and Critical Thought at University of Edinburgh in general and the reflections provided by Lotte Segal and Mihaeala Mihai in particular were tremendously valuable. Many thanks for Sima Shakhsari, who invited me to be part the symposium "Violence and the Shifting Politics of Knowledge Production in the Middle East." I would like to thank Lila Abu-Lughod, Minoo Moallem, Chiara De Cesari, Maya Mikdashi, Asli Zengin, and Rema Hammami for engaging thoughtfully with chapter 5 in this book. The conference on the twentieth anniversary of the US invasion of Iraq, which Haytham Bahoora organized at the University of Toronto in 2023, was a great opportunity to be in conversation with many scholars of Iraq on citizenship practices in Iraq and worldwide, including Haytham Bahoora, Mona Damluji, Qussay Al-Attabi, Bridget Guarasci, Kerem Uşşakli, Orit Bashkin, Sinan Antoon, Rijin Sahakian, Nada Shabout, Sara Farhan, Sara Pursley, Alda Benjamen, Camille Cole, Gabriel Young, Zaynab Quadri, Ruba Ali al-Hassani, and Rand Saleh. I'm also grateful for John Ghazvinian and Ibrahim Bakri for inviting me to share my work with the regional scholars affiliated with the University of Pennsylvania's Middle East Center, including Sara Vakili, David Heayn-Menendez, Ahmad Shokr, Sean Yom, Nada Matta, Megan Brown, and Samer Abboud.

In addition, I'm tremendously indebted to Brie Gettleson for her friendship, tireless assistance, and generosity with her time. Even after she left the main library at Haverford College, she kept finding sources I needed for this book. Brie is a remarkable talent and asset who can figure out exactly what I'm looking for. Having a librarian friend who is trained as an anthropologist is a rare gift. I also thank Ella Shohat for her generous comments and enthusiasm about this project. Members of the Middle East Section at the American Anthropological Association provided a much-needed community and support during the genocide in Gaza, and I'm eternally thankful for the incredible generosity of Amahl Bishara, Lara Deeb, Maya Wind, Eda Pepi, Nadia Guessous, Narges Bajoghli, Krista Lewis, Nada Moumtaz, Nell Gabiam, Kali Rubaii, and Timothy Y. Loh. Aamer Nazih Ibraheem, Adrien Zakar, Candace Lukasik, Abdulla Majeed, Alma Rachel Heckman, Patrick Weil, and Sanaz Raji have engaged with this book in different ways and offered valuable feedback. I am also grateful to Khairuldeen Makhzoomi for lending me his copy of Nassim Qazaz's anthology. Parts of this book were developed from articles originally published as "On Iraqi Nationality: Law, Citizenship, and Exclusion," in the *Arab Studies Journal*; "Precarious Citizens: Iraqi Jews and the Politics of Belonging," in *Political and Legal Anthropology Review*; and "The Denationalization of Iraqi Jews: The Legal and Rhetorical Production of Otherness," in *Palestine/Israel Review*.

I'm very grateful for my community of friends and colleagues at Haverford College, especially Joshua Moses, Linda Strong-Leek, Sarah Horowitz, Anna West, Zolani Ngwane, Ezgi Guner, Xerxes Minocher, Michael D'Arcy, Zeynep Sertbulut, and Emily Hong. Since becoming the director of the John B. Hurford '60 Center for the Arts and Humanities, I've been lucky to have a dream team whose expertise, generosity, and assistance have made my transition into this administrative role while finishing this book a breeze—namely, James Weissinger, Kelly Jung, Matthew Callinan, Manasi Eswarapu, and Kerry Nelson. Kelly Kane—the rock of the Department of Anthropology—has always been a reliable ally. Not only is she an amazing person to work with, but she has been a steadfast supporter of my work and is always willing to help. In addition, I'd like to thank Margaret Schaus, Deadra Brown, and Rob Haley at the main library at Haverford College for their support throughout the years. My friendships with Nilgun Uygun and Ulla Kjellstrand have been a refuge over the decades and a source of unconditional love and care especially during dark times—thank you! Vicki Wurman has been a pillar in my life for twenty years, and her empathy seems boundless. It's truly been a pleasure to work with Kate Wahl on this book. Her detailed feedback and her encouragement made the process of finishing this book more fulfilling and worthwhile. I am also indebted to Sean Mallin, who has been a thorough and dedicated editor, to the anonymous reviewers for their valuable feedback, and to Barbara Armentrout for her superb and meticulous work on this manuscript.

I would like to extend my gratitude to my immediate and found families—in particular, my maternal aunts Maream Sharara-Shaw (and her husband, Jim Shaw) and Balkis Sharara Chadirji. This project came together as a book during COVID-19 as uncertainty and anxiety gripped the world. Though they had to care for Adrian, their new baby, Christina Verano Sornito-Carter and Jon H. Carter have kept me buoyant by regularly sending me cute pictures and videos of my godchild. Adrian's sweet laughter and adorable antics have brought so much joy to me over the past five years. Whenever I'm struggling because of the bleak times in which we live, I look at Adrian's photos and videos and I forget about all the trouble and smile for a fleeting moment. I am also indebted to Alistair Stewart and Stephanie Todd, who are phenomenal hosts whose company, care, and love, and delicious meals have made Scotland feel like home. Many thanks to Graeme Stewart, Karin Stewart, and Megan Stewart for their kind hospitality. Catie Stewart, Mahri Stewart, and Anna Stewart have been so welcoming, caring, and enthusiastic about my work since they came into my life. Last but not least, my thanks to Andrew Stewart, my remarkable partner, who goes out of his way to enable me to focus on my research and writing, who patiently listens to me whenever I'm in doubt about my work, and who happily reads and edits anything I write. More importantly, his restless energy and adventurous spirit frequently encourage me out of my comfort zone. Andrew has helped me to relinquish my strict routine, which has allowed me to be more productive and flexible in terms of my writing habits. Since we met, life has become gentler and more fulfilling. I truly cannot thank him enough.

POLITICAL UNDESIRABLES

INTRODUCTION

BETWEEN UPROOTEDNESS AND RECLAMATION

POLITICAL UNDESIRABLES IS ABOUT the legal making and unmaking of citizenship in Iraq, focusing on the mass denaturalization and deportation of Iraqi Jews and Iraqis of Iranian origin, *taba'iyya*. Since the formation of the modern state of Iraq under British Mandate in 1921, practices of denaturalization and expulsion of citizens became forms of state and colonial governmentality mobilized by ruling elites in order to curb political dissent and suppress opposition. Though politicians and legislators generally tout citizenship as an equal right enjoyed by all citizens, citizenship has always been conditional and precarious. During times of political upheaval, state officials can use citizenship laws to strip political opponents of their citizenship, rendering them stateless. Like education and military service, citizenship laws can serve as a mechanism to discipline the population, enforce commitment to the state's political order and normative values, and eliminate subversive and oppositional elements through charges of disloyalty and treason. As such, citizenship has always been a precarious right that can be taken away if a person is deemed a threat to national security.

This book is concerned with the denaturalization of native citizens, taking Iraq as a case study, since this legal practice metamorphosed into a collective punishment of certain communities during times of political uncertainty and authoritarian rule. The scholarship on citizenship and displacement often examines the ways authorities—whether national or colonial—employ discourses of foreignness and national security to justify the denaturalization and deportation of naturalized citizens.[1] In this framework, the citizenship of native citizens is often assumed and hailed as an inalienable right equally enjoyed by all inhabitants who are native-born or enjoy blood genealogy. The emphasis on inalienability and equality often obfuscates how citizenship is a contingent right that is closely tied to loyalty to the state, as defined by ruling elites. In this book, I approach citizenship practices as governing techniques aimed at constructing obedient political subjects, and denaturalization as a mechanism to get rid of citizens who pose a challenge to existing political and economic arrangements. While doing the research for this book, the term *undesirables* often came up in descriptions of citizens who lost their citizenship because they opposed colonial and national ruling elites.[2] The term evokes the idea that some citizens can become undesirable members of a polity for their political views and activism. The rhetoric of betrayal of the state and/or threat to national security enshrined in the codes of many democratic and authoritarian countries constitutes citizenship as a privilege that is interlinked to loyalty to the state rather than a right enjoyed unconditionally.

Writing on the denaturalization and expulsion of native-born citizens during the first half of the twentieth century, Patrick Weil remarks that "the Soviet Union revoked the citizenship of 1.5 million individuals. The Nazi regime denaturalized forty thousand people and revoked the citizenship of another forty thousand native-born citizens. In France, between 1940 and 1944, the Vichy regime ... stripped the citizenship of five hundred native-born French nationals."[3] However, denaturalization has also been legalized and practiced in democratic countries. During World War I, the United Kingdom and France issued denaturalization policies targeting native-born citizens whose political views were deemed subversive.[4] In 1940, the US government passed the Nationality Act, which "expanded the automatic loss of citizenship to include several new categories of American-born citizens, including those who engaged in foreign military service, voted in foreign elections, or were convicted of treason or of desertion from the armed forces of the United States."[5] Moreover, denaturalization and deportation were practiced widely by European colonial powers all over the world to deal with individuals who posed a threat to the status quo under the pretext that they were foreigners.[6]

Denaturalization and deportation have emerged as governing techniques in recent decades as well.[7] The Bahraini authorities stripped political critics of their nationality in 2014, 2015, and 2016. In 2016, cases of denaturalization and deportation in the country increased around tenfold according to Amnesty International. The Bahraini authorities cited "illegal acts," which included advocating for regime change and defaming "brotherly countries," as the reasons for deportation. Moreover, the Bahraini regime made a legal amendment that targeted "anyone whose acts contravene his duty of loyalty to the kingdom."[8] Likewise, the Dominican Republic provoked international censure when the constitutional court stripped thousands of Dominican-born citizens of Haitian descent of their nationality in 2013. This measure was controversial because it was embedded in anti-Haitian racism and it undermined "the tradition of birthright citizenship and Inter-American human rights system."[9] In 2023, the Israeli government issued a law that revokes the citizenship of Palestinian citizens of Israel who have been convicted of terrorism and have received financial aid from the Palestinian Authority. Claiming that those affected "have betrayed the Israeli state," this law meant that political activism could entail the loss of citizenship for Palestinians.[10] Around the same time, the Nicaraguan government denaturalized and deported around three hundred Nicaraguans as Daniel Ortega aimed to suppress free speech and political opposition to his regime. The Nicaraguan regime designated these denaturalized deportees as "traitors to the motherland."[11]

Following 9/11, the question of citizenship in Europe, in particular in France and the United Kingdom, has raised heated debates. In Britain, the most recent Nationality and Borders Bill states that "maintaining our national security and keeping the public safe are the government's top priorities" and that "removing someone's British citizenship, also known as deprivation of citizenship, is used against those who obtained citizenship by fraud and against the most dangerous people, such as terrorists, extremists and serious organised criminals." While noting that the deprivation of citizenship in the UK has been possible since the 1914 British Nationality and Status of Aliens Act, this bill asserts that "deprivation of citizenship where it is conducive to the public good is reserved for those who pose a threat to the UK or whose conduct involves very high harm, for example in response to activities such as those involving: national security including espionage and acts of terrorism; unacceptable behaviour such as the 'glorification' of terrorism; war crimes; serious organised crime."[12] According to Free Movement, a website run by British lawyers, around 175 British citizens have lost their citizenship on national security grounds since 2006.[13] The most controversial case is that of Shamima Begum, who had been sixteen when she joined the Islamic State in Syria in 2015 and was stripped of her British citizenship, thus becoming stateless and living in a refugee camp in Syria following the fall of the Islamic State. Critics of the British judicial system's decision argue that British courts disregarded the facts that Begum was a victim of child trafficking, that there had been no due process since only the home secretary has the power to revoke citizenships, that Begum had the right to a trial in Britain, and that many countries—including the United States, Canada, Holland, and Finland—had repatriated citizens who joined the Islamic State.[14] Noting the unequal citizenship hierarchy it establishes, Zoe Williams maintains that this bill "means any one of us with a foreign-born parent has a more contestable and precarious citizenship than those without. You don't need to have joined a terrorist death cult to find that chilling."[15]

In all these cases from the past and the present, the ruling elites mobilized the rhetoric of the threat to national security and/or betrayal of the state, the homeland, the fatherland, or the motherland as a justification for denaturalization and deportation. Given the current rise of nativism, right-wing nationalism, and authoritarianism all over the world, citizenship can become a tool to silence opposition and produce precarity through denaturalization. As such, citizenship is not only a mechanism to differentiate between citizens and migrants/aliens, as state officials can employ it to silence citizens as well. In this framework, citizenship is often constructed, granted, or denied through obscure written records and ambiguous laws. Even in the cases of citizenship granted at birth (jus soli, or law of soil) or by blood (jus sanguinis, or law of blood), uncertainty about the boundaries of citizenship's legal recognition with regard to political, psychological, and personal meanings remains a pressing issue for certain groups.[16] The disparities between ideologies of citizenship and their daily operations are tied to the construction of racial, ethnic, class, political, and religious differences within a state. Laws emerge as an apparatus to police citizenship, with the effect of granting or denying citizenship based on the state's desire to keep certain subjects outside the parameters of legal membership.[17]

The question of denaturalization and expulsion under the modern state of Iraq throws the precarity of citizenship rights into relief since Iraqi ruling elites under different governments targeted and uprooted whole communities, not just individuals. While this book is concerned with citizenship as a right, it also focuses on the ways Iraqi deportees challenged official discourses that rendered them as the Other who is intent on undermining the Iraqi state, and asserted belonging to Iraq while in exile. This book makes use archival documents, ethnographic research, and literary and autobiographical works in order to explore the legal construction of Iraqi citizenship by Iraq authorities as well as the politics of reclamation invoked by Iraqi deportees in order to document a shared political and cultural landscape with fellow-Iraqis, and to chronicle the hardships concomitant with expulsion. I have conducted archival research in the British Library and National Archives in London, the Library of Congress in Washington, DC, and the Hoover Institute at Stanford University in Palo Alto to trace the legal evolution of citizenship laws and amendments in the twentieth century and the early twenty-first century. I also conducted ethnographic research with Iraqi Jews and *taba'iyya* in London (2006–2024) about life in Iraq before exile, the impact of the deportation on their lives, and the ways they constructed an Iraqi identity. In addition, I analyze memoirs published by Iraqi Jewish writers and a novel published recently by an Iraqi author whose family was deported during the 1980s. Through a legal, ethnographic, and literary reading, I explore the ongoing legacy of Ottoman rule, the British Mandate, and the project of state formation by Iraqi ruling elites through citizenship practices in the country; moreover, I examine the ways Iraqi deportees constructed an Iraqi subjectivity that critiques Iraqi officials' claims that they were foreign and disloyal to Iraq.

The Right to Uproot

This book approaches citizenship as a murky legal status, which can function as a retributive tool of governmentality during political crises. A historical overview of the modern state in Iraq shows that denaturalization and deportation have been an integral part of rule in the country throughout the twentieth and twenty-first centuries. A legal reading of Iraqi citizenship laws and amendments reveals that the state retains the right to dispose of unwanted citizens. I employ the right to uproot as a concept to highlight the all-encompassing violence engendered by the loss of citizenship, and to draw attention to the inherent contradictions in citizenship rights and to a consistent pattern of governance with different historical reconfigurations. On the one hand, this book examines how different denaturalization legislations build upon each other and employ the same rationale of betrayal of the state and foreignness in order to render some citizens deportable. On the other hand, it focuses on the denaturalization of Iraqi Jews and *taba'iyya* as two examples when the loss of citizenship was mobilized by ruling elites to inflict collective punishment upon, and eradicate, whole communities. While the individual cases of deportation—such as Shi'i scholars, Assyrians, and communists—

provide insights into citizenship legislations, the mass expulsion of Iraqi Jews and *taba'iyya* exposes the multi-layered conditions of dispossession that these two groups endured. In short, the right to uproot encompasses three processes, namely visible and invisible violence, the double binds of citizenship laws, and a persistent policy of discipline and punishment.

Rather than the right to denaturalize or deport, which mainly coveys ruling elites' power to revoke citizenship, the right to uproot connotes multiple forms of violence whose aim is to inflict as much harm as possible, especially when expulsion targets a whole community. For instance, both Iraqi Jews and *taba'iyya* were unexpectedly and violently removed from their homeland without having any opportunity to plan for such a rupture. They also lost their jobs, had their assets and property confiscated, and were deported to countries where they were seen as the Other. In the case of the *taba'iyya*, young women were raped or sexually assaulted, young men between the age of eighteen and twenty-eight were separated from their families and disappeared in the regime's prisons, and families were separated, as some fled Iraq beforehand or were forgotten by the regime but had no way to contact their deported relatives. In short, these patterns of violence entailed economic dispossession, legal precarity, physical violation and psychological abuse, disruption of social and family networks, and political disenfranchisement. Moreover, the right to uproot involves the denial of Iraqi deportees' cultural and political belongings. Iraqi denaturalization laws portrayed citizens who were stripped of their citizenship as subversive outsiders who posed a threat to national security and unity. The invocation of foreignness functioned at once to erase Iraqi deportees' sense of rootedness in Iraq, and to re-write their history in a distorted way.

In this framework, the right to uproot highlights the foreclosure of "the right to have rights." Echoing Susan Bibler Coutin's concept of dismemberment, the right to uproot "refers to the separation of persons from history, the literal injury or destruction of bodies, the embedded nature of structural violence . . . and the denial of membership, either by forcing people to flee their country of citizenship or by preventing them from being granted membership in the country where they reside."[18] The right to uproot signals a legal process of denationalization and the lived realities of dispossession engendered by sudden ruptures. In addition, the right to uproot invokes Hannah Arendt's famous phrase "the right to have rights." Meant to critique the concept of human rights as enshrined in the Universal Declaration of Human

Rights, Arendt, who became a stateless refugee under Nazi Germany, argued that in order for individuals to have human rights, they must be members of a political community.[19] In their engagement with Arendt's phrase, Stephanie DeGooyer, Alastair Hunt, Lida Maxwell, Samuel Moyn, and Astra Taylor remark that "only as a citizen of a nation-state can a person enjoy legally protected rights to education, to work, to vote, to healthcare, to culture, and so on. Hence, Arendt declared that before there can be any specific civil, political, or social rights, there must be such a thing as a 'right to have rights.'"[20] Furthermore, these authors critique the current use of "the right to have rights" by activists who perceive the phrase as a poetic name for human rights and emphasize that Arendt's insight was constituted in the realization that the one right that is needed is the right to be a citizen of a nation-state, or at least a member of some kind of political community.[21]

Moreover, the right to uproot demarcates the limits of citizenship rights since they are a prerogative controlled by the state rather than being inalienable rights. In Iraq, the state has always acted as the sole arbiter of citizenship rights: Iraqi ruling elites under different regimes would declare treason, threats to national security, and foreignness as grounds for denaturalization, but they were the ones who had the power to dictate which actions were subversive and which communities or individuals were foreigners, with intentional and blatant disregard for historical accuracy and lived realities. While in some countries, citizens whose citizenship is revoked have the right to appeal in courts, Iraqi Jews and *taba'iyya* had no recourse to challenge the state's decisions legally. The right to uproot connotes the ultimate power that the state enjoys in granting or revoking legal membership. It is this very double bind of state power that renders citizenship rights as precarious, conditional, and contingent. Here, citizenship emerges more as an elusive privilege dictated by the state rather an absolute right. The right to uproot speaks to the state's ultimate power to employ denaturalization and deportation as mechanisms to dispense with political undesirables and inflict as much harm as possible and to constantly shift the parameters of citizenship, based on political calculations brought about by changing domestic or geopolitical landscapes.

Another aspect of the right to uproot is that it constitutes a structure rather than an event. Since the establishment of the modern state of Iraq in 1921, different Iraqi governments, whether during the monarchical or republican rule, have employed denaturalization as a mechanism to discipline Iraqi citizens who were designated as threats or traitors. Rather than an exception, the right to uproot has connoted a consistent strategy of rule in the twentieth and twenty-first centuries in Iraq. The comparative approach in this book does not intend to draw simple parallels but to problematize discourses of singularity and showcase coherent legal practices. A legal analysis of Iraqi denaturalization legislation shows that the expulsion of Iraqi citizens is not marginal but integral to state governance. The tendency among both some Iraqis and scholars of Iraq to think of monarchy as more moderate and democratic than the republican rule has engendered a perception that the different instances of deportations—namely, of Shi'i scholars, Assyrians, Jews, communists, and finally *taba'iyya*—are unconnected and singular. However, the legal records show that denaturalization laws built upon and invoked each other. Moreover, though denaturalization has been a prevalent governing technique throughout the history of the modern Iraqi state, each case of denaturalization has been informed by and rooted in different historical articulations, such the project of nation-building, ruling elites' anxiety over citizens' political activism, a continuously shifting geopolitical scene, or the rise of authoritarian rule.

In other words, the right to uproot calls attention to the fact that the state remains the ultimate arbiter of citizenship rights and that this absolute power is usually concomitant with other prerogatives, such as the right to confiscate property and documents, separate families, disappear, violate, and kill. This book traces how a British colonial practice—namely, deportation—was transformed under national rule into an enduring strategy that led to mass expulsion of entire communities—Iraqi Jews and *taba'iyya*—and the vilification of identities that have been informed by hybridity, regional networks, and progressive political demands that aimed to change the status quo. *Political Undesirables* unveils the connectedness of historically different configurations of denaturalization campaigns and to a consistent rationale that was appropriated and mobilized by ruling elites during the monarchical and republican rule in Iraq.

An Archive of Dispossession

Iraq was part of the Ottoman Empire from the early sixteenth century until War World I, when Britain invaded Basra in 1914, Baghdad in 1917, and Mosul in 1918. Following the end of the war, the League of Nations put Iraq under British Mandate in 1920. From the start of the invasion of Iraq in 1914, British colonial officials resorted to deportation as a mechanism to get rid of Iraqi figures who opposed the British rule and demanded independence, especially the expulsions of Sayyid Talib al-Naquib, a notable from Basra, to Bombay in 1914; ten religious scholars from Karbala to Henjam Island in 1920; and a few Iraqi nationalists to Henjam in 1922.[22] However, the instance of deportation that caused tremendous controversy in Iraq took place in 1923, when British officials deported Shaykh Mahdi al-Khalisi to Persia for his opposition to the Anglo-Iraqi Treaty of 1922 and for issuing a fatwa against participation in the election to rectify it. This treaty, which was supposed to last for twenty years, granted Britain considerable control over Iraqi affairs.[23] Though Khalisi was from an established Arab family, he and other prominent ulema were expelled "on the basis of a decree that invested the government with the power to deport 'aliens' for political offences."[24] None other than King Faysal I, who hailed from Mecca and was installed as the king of Iraq by the British in 1921, signed the decree, which was met with a heated debate over his foreign origin.[25] While all these individual instances took place before the enactment of the Iraqi Nationality Law of 1924, they set a legal precedent that granted the ruling elites the power to deport political undesirables and to employ foreignness as a justification, in the case of al-Khalisi.

The Iraqi Nationality Law of 1924 (Law 42), which was signed by the Iraqi prime minister and the ministers of justice and the interior, set legal routes for the inhabitants of Ottoman Iraq to acquire Iraqi citizenship.[26] The first route decreed that a person had to be an Ottoman subject as of August 6, 1921, and a habitual resident of Iraq as of August 23, 1921. By setting a specific date for residence in the country, this law integrated King Faysal as historically rooted in the nascent nation-state of Iraq.[27] The second legal route for inhabitants who did not hold Ottoman nationality specified that a person's father had to be born in Iraq in order for the person to acquire Iraqi citizenship.[28] In addition, the law delineates conditions for naturalization and loss of citizenship. Iraqi citizens could be stripped of their citizenship if they got naturalized in another country, served in the army of a foreign government, or decided to relinquish it. Although this law foreclosed the possibility of dual citizenship, it also sanctioned marital denaturalization in that an Iraqi woman who married a foreign man would lose her citizenship. While the law does not declare citizenship rights as inalienable, it also does not mention threats to national security or disloyalty to the state as grounds for the loss of citizenship.

On August 15, 1933, the Iraqi government issued its first denaturalization decree (Law 62), which granted the Cabinet the right to strip Iraqis whose family did not reside in the country before World War I of their citizenship if "they took—or attempted to take—an action that posed a threat to the state's security and safety."²⁹ Following the publication of this decree, the Iraqi authorities deported the Assyrian patriarch, along with his entire family.³⁰ The relationship between the Iraqi government and the Assyrian community in Mosul (a Christian ethno-religious group) had deteriorated drastically after members of the community started demanding autonomy. In May 1933, the Assyrian patriarch—Mar Eshai Shimun—had resumed discussions with the Iraqi and British authorities over his community's rights to have a designated autonomous area in northern Iraq as delineated by the League of Nations Mosul Commission in 1923.³¹ Following the collapse of the negotiations, the Iraqi authorities detained the patriarch, and some Iraqi newspapers published a series of vilification articles against the Assyrians. In August 1933, the Iraqi army waged a military offensive against the Assyrian village of Simele and the surrounding areas. This campaign led to the destruction of a hundred Assyrian villages and the death of at least three hundred in Simele. Shortly after that, the Iraqi authorities expelled the Assyrian patriarch and his immediate family on the grounds that he was a foreigner who constituted a threat to Iraq's security. As such, the denaturalization decree of 1933 set two precedents by giving Iraqi authorities the power to determine who was a citizen based on residence prior to World War I and by linking citizenship with loyalty to the state.³²

Another significant law enacted at the time amended Baghdad's Penal Code in 1938 (Law 51). This decree, which was issued by the king of Iraq and the Iraqi parliament, made advocacy of certain ideologies punishable offenses. The articles in this decree mandate that any person "who circulates any Bolshevik socialist principles (communism), anarchism, exhibitionism, or any other ideology that aims to change the government, or disturb social values as outlined the Basic Law" would be sentenced for life with hard labor or for seven years, have to pay a fine, or be subject to both forms of punishment; a person who used force or threat to circulate these ideologies would be sentenced to life with hard labor or for fifteen years; a person who was serving in the military and propagated these ideologies could be sentenced to death, life with hard labor, or fifteen years; and any Iraqi who was a member of an organization, whether in Iraq or abroad, that embraced these ideologies would be subject to the same punishments stated in this law. The criminalization of leftist activism speaks to the transformation of the Iraqi political landscape when the Iraqi Communist Party's inclusive agenda and demands for social justice, gender equality, and independence appealed to Iraqis from various socioeconomic, ethnic, gender, and religious backgrounds. Moreover, this decree was one of many repressive measures that the Iraqi and British authorities took at the time to quell the increasing popularity of communism, including closures of newspapers and the imprisonment of prominent political figures who challenged the status quo. While this decree did not include denaturalization as a punishment, it did set a precedent that constituted revolutionary ideas and activism as crimes.

The two laws not only had immediate goals, but they also had far-reaching consequences in the 1950s when Iraqi ruling elites expanded and reinterpreted them to mete out collective retribution upon Iraqi Jews in 1950–1951 and to strip Iraqi communists of their citizenship in 1954. With the establishment of the state of Israel in 1948, Iraqi Jews came to occupy a more precarious position. An anti-Jewish campaign in Iraqi ultranationalist newspapers culminated in a law (Decree 1 of 1950) that was an amendment to the denaturalization decree of 1933. Signed by the interior minister and the prime minister, this decree granted the Iraqi Cabinet the right to strip Iraqi Jews of Iraqi nationality if they wished to leave Iraq for good. By invoking denaturalization decree of 1933 to justify the denaturalization of Iraqi Jews, Iraqi authorities not only designated them as a threat to the state but also defined them as foreigners who had recently arrived in Iraq. A year later, the Iraqi authorities issued another law that confiscated the properties of Iraqi Jews who decided to leave Iraq. These two laws rendered Iraqi Jews stateless and penniless overnight. The expulsion of Iraqi Jews constituted the first instance when citizenship laws were amended and reconfigured in order to uproot a whole community because of geopolitical and local concerns.

The denaturalization and deportation of Iraqi Jews in 1950–1951 was followed by another expulsion decree a few years later. In 1954, the Iraqi Cabinet issued an amendment to Baghdad's Penal Code of 1938. This newest ruling (Law 17 of 1954) granted the minister of the interior the power to denaturalize, arrest, and deport anyone convicted by the 1938 decree. What is noteworthy about this short directive is the relatively extensive explanation at the end of the document, which at once criminalizes communism and defines the parameters of citizenship. On the one hand, the reasoning offered for this legislative modification maintains that "communism and all the organizations associated with it . . . or inspired by it take their orders from higher communist centers outside Iraq." On the other hand, it stated that "citizenship in any state is an expression of citizens' loyalty towards the homeland, its religions, traditions, and heritage. It also attests to citizens' dedication to protect their country's independence and work to raise its high status, which completely goes against the belief in communist ideologies."[33] Citing the Iraqi Nationality Law of 1924 and the amendment to Baghdad's Penal Code of 1938, the explanation further clarifies that since the Iraqi Nationality Law dictates that the minister of the interior has the right to strip Iraqis of their citizenship if they serve in a foreign country's army, and since adherence to the communist doctrine amounts to serving the interests of a foreign country, the Iraqi government has the power to strip Iraqi citizenship from communists.[34] Based on this law, the Iraqi government stripped prominent communists—who were leading public figures, poets, and writers from different ethnic and religious backgrounds—of their citizenship.[35] This law at once expanded the punishments dictated in the 1938 decree, considered advocacy of leftist ideologies tantamount to loyalty to a foreign state, and linked citizenship rights to allegiance to one's country.

These three instances of denaturalization and deportation in Iraq following the enactment of the first Iraqi Nationality Law of 1924 rendered citizenship rights precarious, contingent, and conditional privileges closely tied to the ruling elites' anxiety about political dissent and aspirations that challenged the existing political status quo. While each instance of expulsion is embedded in specific historical contexts—namely, Iraqi officials' concerns over Assyrians' demand for autonomy, Iraqi Jews' involvement in leftist and Zionist circles as well as the establishment of the state of Israel, and communism's increasing popularity in the country, these different cases constitute a consistent strategy to dispense with political undesirables. This strategy systematically mobilized the rhetoric of national security threats, disloyalty, and foreignness not only to justify practices of denaturalization and deportation but also to vilify Iraqi citizens as the internal enemy. In this framework, the monarchical reign in Iraq institutionalized the loss of citizenship as a legitimate mechanism to punish political opponents. The expulsion of Iraqi Jews in particular reflects how this practice, which was initially employed to get rid of certain Iraqi individuals, could transform into a collective punishment upon a whole community.

After the fall of the monarchy and the departure of the British in 1958, Iraq became a republic. During the reign of Abdul Karim Qasim, who was one of the leaders of the coup that toppled the monarchy and who became the prime minister of Iraq, no denaturalization laws were enacted. In fact, Qasim revoked some of the articles in the denaturalization law of 1951 that discriminated against Iraqi Jews, arguing that they were Iraqi citizens who had suffered unfairly and tremendously under the monarchy and should be treated as equal citizens.[36] On February 8, 1963, backed by the CIA, the Ba'th Party—an anti-imperialist, socialist, and Arab nationalist party established in 1947—staged a coup d'état that toppled Qasim. While the short-lived reign of the Ba'th Party relied on a brutal campaign of terror to deal with political opponents, especially Iraqi communists, it enacted two noteworthy pieces of citizenship legislation. The new regime issued a few laws that reinstated and reinforced punitive measures taken against Iraqi Jews under the monarchy.[37] It also enacted a law that stripped twelve notable communists of their Iraqi citizenship.[38]

The Ba'th Party was ousted in a coup in November 1963, but it managed to regain power in another coup in 1968. The 1960s and 1970s in Iraq witnessed the consolidation of authoritarian rule and the use of violence to deal with anyone the new ruling elites deemed to be a threat, including Kurds, Jews, communists, the Shi'i religious establishment, and even moderate voices within the Ba'th Party.[39] The rise of Saddam Hussein to power in 1979, when he became the president of Iraq, ushered in a reign of terror and the outbreak of the Iran-Iraq War. At the time, he mobilized the Iraqi Nationality Law of 1924 to cast doubt upon the Iraqiness of Iraqis whose ancestors held Persian nationality under the Ottomans and embarked upon a campaign of mass expulsion of *taba'iyya*.[40] In a brief law (Law 666 of 1980) signed by Saddam Hussein, the Revolutionary Command Council "stripped Iraqis of foreign origin of their citizenship if they are found to be disloyal to the country, the people, and the [1968] Revolution's superior social and nationalistic goals."[41] This law was followed by further decrees whose purpose was to inflict as much harm as possible on Iraqi deportees. For instance, the guidelines that were issued by the minister of the interior regarding the implementation of Law 666 called for the detention of *taba'iyya* men between the ages of 18 and 28 until further notice. The fate of these disappeared men became a source of agony for their families for decades. In addition, another ruling issued by the Revolutionary Command Council dictated that any Iraqi man married to a *taba'iyya* woman would get 2,500 Iraqi dinars when he divorced her if he was a civilian, and 4,000 Iraqi dinars if he was in the military.[42] Other retributory measures against *taba'iyya* included the confiscation of assets and documents and sexual violence against young women.

After the fall of Saddam Hussein's regime in 2003 following the US invasion, the Iraqi government issued a new nationality law in 2006 (Law 26). While this law broke new ground in gender terms, it did not constitute a break with the previous citizenship practices in Iraq, and it affirmed the precarity of citizenship. On the one hand, the law set new precedents in gender equality in that Iraqi women had the right to pass down their Iraqi citizenship to their children born to foreign fathers and to their foreign husbands and to retain their Iraqi citizenship if they married foreigners. On the other hand, the new law granted differentiated treatment to citizens who were denaturalized and deported under previous regimes. It allowed *taba'iyya* and their children to reclaim their citizenship and their confiscated property, and it outlawed denaturalization of native Iraqis as a form of punishment. However, the law exempted Iraqi Jews and their children from the right to reapply for Iraqi citizenship. The law did not even mention Iraqi Jews; rather, it stated that Iraqi citizens who had lost their citizenship according to Law 1 of 1950 and had lost their property according to Law 12 of 1951 could not reclaim their citizenship or assets.

This legal overview of citizenship practices in Iraq reflects the ways ruling elites employed the right to uproot citizens they considered to be subversive. Not only did the different denaturalization laws constitute a coherent policy of rule, but they also spoke to how this right to uproot engendered conditions of precarity and dispossession at the legal, political, cultural, economic, and social levels. Tellingly, Iraqi Jews use the term *tasqit* and *taba'iyya* employ *tasfir* to delineate their mass expulsion. *Tasqit* means the forced loss of citizenship, and *tasfir* refers to the forced removal from one's homeland. In this framework, *tasqit* and *tasfir* gesture towards ruling elites' absolute power to act as the sole arbiter of rights and connote sudden and violent uprootedness and ongoing historical ruptures. However, Iraqi Jews and *taba'iyya* have challenged discourses of state vilification, documented the all-encompassing impact of exclusion, and asserted belonging to Iraq through the right to reclaim.

The Right to Reclaim

Though the right to uproot grants ruling elites the power to define legal membership in the polity, it cannot preclude alternative understandings of citizenship. Despite myriad forms of alienation and dispossession, Iraqi Jews and *taba'iyya* have exercised the right to reclaim in order to assert rootedness in Iraq. While citizenship organizes a relationship between the state and citizens, it is also embedded in relations among citizens.[43] The right to reclaim speaks to citizens' capacity to challenge the state's exclusionary discourses and advance their sense of belonging through different avenues—such as political activism, literary productions, emotional attachment, and reminiscences about the past and collective life. The fact that expelled citizens often have little recourse to thwart denaturalization legislation during times of political oppression does not foreclose the possibility that they can devise various mechanisms to inhabit forms of belonging that transcend legal definitions and categories. Deborah Thomas invites scholars to move away from thinking of citizenship as solely a set of rights and to instead approach it "as a set of performances and practices directed at various state and non-state institutions or extraterritorial or extralegal networks—networks that are global, national, regional, and local—over time."[44] This approach to citizenship focuses on "the creative and dynamic ways people make new worlds out of their own 'bare life' instead of assuming that what marginalized citizens want is merely the extension of rights."[45] Though the state can deny legal membership and enact unspeakable violence, it cannot achieve absolute control over the way people construct alternative notions of the self, homeland, and history.

In this context, the right to reclaim is situated in conceptual, historical, and methodological configurations. Conceptually, the right to reclaim is premised upon denaturalized citizens' power to disengage belonging from ruling elites' exclusionary understandings of citizenship and subvert official discourses that vilify regional networks, hybrid identities, and political aspirations. If the right to uproot asserts the mandate of state institutions, the right to reclaim thwarts this power by laying bare systems of erasure and oppression and foregrounds a shared history with fellow citizens. As such, the right to reclaim constitutes a refusal of the state's exclusionary practices and reflects efforts to articulate a complex and nuanced sense of identity. It expands the scope of citizenship beyond a legal status through inhabiting and imagining forms of belonging engendered by social relations, shared political visions, family roots, economic mobility and prosperity, and artistic and literary expressions. If Iraqi ruling elites under different regimes weaponized laws to get rid of political dissidents by resorting to simplistic binaries to frame whole communities as enemies within, the right to reclaim afforded deported Iraqis the ability to write themselves back into Iraq's social, political, and literary landscapes. Reclamation not only entails affirming a right to one's homeland and rejecting the state's discourses. It also establishes the experiences of denaturalization and deportation as integral to Iraq's history. Documenting these experiences of forced displacement becomes an indispensable mechanism to construct an archive of dispossession that is part of the modern history of the Iraqi state.

Furthermore, the right to reclaim is informed by historical sensibilities and lived realities. In the first half of the twentieth century, a younger generation of Iraqis were inspired mainly by leftist ideologies and modernist trends in literature and art.[46] At the time, Iraqis debated the social and political conditions in the country, and oppositional political thought circulated in communist cells, reading clubs, literary salons, newspapers, cafés, and labor and student organizations.[47] A defining feature of this public sphere was a progressive discourse that developed around notions of political independence, equality, economic prosperity, social justice, democracy, and women's rights. Iraqi Jews, along with other fellow-Iraqis, played an important role in these political and cultural landscapes and imagined a utopian future of sovereignty and equality. At the time, Iraq was not only a hub for revolutionary activism, but it also offered more opportunities for upward mobility. A good segment of people who historically had moved back and forth between Ottoman Iraq and Iran—for trade, religious networks, and marriage connections—and decided to settle in Iraq after 1921 identified as Iraqis like all the residents of Ottoman Iraq who began to embrace an Iraqi identity following the fall of the Ottoman Empire and worked hard to provide a better future for their children. The offspring of these Iraqis, who began to enjoy educational opportunities and economic security, had their dreams cut short by denaturalization and deportation in the 1980s. In short, the right to reclaim—as a mechanism to counteract official reductionist rhetoric—invokes these lived experiences that were based on imagining inclusive and egalitarian politics, vibrant cultural scenes, and utopian and just futures.

However, these historical encounters also have shaped the ability to enjoy or utilize the right to reclaim. While Iraqi Jews have produced a plethora of academic and literary works about their lives in Iraq and denaturalization, *taba'iyya* have left little documentation about what their community has suffered. This disparity is due to different historical experiences, especially in terms of access to education and jobs. The Alliance Israélite Universelle—an organization of French Jews who aimed to Europeanize Middle Eastern Jews by providing them with a secular French education and opened modern schools in Ottoman Iraq for boys in 1864 and for girls in 1893—enabled Iraqi

Jews to be more educated than their Muslim neighbors in the first half of the twentieth century. Although the Alliance prompted the secularization of the Jewish community, it also facilitated their economic and social prominence through their knowledge of English and French, which allowed for the integration of the community into the newly established Iraqi state.[48] Moreover, the opening of more Jewish schools—such as Shamash and Frank 'Aini—and the expansion of state schools in the first three decades of the twentieth century created a generation of young Iraqi Jews who took part in the country's political and literary landscapes. Unlike Iraqis Jews, taba'iyya along with other Shi'i Iraqis have endured historical marginalization under the Ottoman and the modern state of Iraq.[49] Given the lack of access to state schools under the Ottomans, Iraqi Shi'is took up professions that were not related to the state, such as trade, crafts, and agriculture. With the establishment of the modern state of Iraq, the British were suspicious of Shi'i scholars, given their opposition to British colonial rule while the new Iraqi ruling elites had a vexed relationship with Shi'i Iraqis, whom they suspected of loyalty to Iran. Despite these political tensions and exclusion from state bureaucracy, some Shi'i Iraqis benefited from the expansion of modern education, and an educated class that contributed to the Iraqi political and literary scenes emerged. However, given the realities of historical marginalization, a good number of Shi'i Iraqis—especially those who held Persian nationality under the Ottomans—still perceived trade as the avenue to make a living and attain socioeconomic mobility. While the offspring of this older generation began to attain education and enjoy a middle-class life, the campaign of expulsion in the early 1980s disrupted this new trend.

The right to reclaim has also methodological implications. If official archives (legislation and newspapers) elucidate the workings of the right to uproot, autobiographical archives (memoirs, historical novels, and ethnographic interviews) foreground the right to reclaim, which derive their richness from stories and accounts told by expelled Iraqis. The concept of autobiographical archives as politics of reclamation represents the latest reconfiguration of my engagement with storytelling as a technique to excavate the modern history of Iraq as lived by Iraqis and to center their voices.[50] Rather than relying on ethnographic research solely, I make use of memoirs and a historical novel. First, unlike ethnographic interviews, which are informed by the anthropologist's interests even though they involve a high level of exchanges and debates, memoirs and historical novels are dictated by expelled Iraqis' agendas and visions. The discussion of autobiographies and a novel in this book aims not only to celebrate written works by Iraqi deportees, which have received little scholarly attention, but also to approach these works as ways to get a glimpse into the stories the deportees wanted to write and tell themselves. For instance, the three memoirs discussed in this book are written with the intention to disrupt mutually exclusive binaries of ethnonationalism that rendered the category of the Arab Jew an oxymoron. The memoirs by Sasson Somekh and Nissim Rejwan—which were two of a number of autobiographies written by Iraqi Jews following the fall of Saddam Hussein's regime in 2003 when hope for a better Iraq conjured up memories of coexistence and solidarity in the past—portray vibrant literary and political scenes that Iraqi Jews, alongside other Iraqis, took part in. In his recent autobiography, which won the 2024 PEN Hessell-Tiltman Prize, Avi Shlaim reads his family's life in Iraq as an opportunity to imagine an alternative future Palestine/Israel informed by the past and to implicate Zionist emissaries in the expulsion of Iraqi Jews. Not only do these three memoirs reclaim the category of the Arab Jew, but they also dismantle claims about inherent anti-Semitism in Arab majority countries. Second, I offer a close reading of Hawra al-Nadawi's historical novel, given the lack of literary or autobiographical works by *taba'iyya* and given that my first book has an ethnographic chapter with a long-term interlocutor whose family was deported to Iran in the 1980s. Third, this book still makes use of ethnographic research I conducted with Iraqis in London between 2006 and 2024 to shed light on forgotten, repressed, or erased histories, in particular Iraqi Jewish women's involvement in leftist circles in Iraq and gender-based violence that *taba'iyya* young men and women were subjected to during the deportation campaign.

If the right to uproot serves a social engineering project whose goal is to discipline citizens, the right to reclaim draws attention to radical political projects, hybrid identities, shared cultural and literary scenes, and connected geographies. As ruling elites mobilized law to criminalize these alternative arrangements and progressive aspirations since they constitute threats to the status quo, ruminations on lived realities in the past and diasporic networks in the present by expelled Iraqis serve to unsettle simplistic and defamatory discourses. In this framework, the right to reclaim shows that citizenship always exists as a site of contestation rather than a prerogative of the state. The right to reclaim serves as an autobiographical archive that documents a myriad of tender, heartbreaking, and tragic stories about a vanished world. The personal accounts in this book speak to the fact that ruling elites can uproot citizens but they cannot erase histories and memories.

Though the denaturalization and deportation of Iraqi Jews and *tabaʻiyya* were separated by three decades and took place under different political eras, they reveal a pattern of governance predicated upon dispossession through revocation of citizenship and show how a legal practice that first was enacted with the purpose of targeting certain citizens metamorphosed into campaigns of mass expulsion. British officials' reliance on deportation to silence political dissidents established a legal precedent to mobilize citizenship as a tool of collective punishment, which Iraqi ruling elites under different governments embraced and built upon. Still, Iraqi Jews and *tabaʻiyya* have exercised the right to reclaim, whose purpose has been to write them back into Iraq's political and cultural spheres, document their lived realities upon deportation, and maintain social relations informed by past experiences of solidarity, coexistence, and shared political visions. Both communities had to "continue to remember, process, and work through cultural and political shifts that quietly inscribed ruptures in their experiences of the self and the world around them."[51] Orkideh Behrouzan argues that alternative histories of loss are written in the psychological afterlife of social rupture and that these alternative histories "create cultural forms that outlive wars and social crises" and engender generational identities, which outlast crises.[52] Through memories about life and struggles in Iraq, Israel, and Iran, Iraqi deportees have had to write a revisionist history about their lives. Despite political crises, they fashioned an alternative space in which an inclusive and multifaceted Iraqi identity—whether articulated as Arab Jewish or Iraqi Jewish, Arab-Iraqi, or Kurdish-Iraqi—was a possibility.

ONE

THE DENATIONALIZATION OF IRAQI JEWS

THOUGH IRAQI JEWS BECAME an integral part of the political, economic, and literary scenes after the establishment of the modern state of Iraq, they increasingly occupied a precarious position in the 1930s. According to Orit Bashkin, from 1929 on, "a dangerous trend took hold in Iraq: whenever there were troubles in Palestine, they would be echoed in Iraq as events that affected the relationship between Jews and Muslims."[1] In 1929, the Palestinians revolted against the British. After the failure of the revolt, Iraqi writers in ultranationalist publications began to associate Judaism with Zionism. The collapse of the Arab Revolt in Palestine (1936–39), the arrival in Iraq of the Palestinian leader Hajj Amin al-Husayni and other Palestinian exiles in 1939, the increased Jewish migration to Palestine, and pro-Nazi propaganda in Iraq complicated the position of Iraqi Jews. The incendiary anti-Jewish rhetoric culminated in the Farhud (pogrom) following the failure of Rashid 'Ali al-Kaylani's coup in 1941. Over the span of two days, Jewish shops and houses were attacked by angry mobs.[2] It was estimated that between 135 and 189 Jews were killed, and that between 700 and 1,000 were injured. Around 550 stores and 900 apartments were looted.

Following the pogrom and the British reoccupation of Iraq during al-Kaylani coup, anti-Jewish campaigning subsided until the establishment of the state of Israel in 1948. At the time, ultranationalist groups and Iraqi ruling elites "singled out" Iraqi Jews as "a major problem" whose loyalty to Iraq was suspect.[3] In March 1950, citing concerns over national interests and disloyalty of Iraqi Jews, the Iraqi government passed a law giving Iraqi Jews the option to emigrate to Israel on the condition that they renounced their Iraqi citizenship. After the bombing of Jewish institutions in Baghdad in 1950–1951, around 130,000 Iraqi Jews left for Israel. Throughout these political developments, Iraqi officials and ultranationalist writers employed essentialist binaries to depict Iraqi Jews as the Other and conflated religion (Judaism) with a modern political movement that emerged in Europe (Zionism). In this framework, citizenship emerges as a contingent process that is closely linked to imperial policies, struggle over power, and nativist ideologies. Petryna and Follis propose the idea of "fault line of survival" to argue that the distinction made by the formal definition of citizenship between those who belong and those who do not belong has life-and-death implications.[4] Like a fault line in the earth's surface, fault lines of survival "can change as a result of dramatic shifts in political systems in domestic and international spheres."[5] Therefore, citizenship becomes intricately tied to shifting forms of legality, belonging, and nation-building, which interpellate different groups into mutually exclusive categories.[6]

This chapter examines the ways Iraqi Jews were portrayed as foreigners who did not belong to the national realm through a discussion of articles in ultranationalist newspapers and laws of denaturalization. This process of negation undermined the notion of citizenship for Iraqi Jews. If Iraqi Jews appeared in the official history of Iraq, they did so only as eternal enemies. While denaturalization laws constituted a legal process of denationalization, the anti-Jewish rhetoric in ultranationalist press entailed the de-Iraqization of Iraqi Jews—namely, the denial of their cultural and political belonging. Though Iraqi Jews were citizens of the Iraqi state and played an active role in the country's political and cultural landscapes, legal membership in the modern state of Iraq did not confer inclusion. Rather, their very citizenship raised national anxiety over the presence of the Other within the nation among the ruling elites after 1948 in particular.

Scholarship on Iraqi Jews includes a vast body of works that provide revisionist readings of different aspects of Iraqi Jews' lives in Iraq. This historiography aimed to dismantle Orientalist and Zionist discourses, which perceived Jews from the Middle East as victims of persecution, and to emphasize the existence of leftist and liberal voices within the Iraqi society that challenged fascist views.[7] In addition, this scholarship shed light on the process of Orientalization that Iraqi Jews experienced in Israel when they found out that Ashkenazi Jews perceived their Arabic culture as "primitive and degenerate" and racialized their Arabness to denote foreignness and non-European racial identity.[8] These scholarly debates also interrogated reductionist binaries (such as Jews vs. Arabs) and examined the reconfigurations of concepts such as "Arab" and "Semitic."[9] Moreover, this academic literature examined Iraqi Jews' integration into the Iraqi political and cultural scenes and provided detailed and nuanced accounts of the Farhud in terms of the beginning of the attacks, the failure of the British to intervene, and the protection Muslim friends offered to their Jewish neighbors.[10] Furthermore, this scholarship was complemented by rich literary works and memoirs that dealt with different aspects of Iraqi Jews' lives in Iraq, including belonging, the process of modernization, their role in administrating the newly established Iraqi state, their contribution to the Iraqi and Arab literary scenes, the double process of misrecognition they encountered in Iraq and Israel, and the endorsement of progressive politics, including political independence, social equality, and women's rights.

This chapter, by contrast, endeavors to focus on a specific issue that has received little attention by examining laws, discourses, and political calculations. Under the monarchy, the denaturalization legislations in 1950 not only stripped Iraqi Jews of their citizenship but also portrayed them as outsiders who did not belong to Iraq. Moreover, this chapter discusses the anti-Jewish rhetoric in the ultranationalist press in order to show how denaturalization laws codified and lent legitimacy to these Othering discourses. Though ultranationalist authors did not represent the majority of Iraqi society, their narrative was embraced and reproduced by Iraqi officials when they enacted denaturalization legislation. In short, the story of Iraqi Jews' exodus and dispossession in the early 1950s speaks to the confluence of different actors with conflicting political agendas and aspirations. For instance, the British Mandate in Palestine and Iraq—which promised European Jews a Jewish homeland in Palestine and facilitated the expulsion of Iraqi Jews respectively—speaks to the question of imperial intervention. In addition, local politics in Iraq—namely, the involvement of Iraqi Jews in the Iraqi Communist Party—shaped Iraqi officials' expulsion plans. As Iraqi Jews became caught up in the cauldron of imperial and national projects, their political aspirations and mobilizations rendered them political undesirables in the eyes of Iraqi ruling elites. Under the Ba'th rule in the early 1970s, the remaining Iraqi Jews confronted another phase of anti-Jewish campaigning in the aftermath of the 1967 War, which reproduced discourses of vilification similar to those that had emerged under the monarchy and which visited more horrific treatments upon them—namely, mass arrest and public executions.

The first part of this chapter examines articles that portrayed Iraqi Jew as the enemy within after 1948. I rely on *Watha'q wa mutqtafat min al-sahafa and al-masadir al-Iraqiyya 'an yhood al-Iraq fi al-asr al-hadith* (Documents and Excerpts from Iraqi Newspapers and Sources about Iraqi Jews in the Modern Age), collected and edited by Nassim Qazaz, and revised by Shmuel Moreh (2013) to discuss the anti-Jewish rhetoric in ultranationalist press.[11] The second part of this chapter offers a legal reading of laws that stripped Iraqi Jews of their nationality and property, which were published in *Al-Waqa'i' al-'Iraqiyya* (Iraq Government Gazette). It also discusses Abd al-Razzaq al-Hasani's *Ta'rikh al-Wizarat al-Iraqiyah* (The History of Iraqi Ministries), which is a chronicle of different ministries under the monarchy. The eighth volume of this work provides a discussion of the denaturalization of Iraqi Jews and reproduces anti-Jewish sentiments expressed in legislation and ultranationalist newspapers. The third part of this chapter explores the consolidation of the notion of Otherness for Iraqi Jews who stayed in Iraq until the late 1960s and early 1970s. These processes of negation exposed the intricacies of citizenship and the construction of Iraqi Jews as noncitizens.

Discourses of Othering

The establishment of the state of Israel in 1948 reignited anti-Jewish discourses in ultranationalist newspapers in Iraq. Articles in *al-Yaqdha* and *al-Nahda* published after 1948 portrayed Iraqi Jews as the enemy within who trained one another to bear arms against the Arabs in Iraq and Palestine, migrate to Israel illegally, undermine the Iraqi state, and spy on behalf of Israel. One writer in particular, Salman al-Safwani, wrote fiery articles about the destructive activities of Iraqi Jews. He depicted Iraqi Jews as Zionists who remained loyal to the state of Israel rather than Iraq. In one article, titled "We and the Jews," Safwani accused the Jews of the Arab countries in general and of Iraq in particular of playing an important role in supporting "the Jewish gangs in Palestine" by donating money and sending young men and women to fight Arabs in Palestine.[12] Moreover, according to Safwani, Jews aimed to undermine Arab countries by "destabilizing the markets, controlling prices, stopping people from working, and suspending monetary transactions."[13] Safwani condemned "the devilish means and ways" to which the Jews resorted and called upon Arab governments to limit their ability to import and export. Seeing himself as representing "the Arab public opinion," he remarked, "It is really shameful that a person walks the streets in Baghdad on a Saturday, and he think he is in Tel Aviv. . . . Why? Because the Jews are the masters of the markets, and they hold the keys of the economic situation. When it is Saturday, they close down." He ended the article by calling upon the Iraqi people and government to protect national wealth, give national companies licenses to import and export, and replace Jewish money exchange with national money exchange. While this article posited the Jews as the other of Arabs, it also reproduced anti-Jewish discourses that perceived Jews as conspiring to destroy Arab countries through control of the economy and support of the state of Israel.

On June 24, 1949, *al-Yaqdha* published a commentary on an anecdote about a Jew making fun of a soldier who went to fight in Palestine and saying, "They went to Palestine and threw it away and came back." The anonymous writer of the commentary asserted that this was not the first time a Jew ridiculed and disparaged Arabs, and referred to another Jew writing on some official documents "a stamp to save donkeys" instead of "a stamp to save Palestine." The writer read these remarks as reflecting "the psyche of Jews in Iraq and Arab countries towards the Arabs, who unfortunately still think highly of these enemies (as citizens). We hope these incidents would wake up the sleepers among our nation and urge our government to protect our dignity."[14] Although this commentary depicted Iraqi Jews as the enemy even though they were citizens, it again emphasized the idea that Arabs and Jews were different. In this framework, Jews in Iraq could only be loyal to Israel. This characterization relied on the premise that Judaism and Zionism were closely linked and that Jews could not be loyal citizens in Arab countries.

Another writer, Adnan Firhad, penned an article titled "Local Zionism and Its Danger to the Safety of Arab Countries" in *Al-Nahda* in August 1949.[15] He wrote about a letter sent by the Arab Higher Committee to Arab countries warning them of the dedication of Jews in Arab countries to Zionism and of "the devilish ways" they devise to move to Palestine and to smuggle their money. Firhad asserted that the committee would not have sent such a letter unless it was certain of Jewish plans to serve Israel and expand their influence in Arab countries. Remarking that this was not the first time Jews in Arab countries rushed to support Zionism, he declared that "Jews were not, and will not, be loyal citizens who know the duties of citizenship at any time because they are 'a minority' that aims to gather all its diasporas to build a strong front that stands up to international trends. There is no doubt that 'the state of Israel' today is the destination of all the Jews in the world in order to establish this entity and seek reunion." Firhad called upon Arab countries to intensify their surveillance of the movements and activities of Jewish people in order to safeguard themselves from danger. He further argued that "Arab countries would not be able to eliminate the state of Israel before it first succeeds in eliminating 'the Zionist fifth column' in Arab countries, who works day and night with all the means available to it to establish a strong Zionist network in each country . . . with the aim of controlling Arab countries economically first, and then politically and militarily."

Towards the end of the article, Firhad commented on the relationship between Judaism and Zionism. He asserted that he did not believe in the claim that Judaism was a religious creed while Zionism was a colonial movement, since he did not care as much about appearance as about essence and intentions. To him, there was no doubt that Judaism and Zionism both aimed to serve Israel. Not only did Firhad erase the fact that Iraqi Jews had been part of the political and cultural landscape in Iraq and that the majority of Iraqi Jews did not endorse Zionism, but he also ignored the fact that Iraqi Jews mostly identified as Iraqis and worked to combat Zionism through establishing the League for Combating Zionism. Firhad ended the article by associating Zionism with communism in Iraq, arguing, "What aggravates the situation is that the Jews succeeded in finding local press that serves their interest in the Arab countries and especially Iraq. The government has unfortunately failed to stop it. On the contrary, some politicians encouraged it to continue in challenging the feelings of the people and to broadcast Zionist propaganda openly." He finally named *al-Shaʻb*, the Iraqi Communist Party's newspaper, as carrying the banner of defending Zionism, while also questioning the patriotism of loyal men in the national press.

An article in *al-Yaqdha* about a demonstration by Iraqi Jews in Baghdad against their persecution portrayed Jews as "the Jewish fifth column" and Jews and communists as "the communist Jewish fifth column." The anonymous writer of the article emphasized that Jews were conspiring against Iraq and shouting slogans like "Long live the Israelite sect," "Glory to our dead in Palestine," "Jews are the chosen people," and "Down with Arab fascism."[16] The depiction of Iraqi Jews as a fifth column was accompanied by further assertions that they were not citizens of Iraq. Nour al-Din Dawoud wrote an article in *al-Nahda* titled "It Is Time We Cleanse Our Country from Elements of Treason, Sedition, and Riots," about the legal status of Iraqi Jews.[17] He asked his readers to consider the following premises: first, the Iraqi Essential Law prohibited the exile of Iraqis outside Iraq, but it did not force the country to accept foreigners or those who claimed another foreign citizenship in the country; second, most Jews in Iraq did not hold Iraqi citizenship, and many could not prove descent from Iraqi parents because they had snuck into Iraq from Iran, Turkey, Poland, Germany, and other countries after World War I; and third, the constitution of Israel considered all Jews in the world as citizens of Israel unless they renounced this citizenship within a year. Dawoud argued that no Iraqi Jews objected to being a citizen of Israel and that it was necessary to differentiate between Jews who professed loyalty to Iraq and those who did not by calling upon them to show their Iraqi nationality certificate. He further called for the deportation of Iraqi Jews who could not prove their Iraqiness and for their property to be confiscated except for an amount of money that would enable them to get by for a month.

In addition to articles and editorials, *al-Yaqdha* also had a gossip and news column on page 2, which included short anonymous pieces on "Iraqi Jews' crimes and propensity for wrongdoings." This rumor column traded in anti-Semitic rhetoric, reiterating conspiracy theories about Iraqi Jews' control of the economy, support of Israel in alliance with the communists, and collaboration with Israel; and calling for the expulsion of Jews from Iraq.[18] The basic assumption in *al-Nahda* and *al-Yaqdha* was that all Iraqi Jews were Zionists and should not be treated as equal citizens. Moreover, writers in these newspapers called for the expulsion of Jews from their jobs in ministries and public institutions, though most newspapers in Iraq did not publish such anti-Semitic articles against Iraqi Jews.[19] Furthermore, the Iraqi government had a long history of censoring communist and leftist newspapers for their critical articles on social and pro-British policies, while it did not censor articles in *Al-Yaqhda* and *al-Nahda*. This state of affairs indicated to Iraqi Jews that the government supported the nationalists' views. Rabbi Khaduri complained that the Iraqi government failed to restrain attacks on Jews in the press.[20]

Denaturalization of Iraqi Jews

In the late 1940s, Iraqi Jews confronted three processes of dispossession: repression and loss of livelihood, defamatory rhetoric in ultranationalist Iraqi press, and the enactment of denaturalization laws, which rendered them stateless and destitute overnight. At the time, Iraqi authorities, in an attempt to underscore their fight against illegal Zionist activities, meted out collective punishment to the Jewish community. They arrested Jews who were not involved in Zionism and came to treat Jews as second-class citizens. British officials in Iraq described the summer of 1948 as a period of "anti-Jewish campaign," when Jews were accused of disrespecting both Iraqis and Palestinians. At the same time, the parliament outlawed Zionism, making it punishable by imprisonment (with a seven-year sentence) or, in extreme cases, by death. Many Jews lost their jobs in government ministries. The Iraqi authorities also authorized the search of Jewish homes to look for Zionist propaganda, unofficially banned the sale of real estate to Jews, and assigned Jews in the army to noncombatant roles.[21]

This anti-Jewish campaign and the increased activity of the underground Zionist movement led to the illegal migration of a limited number of Iraqi Jews to Israel in the late 1940s. Illegal migration was the only possible avenue for Iraqi Jews who wished to leave for Israel since the Iraqi government had enacted a law in 1946 that decreed that any Iraqi Jew who wished to go abroad had to deposit 2,000 dinars. This amount of money, which represented a fortune at the time, would be forfeited if the person failed to return. On May 15, 1948, this amount was increased to 5,000 dinars.[22] After 1948, the Iraqi government faced increased international pressure, exerted by Israel and the United States, to allow the free movement of Iraqi Jews. Given this pressure and continuing illegal migration, the Iraqi authorities came to the conclusion that passing a law to legalize migration to Israel was the only way to stop illegal flight. According to Avi Shlaim, the Iraqi authorities sought the advice of the British ambassador before the enactment of any laws. He remarks that "the Iraqi cabinet asked Salih Jabr, the minister of the interior, to seek the advice of the British government. Jabr went to see the British ambassador in Baghdad and was informed that the British not only agreed that Iraq's Jews should be permitted to move to Israel but that they had already drafted a law to make it possible."[23] These different considerations resulted in the enactment of Decree no. 1 of 1950, also known as *tasqit al-jinsiyya* (denaturalization law) among Iraqi Jews.

The law, which was the product of negotiations between the Iraqi prime minister (Tawfiq Suwaydi) and Zionist emissaries, was presented as a liberal act since the Iraqi authorities offered Iraqi Jews the option to leave the country legally.[24] Decree no. 1 of 1950, which contained seven articles, was published in the Iraq Government Gazette and signed by the interior minister and the prime minister on March 9, 1950. Article 1 granted the Iraqi Cabinet the right to strip any Iraqi Jew of his Iraqi nationality if he wished to leave Iraq for good after signing a document in front an employee from the ministry of the interior to this effect.[25] Article 2 states that any Iraqi Jew who leaves or attempts to leave Iraq illegally will be stripped of his nationality by a decree from the Cabinet. Article 3 dictates that any Iraqi Jew who left Iraq illegally will be considered to have left the country for good if he does not return within two months after the enactment of this law and will be stripped of his nationality. Article 4 empowered the minister of the interior to deport anyone who was stripped of their Iraqi citizenship according to Articles 1 and 2 unless the person can present reasons for his temporary stay outside the country. Article 5 states that this law will be valid for a year after its issuance and that it can be annulled at any time during this time by a royal decree published in the official gazette. Article 6 makes this law effective once it is published in the official gazette, and Article 7 entrusts the minister of the interior with implementing the law.[26]

On the surface, these articles define the legal conditions for a lawful departure from Iraq and for retributions in case of illegal flight though both forms of migration entail the loss of Iraqi citizenship. However, a close reading of the law reveals some sinister connotations, especially the title of the law and the rationale provided for its enactment at the end of document. The title of the law is "An Appendage to the Denaturalization Decree of 1933 [Law 62]." On August 15, 1933, the Iraqi government passed Law 62, which gave the Cabinet the right to strip Iraqis whose family did not reside in the country before World War I of their citizenship if "they took—or attempted to take—an action that posed a threat to the state's security and safety."[27] Using this law, the Iraqi authorities deported the Assyrian patriarch along with his family on the grounds they were not Iraqis. By making the denaturalization decree of Iraqi Jews an appendage to the 1933 law, the Iraqi authorities not only designated Iraqi Jews as a threat to the state's security and safety, but they also defined Iraqi Jews as foreigners whose family had recently arrived in Iraq, rather than an established community with deep historical roots in the country. This law legally enshrined the process of de-Iraqization of Iraqi Jews as laid out in ultranationalist presses.

The second issue is related to the rationale for the law. A statement at the end of the law reads:

> It was noted that some Iraqi Jews have resorted to different illegal ways to leave Iraq for good, and some had already left illegally. Having subjects who are forced to stay in the country and compelled to keep their Iraqi citizenship will definitely result in consequences with far-reaching repercussions for national security, and will create social and economic problems. Therefore, it was crucial not to stand in the way of those who desire

to leave Iraq for good, and to strip them of their Iraqi nationality. This law was enacted to achieve this purpose.

Given the fact that the number of Iraqi Jews who left Iraq was limited, this reference to concerns over national security and economic and social problems reiterates the idea that Iraqi Jews represent a threat to the Iraqi state. As such, the rationale and the title of the law work to insinuate that Iraqi Jews were foreigners who posed an existential threat to the state of Iraq. The Iraqi prime minister who signed the law was Tawfiq Suwaydi. Interestingly, Suwaydi had close Iraqi Jewish friends and he had attended the Alliance Israélite Universelle, a Jewish school in Iraq established by French Jews in 1864.[28] Seen as being "well-disposed towards the Jews," his decision to relegate the organization of migration of Iraqi Jews to Jewish leaders in Iraq was read as a sign of his goodwill towards Iraqi Jews.[29] That someone like Suwaydi signed a law that vilified Iraqi Jews reflects the fact that the anti-Jewish rhetoric in ultranationalist newspapers was institutionalized by the state through this wording of the law.

While a legal analysis of the law can reveal the exclusionary state rhetoric at a specific historical moment, an autobiographical reading about the meaning of the law for Iraqi Jews shows the way laws can be reconfigured and reinterpreted by people in power once a government changes. Avi Shlaim's detailed conversations with his mother show how Iraqi Jews perceived the law. According to Shlaim's mother, "Many of the Jews who registered under the law had not finally made up their mind to surrender their Iraqi citizenship; they simply wanted to give themselves a way out should the situation became intolerable. In other words, it was an option rather than an irrevocable decision. Moreover, they assumed, reasonably enough, that even in the event of leaving, their property rights would not be affected."[30] Still, the majority of Iraqi Jews had no desire to leave Iraq, and "very few Jews registered to relinquish their Iraqi nationality" after the enactment of the law on March 9, 1950.[31] In addition, Iraqi officials did not think many Jews were interested in leaving Iraq for Israel. In fact, by enacting this law, they were motivated by the desire to get rid of radical Jews—namely, communists and Zionists—as well as poor Jews, and they estimated that around ten thousand Iraq Jews would take advantage of the law.[32]

Two events changed the course of history for Iraqi Jews at the legal and economic levels. First, Jewish centers in Baghdad were bombed five times: on April 8, 1950; January 14, 1951; March 14, 1951; May 10, 1951; and June 5–6,

1951. These bombings have been a source of controversy and heated debates for the past seven decades in Iraq and Israel and among the Iraqi Jewish diaspora. The controversy revolves around the identity of the perpetrators—namely, whether the Iraqi government or Zionist emissaries were behind the bombings. (This debate is beyond the scope of this chapter, and I will visit Avi Shlaim's discussion of it in the next chapter.) However, the bombings had a huge impact on the Iraqi Jewish community when 105,000 Iraqi Jews had registered to leave Iraq by the beginning of March 1951. Seventy thousand of them were still in Iraq.[33]

The other crucial event was the change in the Iraqi government. In September 1950, the veteran Iraqi politician Nuri al-Said replaced Suwaydi as a prime minister.[34] Bashkin remarks that al-Said "immediately took steps so that Jews would leave Iraq as rapidly as possible."[35] Al-Said's government issued a law that rendered Iraqi Jews destitute and penniless. On March 10, 1951, the Iraqi Cabinet issued Law no. 5 of 1951. Article 1 offers definitions of two terms. According to it, the term "the Iraqi who is stripped of his Iraqi nationality" refers to "an Iraqi who lost his citizenship according to Law 1 of 1950." The term *property* is defined as "immovable assets, including insurance policies, rent revenue, mortgage, cash, foreign currencies, transfer policies, debts, shares, or any material right."[36] The most important article in the law, namely Article 2, dictates that the denaturalized person's property and assets will be frozen, that the person cannot dispose of them, and that guidelines concerning managing these assets will be issued later on. Moreover, Article 2 established a special governmental body to overlook and manage denaturalized people's assets. The second item in Article 4 states that any person who violates this law will be subject to a two-year prison sentence or fine that cannot exceed 4,000 dinars.

On March 22, 1951, the Iraqi Cabinet issued Law no. 12 of 1951, which is an appendage to Law no. 5 of 1951.[37] Article 1 dictates that any Iraqi Jew who had left Iraq since January 1, 1948, would have his property frozen and managed according to Law no. 5 of 1951. Article 2 contains four subheadings that granted Iraqi Jews impacted by Article 1 the option to return to Iraq within two months after Iraqi embassies and consulates publicized this law in newspapers published in the capitals where they were located; moreover, this article specifies that any Iraqi Jew who did not return to Iraq would be considered to have left Iraq for good and would be stripped of his citizenship and subject to Law 5 of 1951, whereas if he returned in time, he would have his frozen property back after processing fees were deducted. Article 3 details the exemptions to the loss of citizenship within two months, including staying abroad for medical reasons or education. The rest of the articles restate measures concerning loss of citizenship and the confiscation of properties.

Shlaim advances two reasons for al-Said's positions towards Iraqi Jews. He argues that

> Nuri had not displayed any anti-Jewish sentiments in the past. On the contrary, he was associated with Faisal I's policy of befriending the Jews, a policy that Gertrude Bell had strongly recommended to both of them. But the large number of Jews who had participated in the Communist demonstrations against the Portsmouth Treaty in January 1948 was said to have incensed Nuri.... Popular protests forced Nuri to repudiate the new treaty, but they also turned him against the rebellious Jews. It was even rumored that he swore to reduce the Jews to pauperism, to the selling of chickpeas in the streets of Baghdad.[38]

In addition, Nuri al-Said feared that the Iraqi economy would suffer tremendously if Iraqi Jews transferred their capital abroad.[39] Hence, he "reversed Suwaydi's accommodating policy towards the Jewish community" and called for a special session of the Cabinet in order to pass Law 5 of 1951. Because this law took effect immediately, banks "were ordered to close their gates for two days, Jewish companies were impounded and Jewish shops were closed and sealed by the police, denying access to their owners."[40] While some Iraqi Jews managed to get some assets by illegal means, the majority of them—especially the 70,000 who were still in Iraq—became stateless, jobless, penniless, and in many cases homeless overnight.[41] In the end, each adult was allowed to take fifty Iraqi dinars and one suitcase. Orit Bashkin estimates that Iraqi Jews lost between US$150 million and $200 million.[42]

The laws of 1950 and 1951 represented the first time when the Iraqi authorities employed amendments to the citizenship law in order to denaturalize and dispossess a whole Iraqi community on political grounds. The denaturalization of Iraqi Jews under the pretext that they represented a threat to national security meant that the Iraqi government endorsed the conspiratorial discourses in ultranationalist circles. Noticeably, this vision of Iraqi Jews was embraced and reproduced by one of Iraq's most celebrated historians, Abd al-Razzaq al-Hasani, who documented the history of Iraqi ministries under the monarchy in eleven volumes. Before citing the denaturalization law, al-Hasani provides a historical overview of Iraqi Jews. He dates the arrival of Jews to the Babylonian captivity and asserts that Islam treated then respectfully since they are people of the Book. Under the modern state of Iraq, according to al-Hasani, Iraqi Jews enjoyed equal rights in all aspects of life. However, al-Hasani wanted "to set the records right" about "Jews in Iraq" as well, in that "they got filthily rich at the expense of others," that they welcomed the British troops who entered Baghdad in 1917, that they assisted the British by "taking positions in the occupier's bureaucracy," and that they refused, along with Christians, to sign a petition that demanded independence."[43] Furthermore, al-Hasani portrays Iraqi Jews as Zionist, who founded "the Zionist Foundation in Mesopotamia" in 1921 in order to support the international Zionist movement, who established literary and athletic institutions whose true purpose was to assist the Zionist movement to collect donations for Jews in Palestine, and who began to flee to Palestine after the establishment of the state of Israel in 1948.[44] Through a sketchy history of Iraqi Jews, al-Hasani reproduced anti-Semitic discourses that considered all Iraqi Jews as Zionists who were loyal to Israel.

After citing the laws that confiscated Iraqi Jews' assets, al-Hasani titles the next section "The Jews' Crimes." Here, he relies on reports from the Iraqi police to discuss the bombings of the five Jewish institutions in Baghdad and accuses Zionist emissaries of coordinating these bombings and collaborating with Iraqi officers trained in Britain and "foreign experts" in order to push Iraqis Jews to migrate to Israel. What is striking about this discussion is al-Hasani's use of words. Rather than distinguishing between European Jews and Middle Eastern Jews, al-Hasani employs the word *al-Yahud* constantly as if Jews, wherever they are, constitute a unified community without any cultural, political, religious, national, or historical differences.[45] Although al-Hasani recognizes that Iraqi Jews were slow to respond to Zionist propaganda, he describes them "as ungrateful to Iraq, which provided them with shelters for thousands of years, and as unfaithful through migration and action."[46] Al-Hasani's eight-volume work was published in 1955, or five years after the denaturalization law and four years after the exodus of Iraqi Jews from Iraq. As such, this body of work, which is considered to be an authoritative account of Iraqi history under the monarchy, reiterated anti-Semitic views, employing reductionist binaries and a simplistic reading of the Jewish presence in Iraq in order to promote the idea that Iraqi Jews were outsiders, rather than citizens of the Iraqi state.[47]

The systemic and encompassing campaign to dispossess Iraqi Jews at the legal, economic, and cultural levels signaled the end of a flourishing community in Iraq. In addition, this campaign shows that their citizenship was not only a privilege granted or revoked by the state but also was a mechanism used to bring about collective punishment and displacement against Iraqi citizens perceived as political undesirables by the ruling elites. Rather than an inalienable right, citizenship in the modern state of Iraq engendered legal, political, and economic precarity. The association of citizenship with national security rendered Iraqi Jews conditional citizens whose legal belonging was dependent on their being docile citizens and on changes in the political landscape in Iraq and the region. Furthermore, the denaturalization of Jews under the pretext that they represented a threat to national security meant that the Iraqi government endorsed the conspiratorial discourses in ultranationalist nationalist circles that portrayed Jews as the enemy within.

Laws and Policies in Iraq after 1958

A few thousand Iraqi Jews remained in Iraq after 1951. Their status within the state improved greatly after the fall of the monarchy in 1958, as their reintegration into Iraqi society was a goal of the new leader Abdul al-Karim Qasim.[48] For instance, in 1960, the Iraqi government issued a law that did away with Article B of the 1951 law on monitoring and managing the property of Jews who had been stripped of their nationality in 1950. The law of 1960 was accompanied by this explanation:

> Iraqi Jews who reside in Iraq have endured tremendous difficulties due to the application of this article [Article 2]. In addition, the continuation of this article goes against the goals of the revolution [of 1958] and the constitution, which ensures the equality among Iraqis with regard to rights and responsibilities. Also, the principle of stripping a person of the Iraqi nationality goes against the spirit of the constitution on the basis that nationality is a natural right for every citizen, a right that cannot be taken from him simply because a person was late in returning to Iraq within the time limit set in the passport.[49]

Qasim's reign represented a reprieve for Iraqi Jews from constant persecution and exclusion. The law of 1960, importantly, recognized Iraqi Jews as full Iraqi citizens who were entitled to the same rights and responsibilities as all other Iraqi citizens and who were entitled to live a life free from exclusion and vilification.

However, the overthrow of Qasim during the CIA-backed Ba'th coup in 1963 jeopardized the position of Iraqi Jews, as the new regime adopted repressive measures towards them. Shortly after the coup, the new ruling elites, who endorsed an Arab nationalist and socialist agenda with authoritarian tendencies, issued a law on March 31, 1963, that annulled the 1960 law and reinstated Article B of the 1951 law, which dictated, "Every Jew who left Iraq with a passport after this law became valid has to return to Iraq within the time limit set in his passport. If he does not come back after this period, the Council of Ministers, on the suggestion of the minister, can decide to strip him of the Iraqi nationality and manage his property according to Law 5 of 1951." The justification for the law was provided at the end of the document: "The conditions under which Law 12 of 1951 was enacted were still valid since a large number of Jews left Iraq without coming back. The denaturalization was carried out since they did not come back and since they proved their disloyalty to Iraq by going to Israel, which necessitates the freezing of their property for the sake of national interests."[50] This law was followed by a series of laws that stripped the nationality of Iraqi Jews who left Iraq between 1960 and 1963 or who acquired foreign citizenship, and they also enshrined the confiscation of their property.[51]

The Ba'th regime also issued new guidelines that restricted the ability of Iraqi Jews to leave Iraq. On August 4, 1963, the Iraq Government Gazette published instructions that dictated that the public security director had to approve the travel of Iraqi Jews abroad, based on certain conditions. The first condition was the need for medical treatment abroad. However, the patient had to provide a medical report explaining why it was necessary to seek medical care abroad, and the patient could stay abroad only for the period of time stated in the report. Second, Iraqi Jews could go abroad for educational reasons and stay abroad for the duration of their study, but they had to renew their passport in an Iraqi consulate annually and provide paperwork showing their ongoing academic enrollment. Third, Iraqi Jews could travel for tourism as long as the government could guarantee that the purpose was strictly tourism, but they could not stay abroad for more than four months. Finally, they could travel to do business abroad, as long as they were registered with the Chamber of Commerce and provided documents related to their business transactions. Again, they could not stay abroad longer than four months. Together, these laws reinstated discriminatory measures against Iraqi Jews, again casting them as citizens who were suspect in their loyalty to Iraq and who had to endure surveillance and restrictions on their mobility in the name of protecting Iraq's national interests.

The vilification of Iraq Jews reached its peak in 1967, after the Six-Day War. The president of Iraq at the time—Abdul Rahman Arif—was a pan-Arabist. *Al-Jimhuriyya* had a regular column called "These Are the Moral Traits of the People of Zion," written by someone who used the name Muwafaq. These columns were a collection of anti-Jewish sentiments expressed by Western writers and by Christian and Muslim figures with the aim of showing that Jews had always conspired against the people they lived with, that they hated Jesus, and that they connived to control the world. In one column, the author cited the character Shylock in William Shakespeare's *The Merchant of Venice*, who demanded a pound of flesh for the merchant's failure to pay his debt, as exemplifying the character of Jews. The writer also cited Jesus as saying, "No man can serve two masters: for either he will hate the one, and love the other; or else he will hold to the one, and despise the other. Ye cannot serve God and mammon" (Matthew 6:24). The argument that Muwafaq advanced was that Jews worshipped money rather than God. The writer also invoked Ben Hecht's *A Jew in Love* as an instance of Jewish hatred of Jesus. Hecht wrote, "One of the finest things ever done by the mob was the Crucifixion of Christ. Intellectually it was a splendid gesture. But trust the mob to bungle the job. If I'd had charge of executing Christ, I'd have handled it differently. You see, what I'd have done was had him shipped to Rome and fed him to the lions. They could never have made a savior out of mincemeat!"[52]

In another column, Muwafaq described the Talmud as a text that revealed seven hidden principles of Jews. These principles included the belief that other races were created to serve the Jews, that the Jews could be hypocritical towards non-Jews, that Jews are allowed to corrupt non-Jews by any means, and that whatever good existed among non-Jews should be destroyed. Muwafaq also quoted Mohammed bin Maslama al-Ansari, a figure in Islamic history, as citing the Prophet Muhammad's call for the murder of Jews. In another column, he alleged that the Jews killed John F. Kennedy after he welcomed students from the United Arab Republic—namely, Syria and Egypt—to study in the United States. In that column, the writer addressed the American people, saying,

> Did you hear, people of America. . . . You want to help the Jew but where is the loyalty? . . . They killed your president in the street and you could

> not speak in spite of your police. This is Judaism, people of America. The Jew sought your help and treated you like a big child by asking you for help but hitting you with a shoe whenever he wanted. He knew you as a naïve tiger so he lived on your blood and messed with your brain, so you imagined that his existence in our land would benefit you. Oh you, poor, ignorant American people, you do whatever international Judaism wants from you.... Oh learn, you ignorant people, that the Jews will destroy America just as they destroyed the Romans and Napoleon.

The writer went on to ask the American people to shake "the Jewish dust" from themselves and stand up to the Jews. These conspiratorial fabrications portrayed the Arab-Israeli conflict not as a political conflict over the land of Palestine but rather as part of a Jewish conspiracy to control the world and inflict pain and destruction on non-Jews.[53]

The publication of these columns coincided with the translation of *The Protocols of the Elders of Zion* into Arabic by Ajaj Nowaihd in Iraq. *Al-Jimhuriyya* published a discussion of the book in a seminar that was televised on November 9, 1967. The seminar, presented by the participants as the first Arab attempt to unveil the Jewish plots against the Arabs, approached the book as an accurate portrayal of the true intentions of the Jews against humanity. One of the participants asserted that Zionists and all the forces that supported them aimed to discredit the book by claiming that it was anti-Semitic and anti-Jewish and also based on fabrications. The interviewer then remarked that the translator had provided evidence that the protocols were factual by citing Western figures who confirmed the accuracy of the book.[54] In another series of articles titled "The Jewish Plan and the International Status Quo," Jihad al-Hassani reflected on the upbringing of Jewish children and remarked that

> Jewish upbringing starts with introducing the child to his religious identity according to the stories of Torah, indoctrinating him with Jewish pride through the grand achievements of Jews, and familiarizing him with the exile and banishment his people suffered at the hands of non-Jewish infidels. The Jewish child is taught rancor and hatred for any non-Jewish people.... The Jewish child is raised with hatred against humanity, which he considers to be his enemy since he descends from the best race, and his belonging to those that God chose to be the masters of the world.

Al-Hassani cast the stories in the Torah and Talmud as twisting the truth and argued that one could not distinguish between Jewish nationalism and the Jewish religion, since what united Jews was the sect and their upbringing. He also asserted that unlike other people, Jews did not have national affiliations, since religion was considered a pillar of nationalism. Al-Hassani implied that Jews did not have any nationalist feelings about the countries in which they lived and their loyalty was only towards fellow Jews all over the world, erasing the contributions Jews made in their homelands.[55]

The vitriolic attacks on Jews in Iraqi newspapers and television portrayed Iraqi Jews as disloyal citizens who worked to undermine the countries in which they lived and who remained loyal to the state of Israel. Implied in these attacks was that the Iraqi regime was justified in enacting laws that discriminated against Jews and jeopardized their livelihoods and safety. On March 3, 1968, the Iraqi government published Law 10 of 1968 in the Iraq Government Gazette, which stripped Iraqi Jews of their ability to dispense of their property. The law prohibited the Department of Tapu and Endowments and the Office of the Notary from processing any transaction related to selling, gifting, renting for more than a year, or mortgaging any property that belonged to a Jew.[56] The law stated that the property could not be subject to any transaction that would take it out of the owner's proprietorship,[57] rendering the real estate owned by Iraqi Jews valueless for their owners, since they could not dispense of it or benefit from it except by renting it out for a year.

Moreover, these attacks on Jews in newspapers opened the door for the use of violence against the remaining Jews in Iraq. Between 1967 and 1969, around three hundred Jews, which constituted 10 percent of the Iraqi Jewish population, were arrested. Moreover, the government confiscated the property of Jews and dismissed them from government jobs.[58] The status quo for Iraqi Jews in Iraq deteriorated drastically after the second Ba'th coup in July 1968. In 1969, the regime publicly executed eleven Iraqi Jews in Baghdad and three in Basra after accusing them of treason and espionage. Another twenty-six Iraqi Jews died in prisons under torture. *Al-Jimhuriyya* published the pictures and details of the public executions.[59] This wave of persecution prompted a considerable number of the remaining Iraqi Jews to flee the country via Iran, since they were not allowed to leave Iraq legally. By 1971, "only fifteen hundred Jews remained in Iraq; a year later this number declined by two-thirds."[60] This mass exodus, in addition to the exodus in 1950–1951, meant that the presence of Iraqi Jews in the country became a relic of the past.

Conclusion

In Iraq, the support of Palestine entailed the disarticulation of an Iraqi Jewish identity. While Jewishness was dissociated from rootedness in Iraq, it was linked to Zionism in that being a Jew was translated as being loyal to the Zionist project of nation-building in Israel and as being a disloyal citizen who was intent on the destruction of Arab countries. The depiction of Iraqi Jews as the enemy within meant the state at once exposed them to physical jeopardy (since traitors and spies could be executed) and erased their history in Iraq and their sense of loyalty to the country of their ancestors. Whether in the late 1940s or in the 1960s, the anti-Jewish and anti-Semitic sentiments expressed in Iraqi newspapers impacted Iraqi Jews by supporting calls for their eradication and uprooting from the land in which they had lived for millennia. These calls were followed by laws enacted by Iraqi statesmen, which dismissed Iraqi Jews from their state jobs, stripped them of their nationality, confiscated their property, and deported them to Israel. Moreover, the campaign of vilification of Jews after 1967 resulted in the death of forty Iraqi Jews through public execution and torture. The calls for the eradication of Iraqi Jews were no longer limited to the efforts to strip them of their nationality and deport them but also included the literal destruction of their bodies since their designation by the state as spies justified their murder.

TWO

HOMELAND EULOGIES

THE PROJECT OF NATION-BUILDING in the Middle East in the first half of the twentieth century presented Iraqi Jews with possibilities to forge new forms of belonging and imagine alternative futures before the onset of the process of Othering and exclusion. On the one hand, the vibrant roles Iraqi Jews played in Iraq's public, political, and cultural spheres inspired them to perceive themselves as citizens of the new nation of Iraq and to adopt a new Arab identity, whether through identifying as Arabs, taking part in the Iraqi literary scene, speaking Arabic, or enjoying Arabic music and cinema.[1] In addition, Iraqi Jews changed the Arab national discourse in Iraq by infusing it with more tolerant and inclusive tendencies.[2] They also took inspiration from Muslim reformers—who called for the liberation of Muslim women and critiqued the Muslim religious establishments—in debating the status of Jewish women and the structure of Iraqi rabbinical leadership. Debates over what it meant to be an Iraqi, an Arab, and a Jew reflected similar concerns among Iraqi writers from Muslim and Christian backgrounds. Ella Shohat remarks that "For Middle Easterners, the operating distinction has always been 'Muslim,' 'Jew,' 'Christian,' not Arab versus Jew. The assumption was that 'Arabness' referred to a common shared culture and language, albeit with religious differences."[3]

Moreover, Iraq held a special significance for Iraqi Jews, who saw their belonging to the land to date back to the days of ancient Babylon.[4] That the Babylonian Talmud was written in Iraq was an essential component of Iraqi Jewish narratives. This rootedness in Iraq was at the core of a belief that Iraqi Jews belonged to the East.[5] Furthermore, Iraqi Jews' perception of themselves as Arabs and Iraqis was situated in debates about modernity and secularism, comparisons to Western Jewishness, and critiques of European colonialism. Like European Jews, Iraqi Jews expressed their concern over the community's need to modernize within the parameters of the nation-state during debates in cafés, schools, and communist cells. These debates spoke to efforts to develop new forms of subjectivity and nationhood. However, Iraqi Jewish authors aimed to differentiate themselves from Western Jews by contending that "Iraqi Jews and Iraqi Muslims and Christians shared an internal domain of Eastern authenticity, which included motifs from Semitic, Islamic, and Arab cultures. This shared Eastern domain was located outside, and often constructed in opposition to, European colonialism."[6]

On the other hand, Zionist and Arab-nationalistic discourses rendered the category of the Arab Jew as an ontological oxymoron.[7] While ultranationalist newspapers and politicians in Iraq perceived Iraqi Jews as a fifth column, the Orientalist discourse embraced by Zionist emissaries in Iraq and later by Israeli officials invoked distinctive categories based on race and color. In this framework, Iraqi Jews were racialized as the inferior Other vis-à-vis European Jews.[8] The confrontation with imperial whiteness and processes of racialization before their exodus to Israel was exacerbated upon arrival in Israel in 1950.[9] Deported and denaturalized Iraqi Jews faced segregation and poverty and experienced downward mobility in Israel. They lived in tents and shacks, had no property or easy access to amenities, and could not find jobs. Moreover, they found out that Ashkenazi Jews perceived their Arabic culture as "primitive and degenerate" and that their Arabness was racialized to denote foreignness and non-European racial identity.[10] While Zionism claimed that it was a liberation movement for all Jews and attempted to make the terms *Jewish* and *Zionist* synonymous, it fashioned itself along a binary of East and West, whereby European Jews were portrayed as rational, developed, superior, and human while the Other—represented by Oriental Jews—was portrayed as underdeveloped and inferior.[11] This double process of uprootedness and negation erased a history of hybridity based on a Judeo-Muslim tradition in the Middle East. Though Iraqi Jews were at first citizens of the Iraqi state and then of the Israeli state, legal membership did not confer inclusion. Rather, their very citizenship raised national anxiety over the presence of the Other within the nation who posed a threat to the state.

However, Iraqi Jews endorsed a politics of reclamation in order to resist the conditions of dispossession and erasure both in Iraq and Israel. In the past few decades, the term *Arab Jew* was invoked by many Jewish writers from Arab-majority countries in order to contest nationalistic binaries of "us" versus "them" and to delink Jewishness from Zionism and Arabness from Arab nationalism. By critiquing exclusionary nationalistic discourses and by reclaiming the "Arab Jew" as a revisionist category constituted in lived experiences, Iraqi Jews at once constructed an archive of loss and of friendship, solidarity, and rootedness in a country that has been at the crossroads of cultural exchange, colonial competition, modernization processes, regional networks, and nation-building projects over the centuries. Iraqi Jews, like the other inhabitants of Iraq, went through a process of Arabization and used Arabic in their everyday conversations and literary productions while still maintaining their communal identity.[12] In the early twentieth century, they began to identify as Iraqis and took part in the vibrant political and literary spheres in the country. This history reverberates today, and the right to reclaim has emerged as a liberatory aspiration. In his recent memoir, Avi Shlaim argues that the history of Arab Jews in the Middle East constitutes a blueprint for imagining a more optimistic and just future in Israel/Palestine.[13]

This chapter makes use of life stories from recent memoirs written by Iraqi Jews and interviews I conducted in London. While these biographical accounts undermine Iraqi ruling elites' characterization of Iraqi Jews as the enemy within, they also constitute individuals as subjects empowered to offer alternative narratives about the past. The narratives about political activism, literary productions, and nostalgic reminiscences about the past shed light on the ways Iraqi Jews aimed to contest simplistic readings of history following the onset of the Arab-Israeli conflict and to write themselves back into Iraq's political, economic, religious, and cultural landscapes. In addition, Iraqi Jews' chronicles about different aspects of their lives in Iraq speak to the experiences of a whole generation of Iraqis who were deeply attuned to anticolonial struggles and social injustices and championed modernity and secularism in the first half of the twentieth century. While the narratives in this chapter are about a specific community, they are part of a larger story about the utopian futures entertained by Iraqis who came of age in the first half of the twentieth century and are also about the legacy of displacement and loss, a fate many Iraqis experienced in the postcolonial state. The first part of the chapter, based on a reading of two memoirs, focuses on the literary scene in Baghdad in the 1930s and 1940s. The second part, based on fieldwork conducted in London with Iraqi Jews, examines young Jews' political activism with the Iraqi Communist Party and the League to Combat Zionism in the 1940s and later on in

Israel. The third part discusses Shlaim's reading of the past in terms of the future in his latest memoir.

Literary Networks

When the nation-state of Iraq was formed under the British Mandate in 1921, there were already many Iraqi Jews who were well-versed in Arabic, familiar with Western literature, and dedicated to emerging forms of Arabic literary modernism.[14] Iraqi Jewish writers experimented with classical and modern forms of fiction, poetry, drama, and journalism and contributed to Iraqi newspapers. The Alliance Israélite Universelle played an important role in the late nineteenth century in transforming the Iraqi Jewish community. It provided young Jews with an opportunity to achieve economic prosperity and social mobility through access to modern education, unlike their Muslim neighbors. Given their fluency in English and French, Iraqi Jews joined the bureaucracy of the newly established Iraqi state. Moreover, the Iraqi Jewish community rejected the Alliance's policy of adopting French as the sole language of instruction, and most Jewish schools retained Arabic as the language of instruction. Therefore, while many Jews became cosmopolitan, they "remained in the Arabo-Muslim cultural orbit."[15] They, moreover, "saw Iraq as their homeland, and many sought to contribute to building up the new state and society, while differing widely on how this should be done. The Iraqi orientation of the Jewish community enabled members of its intelligentsia to become significant figures in the formation of modern Iraqi Arabic culture."[16]

Anwar Sha'ul, Murad Mikha'il, Shalom Darwish, Me'ir Basri, Ya'qub Bilbul, and Nissim Rejwan were among an early generation of Iraqi Jewish writers who played an important role in Iraq's emerging literary scene in the first half of the twentieth century. Other writers who came of age during the 1940s, including Sasson Somekh, Naim Kattam, Shimon Ballas, Sami Michael, and Samir Naqqash, continued writing about Arab and Iraqi issues after their arrival in Israel in 1951. Iraqi Jewish writers and journalists founded Arabic newspapers—such as the *al-Haris* (1920), *al-Misbah* (1924–1929), *al-Hasid* (1929–1938), and *al-Barid al-Yawmi* (1948)—and contributed to other Iraqi newspapers. Through these literary networks, these writers experimented with new genres in Arabic poetry and fiction and discussed issues of concern to all Iraqis, including political independence, social inequalities, and women's rights. Moreover, these literary circles were based on friendships that Iraqi Jewish writers cultivated with fellow Iraqi writers, who all aimed to fashion a new Iraqi self, introduce modernist sensibilities, and demand equality and inclusion. Memoirs by Nessim Rejwan and Sasson Somekh provide accounts of the relationships Iraqi Jewish writers had with Arabic and Arabic literature, the roles that schools and cafés played in providing spaces to interact and debate with fellow Iraqis, and the anxiety these writers felt at the increasing anti-Jewish sentiments in Iraq in the late 1930s and early 1940s, which led to their exodus from Iraq in 1951.

The memoir by Nissim Rejwan, who was born in 1924, portrays the life of a poor Jewish boy in Baghdad and provides an alternative to memoirs by prominent Iraqi Jewish writers who attended prestigious Jewish schools and who belonged to the middle class. In his reflection on his family's economic situation, gender relations, and schooling, Rejwan offers an account of someone who did not have the luxury of a full education and who did not live exclusively in Jewish neighborhoods. His family often lived as subtenants in different Muslim neighborhoods, and Rejwan grew up mingling with Baghdadis from different religious backgrounds who struggled to make ends meet. The family's limited means prompted Rejwan to find jobs at an early age in order to buy books and socialize with his friends. Given that Rejwan was born in 1924, he spent his first fifteen years in a Baghdad not yet marked by anti-Jewish sentiments, and he grew up navigating and moving among different literary, social, and political circles. Indeed, Rejwan's account of life in Baghdad is not only about the hardships under which most Iraqis lived but also about vibrant literary and political scenes. Although Rejwan struggled in school, he embarked on self-education by buying and reading Arabic books and translations of French and English literature before eventually teaching himself English. During this period of self-education, Rejwan met with Iraqi friends in cafés who were interested in literature and discussed literary works with them. He later on began to write literature and film reviews for *The Iraq Times*.

Rejwan asserts that he began reading Arabic books and magazines at an early age. Like other Iraqis of his generation, he was influenced by the historical novels of Jorgi Zaydan and was at first introduced to French and English literature through Arabic translations of romances and novels. Not only was Rejwan an avid reader, but he was also a bibliophile and built a sizeable home library that included the works of famous Egyptian writers, such as Taha Hussein, Ahmad Amin, Muhammad Hussein Haykal, and Tawfiq al-Hakim, among others.[17] Moreover, he collected works by classical Arab writers, such as Ibn Khaldun, Ibn al-Atheer, Ikhwan al-Safa, and Abu al-Faraj al-Isfahani, in addition to classic poets, such as al-Mutanabbi, Al-Ma'arri, and Ibn al-Rumi. After a short period, Rejwan realized that most of the Arabic and Islamic classical writings and contemporary works were monotonous and lacked originality. Sometime in the second half of the 1930s, he discovered "a fresh breeze" coming from Beirut when he began to read the weekly *Al-Makshuf*, which "was launched by an enterprising Lebanese Christian and immediately became an outlet for experimental and avant-garde poetry, fiction, and criticism."[18] Through this weekly, he was introduced to Lebanese writers, such as Khalil Taqiyeddine, Tawfiq Yusuf 'Awwad, Elias Abu Shabaka, Maroun 'Abboud, 'Umar Fakhuri, Constantin Zureiq, Raeef Khuri, and Qadri Qal'achi. To Rejwan, the Iraqi literary scene at the time was very poor, except for prominent poets like Muhammad Mahdi al-Jawahiri, Muhammad Salih al-'Ulum, and Ahmad el-Safi al-Najafi and the Jewish fiction writer Ya'qub Bilbul. Rejwan also started collecting Arabic weeklies, such as *Al-Thaqafa*, *Al-Riwaya*, and *Al-Risala*, to familiarize himself with literary and cultural developments in Iraq. At the time, he discovered the works of the Egyptian writer Salma Musa and his monthly *Al-Majalla al-Jadida*, along with other Egyptian writers who "were considered modernists and innovators, their writings having been 'scientific,' and they having introduced into the Arab cultural scene such new and novel ideas as evolution, socialism, nationalism, and agnosticism."[19] These various weeklies and monthlies and translations of books by publishers in Beirut and Cairo provided Rejwan with the first glimpses of the richness of Western thought.[20]

Rejwan's avid interest in Arabic and Western literature reflected a trend in the Iraqi literary scene at the time, when Iraqi writers and readers engaged with classical and modern Arab authors—brought about by the consciousness for the need for an Arab renaissance—and became curious about Western literature. This literary curiosity was accompanied by political awareness for many of the Iraqi youth at the time. While the Spanish Civil War made Rejwan aware of the struggle between the Republicans and the fascists, who were supported by Nazi Germany, he ascribed his enthusiasm for the Republicans to the passion of "an impressionable lad of thirteen," who was less concerned about Franco's fascism and anti-Semitism and more about "high matters of right and wrong, legitimacy and illegitimacy, human rights and the treatment of prisoners of war."[21] Rejwan also confronted rising sympathy for Nazi Germany and fascist Italy in Iraq when nationalist sentiments reproduced anti-Jewish rhetoric and two Jewish businessmen were shot in the streets of Baghdad in the late 1930s.[22] Rejwan's efforts to understand the political status quo at home and in the world prompted him to learn English and start reading English weeklies and monthlies like *World News and Views* and *Labour Monthly*, which were imported to Iraq thanks to the efforts of a Christian tobacconist with communist leanings.[23] At the time, he also discovered Marxism and began to frequent Marxist circles in Iraq.[24] He met prominent communist leaders, such as Yusuf Salman Yusuf (known as Fahd), Hussain Muhammad el-Shabibi, and Zaki Muhammad Baseem. In addition, Rejwan had opportunities to discuss literature, politics, and women's rights in cafés in Baghdad. His favorite café at the time was Hassan 'Ajami', where he cultivated his "most lasting friendships in the late 1930s" until his shifting intellectual interests and his steady job took him in a different direction.

This shift in his intellectual leanings by the outbreak of World War II meant that Rejwan's library consisted mainly of English books and a limited collection of Arabic books by avant-garde Arab writers of the time, such as Raeef Khuri, Tawfiq Yusuf 'Awwad, and Ibrahim Naji from Egypt and Ahmed el-Sayyid, Abdel Fattah Ibrahim, and Mahdi al-Jawahiri from Iraq. He ascribed this shift to his "encounter with the West, its politics, its culture, and its literature, and prior to my first meetings with Elie Kedourie and, subsequently, with a number of aspiring intellectuals and dilettantes who later came to be known as 'the gang.'"[25] However, this shift did not indicate a rejection of Arabic or Arabic literature. Rather, it was driven by a desire to read modernist forms of literary production, whether in Arabic or Western literature. Here again, Rejwan cultivated close friendships with fellow Iraqi poets and writers who were leaving behind classical Arabic literature, experimenting with free verse, and drawing inspiration from modern Western works. Though his literary growth was marred by Rashid 'Ali al-Kaylani's coup and the Farhud of 1941, Rejwan still thought of the years of 1938–1945 as formative. To him, Baghdad of the mid-1940s and his own experience within the Muslim Arab milieu in which he grew up provided him with "the nearest thing to emotional and intellectual maturity and fulfillment."[26] In his reflections, he came to appreciate "the general atmosphere of 'tolerance' in which we moved, read, loved, and just plain lived."[27]

At the time, al-Rabita Bookshop, which opened in 1946, provided this space of tolerance, growth, and exchange. The bookshop was an offshoot of a cultural association founded by left-leaning intellectuals. The secretary of the association, Khadduri Khadduri, had asked Rejwan to "help with the establishment of the shop, which was to deal with almost exclusively in English-language books."²⁸ After a short interview with the association's chairman, Abdel Fattah Ibrahim, Rejwan got the job. He came to relish his job at the bookshop. "Except for the more specialized works on sociology, economics, and history, which were chosen by Abdel Fattah himself, I have a completely free hand in making the orders, and my various literary predilections and inclinations played a decisive role in establishing the character of the bookshop and the type of clients who frequented it," he reminisced.²⁹ The bookshop became a hub for Iraqi intellectuals of all kinds and created a literary circle for people interested in the latest developments in Western literature. At the bookstore, Rejwan met Iraqi and Arab writers who were experimenting with new forms of writing. In addition to the bookstore, he met with these writers in Café Suisse and discussed with them the latest political developments and literary trends in Western literature, such as works by George Orwell, Franz Kafka, Ezra Pound, and James Joyce. Buland al-Haidari, who later became one of Iraq's leading modern poets, called this literary circle the *shulla* (or gang).

Rejwan was fond of this group in his reminiscences about his life in Iraq not only because it provided a venue to discuss literary works but also because he felt he belonged to it. The establishment of al-Rabita Bookshop and the meetings at Café Suisse took place at a time of turmoil in Iraq and Arab countries. Speaking of the partition of Palestine, the protests against the new Anglo-Iraqi Treaty of 1948 (the Portsmouth Treaty), the defeat of Arabs in Palestine, and the increasing anti-Jewish sentiments, Rejwan remarked that "all these and many more developments occurred without relations between Jews and Muslims in our circle being in the least affected," and the "circle included two or three Jews who somehow seemed to be quite at home in it and shared a high spirit of friendship and camaraderie with the Muslims."³⁰ The circle also included two pan-Arab nationalists, with whom Rejwan maintained a cordial relationship. Reflecting in particular on his relationship with 'Adnan Raouf, Rejwan commented that he shared with Raouf "far too many interests—literature, time-out, and just plain companionship—for him to allow his political views to interfere in our friendship."³¹ This literary network enabled Rejwan to pursue his interests in Western and avant-garde Arabic literature, maintain friendships with fellow Iraqis, and articulate an Iraqi identity situated in the concept of modernity and critical of tradition. Cafés and bookstores in Baghdad provided a space to share these interests with his friends. If Café 'Ajmi enabled him to carve friendships with Iraqis interested in Arabic literature, Café Suisse and Café Brazil became meeting points with friends exploring the latest literary productions in the West.

If Rejwan's narrative sheds light on the experience of a poor, self-taught, young Jewish man who was eager to discover the latest trends in Arabic and Western literature and to build literary networks with fellow Iraqis, the account by Sasson Somekh speaks to the experience of a middle-class Baghdadi Jew who went to Jewish schools and had a strong sensibility as an Arab Jew and a deep attachment to Arabic literature. Somekh, who was born in 1933 and later became a prominent scholar of Arabic literature in Israel, opens his memoir with an acute awareness that his generation was "the last generation of Iraqi Jews who lived side by side with Iraqis of other religions, speaking a common language and participating actively in Iraqi culture."[32] This sense of commonality with fellow Iraqis was accompanied by a feeling of rootedness in Iraq, since the Iraqi Jewish community could date its existence in Mesopotamia to 587 BCE following the destruction of the First Temple in Jerusalem. For Somekh, this rootedness in Iraq for millennia meant that the Jewish community survived and adapted to different empires that had ruled the country, including the Babylonians, Persians, Arabs, Turks, and British.[33] He, moreover, saw his generation and community as undergoing yet other important changes. On the one hand, he was aware of the increased secularization of the Jewish community, which began in 1860s with the establishment of the Alliance Israélite Universelle school system and accelerated in the 1930s and 1940s all over Iraq after the establishment of the modern state of Iraq. On the other hand, he witnessed the increased involvement of young Jews in political movements in Iraq, in particular the Iraqi Communist Party. The latter development represented two trajectories in Somekh's view: "The first involved the desire to act side by side with other Iraqis, and the second stemmed from a growing political awareness."[34]

However, Somekh did not get involved in any political movements. What preoccupied him was Arabic poetry and literature. As a teenager, he wrote Arabic poems and prose and even managed to publish some of his writings in Iraqi newspapers before he had to leave for Israel. Indeed, his memories of Baghdad were tinged by his love for poetry. When he expressed his desire to visit Iraq again, he wrote about the Tigris as the river of his childhood and adolescence as well as the site of his first efforts to write Arabic poetry.[35] When he slept on the roof in the summer—a tradition that Iraqis practiced for generations before the introduction of air conditioning—and looked at the galaxies, he thought of medieval Hebrew and Arabic poetry, which interpreted these constellations as a shepherd and a shepherdess tending their flocks in the mountains.³⁶ Like many Iraqis of his generation, Somekh became an avid reader at a young age, reading Arabic books at first and English books later on. This fascination with books was facilitated by his access to the General Library in Baghdad, his interactions with schoolteachers who instilled in him a love for Arabic literature, and discussions with friends in coffee shops and bookstores. Reminiscing about the General Library, Somekh felt he owed the library gratitude "for the part it played—for better or worse—in forming the world I came to know through reading."³⁷ At the library, Somekh "absorbed some of the best of Arabic literature" and had access to "works and periodicals of modern Egyptian literature."³⁸

After his primary school education at Madame 'Adil's in a modern neighborhood inhabited by middle-class Muslims, Christians, and Jews, Somekh went to the Jewish school, Shamash, where the language of instruction was exclusively in English. While his British teachers there introduced him to English literature, it was his Arabic teachers who left an indelible mark on him by including him in their literary circles and familiarizing him with contemporary political debates. Somekh fondly remembers Muhammad Sharara, my grandfather, as a nonconventional teacher who was not concerned about teaching the curriculum but rather about making his students politically aware of the status quo in Iraq and the world by discussing imperialism, class exploitation, and the "quack parliament" in class.³⁹ In addition, Sharara encouraged Somekh to write poetry and helped him get one of his first poems published in *al-Hadara*.⁴⁰ Somekh particularly admired the prominent Iraqi poet Muhammad Mahdi al-Jawahiri. Once, he bought a collection of al-Jawahiri's poetry and was enthralled by a poem called "The Tigris in Autumn" but found the language difficult since al-Jawahiri was "known as the knight of neo-classical poetry, and he often used expressions derived from ancient Arabic verse." Somekh asked Sharara to discuss the poem with him. Sharara was close friends with al-Jawahiri, since they shared the same leftist ideology and knew each other in Najaf. He suggested to Somekh that they both visit the poet at Hassan Ajami Café next to Shamash. When they went to the café and met with al-Jawahiri, Somekh was so nervous that he could not remember the content of the conversation, although he remembers that "the 'Jewish question' came up. Al-Jawahiri told us of how he once found himself behind bars for daring to side with Baghdad's poor Jews."⁴¹

The meeting with al-Jawahiri was a turning point in Somekh's life in that it "whetted my literary appetite. I had immersed myself in Arabic literature, especially poetry, and had begun to think of myself as a budding poet. My teacher Sharara encouraged me."[42] Sharara asked Somekh to translate some English poems into Arabic with the aim of publishing them. Instead, Somekh wrote his own poems, using a classical structure. One such poem, "Autumn Will Come," was published in *al-Akhbar*. Somekh recalls:

> From then on, literary pursuits filled my life. I spent my days running back and forth between the many cafés on al-Rashid Street, which were the gathering places of young writers and artists—most of them Muslim, secular, and left-wing, and all of them several years older than I was. A world of culture opened before me. Baghdad in the late 1940s was humming with literary activity, and seemed poised to become the center of literature in the Arab world. . . . Poets, fiction writers, painters, sculptors, all in their early twenties, eagerly embraced the new winds blowing from the West. They experimented with modern techniques and used the Arabic language in innovative and refreshing ways.[43]

During a visit to a café in 1949, Somekh met Badr Shakir al-Sayyab, a pioneer of modern Arabic poetry, who brought with him the proofs for his poetry collection *Asatir* (Myths), which heralded "a revolution in modern Arabic poetry." Somekh alerted al-Sayyab to two or three typographical mistakes. Al-Sayyab thanked Somekh and sent him a copy of the book a few weeks later: "In it were the corrections I had suggested. How elated I felt at having contributed, even in such a small way, to Arabic literature!"[44] These literary exchanges with Iraqi authors, artists, and mentors in cafés enabled Somekh to feel like a part of the Iraqi literary scene at the time, even though the position of the Jewish community in Iraq was in jeopardy following the partition of Palestine and the establishment of Israel in 1948. However, his literary circle was not affected by these events. On the contrary, he reminisced that "the year 1950 may have marked the demise of the most ancient Jewish community in the world, but from my perspective, it was a year of literary awakening. Some short pieces of my writing appeared in literary sections of newspapers like *al-Nadeem* and *al-Naba'*."[45] As the uprootedness of the Jewish community loomed in 1950, Somekh vowed "that I would remain loyal to Arabic literature. I took that oath, and I believe have remained true to it."[46] Somekh went on to become Israel's leading authority on Arabic literature and included the Egyptian Nobel laureate Naguib Mahfouz among his Arab friends. Speaking of the importance of the literary scene in Iraq in shaping him, he remarked that his "memory of these writers and poets, all or most of whom were Muslim, remains at the center of my consciousness to this day."[47]

Through literary circles in Baghdad, Iraqi Jews could articulate an Iraqi identity with Arab leanings despite the ruling elites' efforts to designate Jews as disloyal citizens. The friendships and mentorship Iraqi Jews cultivated with fellow Iraqis speaks to a general trend in Iraqi society at the time, when writers, artists, and activists yearned to discover the latest trends in literature and politics and to modernize the Iraqi literary landscapes. Iraqi Jewish writers were part of a vibrant community, which transcended interreligious differences and were concerned about issues of interest to Iraqis from different religious backgrounds—namely, a literary renewal, the status of women, social justice, and the lack of independence. Not only did these circles carve out a space dedicated to inclusion and provide a scathing critique of policies and practices endorsed by Iraqi ruling elites, but they also shaped Iraqi Jews' sensibilities after their expulsion once memories of life in Iraq became a refuge and a venue to forge relations with Palestinians after their expulsion.

In addition to these literary networks, Iraqi Jews played an active role in the political scene in Iraq through taking part in demonstrations against the British colonial rule and the feudal monarchy, joining the Iraqi Communist Party, and advocating for the rights of the poor and women. While the literary circles described above remained dominated by men to a great extent, Iraqi Jewish women played an important role in the Iraqi political landscape through their activities in leftist circles.

Political Activism

Iraqi Jews who came of age in the 1930s and 1940s belonged to a generation in the Middle East that was deeply attuned to anticolonial struggles and social inequalities. The participation of young Iraqi Jews in leftist circles along with fellow Iraqis was echoed in Morocco, Egypt, and Iran, where young Jews joined communist parties to fight against fascism and colonialism, to become involved in national liberation movements, and to assert their belonging to the countries in which they grew up. At the time, Jews from the Middle East found communist parties appealing, given their inclusive ideologies, promotion of equality among all citizens, and dedication to social justice.[48] Jewish men and women took part in the Iraqi political scene. While the experiences of Jewish men in the Iraqi Communist Party and the League to Combat Zionism have been documented in documentaries, memoirs, and scholarly literature, the role Iraqi Jewish women played in these circles has been mainly silenced. When authors have discussed the lives of Iraqi Jewish women, they have focused on the experiences of the urban poor.[49] The story of Jewish women activists has been excluded from the histories of Arab feminism, the Iraqi Communist Party (ICP), and the Israeli Communist Party (MAKI).[50] Some Iraqi Jewish women joined the ICP's rank and file, while a few—for instance, Allen Darwish, Madeline Mir ʿEzer (or Ezra), and Saʿida Mashʿal/Suʿad Khayri—assumed leadership roles. As educated women, they appreciated the communist agenda, which emphasized equality between men and women and advocated equality in the job market and suffrage. As Jews, they found the party's nonsectarian vision of Iraq especially appealing.[51] Like men, "they operated in both Jewish and nonsectarian settings, and understood their actions within communist and Iraqi patriotic frameworks simultaneously."[52]

Iraqi Jewish women were first introduced to communist ideas through family members—husbands, siblings, and cousins—and were further radicalized at high schools and colleges where the ICP was active. The life story of Eileen (1936–2014), whom I interviewed in London, sheds light on Iraqi Jewish women's political roles. Eileen was a cell member, and she participated in demonstrations against British rule, sought to advance the status of Iraqi women, demanded social justice, and eventually was smuggled out of Iraq to Israel by her family to avoid imprisonment. In Israel, she got involved with the Israeli Communist Party, whose members included Palestinians and Jews, and voiced scathing criticism of Zionism and Israeli discrimination against Palestinians and Arab Jews. She left Israel and went to the United Kingdom with her immediate family, where she resumed her relations with Iraqi communist women, helped Iraqi refugees in London, and opposed the sanctions and US invasion of Iraq.

I met Eileen one morning at the end of 2006 at an event organized by the Iraqi Women's League about the increasing gender-based violence and the suppression of women's rights in Iraq following the US invasion in 2003. After the event, an Iraqi communist woman who knew my parents introduced me to Eileen, a widow who was in her mid-sixties at the time. Eileen was warm and happy to meet me, as a fellow Iraqi who had left Iraq only in 1997. She was eager to know what life had been like for me and my family under Saddam Hussein's regime and to hear about my exilic trajectory, which had brought me to London to do research. She invited me and the friend who introduced us to go back to her home for coffee and Iraqi pastries. The conversation during the bus ride revolved around the deteriorating political situation in Iraq and the utopic past when progressive politics premised upon political independence and social justice prevailed. At Eileen's house, I met her sister and brother-in-law, who were also communists. As I listened to Eileen, I realized that she was a pivotal member among the Iraqi communists in London and that the bleak present did not dampen her spirits or her belief in a better future for all Iraqis. As I was about leave, Eileen asked me to keep in touch, to visit her when I wanted, and to know that her house was open to all Iraqis every Saturday, when she would make Iraqi and Iraqi Jewish food in order to entertain her family and friends. After a few visits and encounters at other public events on Iraq, I asked Eileen if I could interview her, and she was delighted to help me with my research in any way she could.

Eileen's political awareness began at home. Her sisters and their fiancés were politically active and had introduced her to communist ideas at an early age. At school, Eileen further encountered communist ideologies and calls for political struggle against colonial rule in Iraq. At the time, British officials were against the expansion of the public school system in Iraq, fearing that overeducation would produce subjects engaged in political agitation and unwilling to do manual labor. Iraqi nationalists, by contrast, saw schools and the family as arenas of social reform and economic development that aimed to produce new Iraqi subjects worthy of sovereignty.[53] Families and schools did not become sites to produce docile and governable subjects. Rather, they emerged as hubs for revolutionary sentiments,[54] and it was at school that Eileen was further exposed to communist and nationalist trends. To Eileen and her sisters, participation in the popular political scene in Iraq was not only a way to demand political independence and social justice but also a mechanism to assert belonging in Iraq in the face of increasing vilification of Jews by the Iraqi government and ultranationalist newspapers in the late 1940s.

Eileen became politically active in her early teens. She joined the youth organization associated with the Iraqi Communist Party, since she was too young to join the party. Her responsibilities included collecting donations for the Iraqi Communist Party, distributing communist pamphlets, teaching illiterate women how to read and write, and participating in demonstrations against the government for its close ties with the British and for its failure to enact social reforms. Eileen recalled an early incident in her activism:

I was in primary school when I got politically active. I always took risks. When I first went to secondary school, my liaison asked me to see the headmistress and ask her for a donation for the national movement. He asked me to say that the national movement needs money. I told him this is impossible, but he insisted. After school was over one day, I went to the office of the headmistress and waited till all the other teachers left the room. I was shuddering with fear the whole time I was waiting. When the headmistress saw me, she asked me to come in. She inquired why I have been waiting for a long time to speak to her. I just told her that "the national movement needs money." She said, "Welcome. Have a seat, my daughter." Then she reached into the drawer, gave me forty dinars, and asked me to give her regards to the movement. Then I met with my liaison and gave him the money.

Eileen's political awareness was national, regional, and international in its scope. While she and her communist comrades wanted to see Iraq enjoy meaningful independence from Britain, she was also inspired by the anticolonial movements in other Arab-majority countries and throughout the Third World. The question of Palestine was particularly pressing for her, since she supported the Palestinian cause. She agreed with her teachers at school who explained the events in Palestine by linking the efforts to establish a Jewish state to colonialism:

The question of Palestine preoccupied me a lot. I didn't like it because it took me away from my roots, my friends, and my people who never persecute me or hurt me. I never felt any affinity with the Jewish question. I saw that colonial powers encouraged the Jewish migration to Israel in an effort to divide people. Our struggle was to get rid of colonialism. I participated in demonstrations in 1946 and worked with the League for Combating Zionism. Eight Iraqi Jews established the league in 1945, after coordinating with the Iraqi Communist Party. The league organized demonstrations to express solidarity with the Palestinians, to call for social reforms, and to demand the removal of foreign troops from Iraq. Thousands of workers and students took to the streets and headed towards the British embassy. The police opened fire on us, and an Iraqi Jew, Sha'ul Tweig, died.

Despite her young age, Eileen found the message of the League for Combating Zionism appealing, since it perceived Zionism as the enemy of Arabs and Jews, and it distinguished between Judaism and Zionism. Moreover, Eileen thought that the demonstrations in 1946 emphasized Jewish-Muslim solidarity, opened up a space of camaraderie among Iraqis from different backgrounds, and reiterated the demands of the national movement, which emphasized equality among people from different religious backgrounds. More importantly, the demonstrations gave Eileen the sense that she was an Iraqi and that she belonged to Iraq. In 1948, Eileen participated in the Wathba against the new Iraqi-Anglo treaty to demand social justice and the end of colonial rule. Like other Iraqis who took part in the protest, Eileen perceived the Wathba as a revolutionary moment that promised equality and independence through the struggle of the people and as an event that enabled her to assert belonging to Iraq through political activism. However, the hopes Eileen felt upon participating in these demonstrations were short-lived, as the establishment of the state of Israel shortly afterward cast its shadow over the Jewish community in Iraq:

> When the state of Israel was established, there was an anti-Jewish campaign in Iraq. The government began to agitate against the Jews. The first thing it did was to fire Jews from state institutions. Then it froze the assets of rich Jewish families. Then there was the case of a Jewish man who was executed in Basra. We began to be treated as Jews, not Iraqi citizens as we felt. The government tried to instill hatred against the Jews among people. But until today, Iraq is my country. I still feel I belong to it. This is the place where I grew up and I will never replace it. The government wanted to implant hatred in late 1948. No matter how much the conservative and Zionist forces in Iraq tried to incite Jews to emigrate, they failed because Jews were nationalists and attached to their patriotism at the time.

This state-sponsored anti-Jewish campaign impacted Eileen's family directly. In 1948, her two older sisters, along with their fiancés, were sentenced to prison for twenty years for their communist convictions, while her aunt was sentenced to five years and her thirteen-year-old brother was sentenced to seven years. By the end of 1948, Eileen's parents were worried that she would also get arrested and sent to prison for her political activism. To avoid this scenario, they smuggled her against her will to Israel via Iran.

Arriving in Israel was a shock to Eileen on many levels. In Israel, Iraqi Jews lived in segregated and poor areas with little control over decisions that impacted their lives and futures. In the early years after their arrival, Iraqi Jews and Jews from other Arab-majority countries lived like refugees: they had no property and assets, could not find jobs, could not feed themselves or their children, did not have access to water without help from the Israeli state, and did not have proper housing. The ruling elites in Israel were guided by national considerations and demographic concerns, rather than by the interests and desires of Iraqi Jews. Iraqi Jews, who were primarily part of an urban and educated community in Iraq, found themselves poor, voiceless, and disrespected. Arriving on her own in the late 1940s, Eileen experienced humiliating conditions in Israel:

> As soon as we landed, the Israeli authorities said, "These are Iraqis so we have to spray them with anti-lice spray." They sprayed us with DDT as if we were animals. They asked if I knew how to sleep on a bed. I lived in a tent for two years. The ground was so low that the tents flooded when it rained. They took pictures of the flooded tents and sent them to Jewish organizations abroad to collect donations. Total humiliation. Disrespect and abuse.
>
> During lectures, the educators told us that the state of Israel was a safe home for Jews, who were persecuted everywhere, and that there is no discrimination against Jews in the newly established state. I told them, "No discrimination? You treat us as Orientals who need cleaning." Once, I went to check out a kibbutz and saw a slogan in English: "Socialism, Equality, Justice, and Zionism." I asked them how they could reconcile equality with Zionism, which is a racist movement that serves the interests of Jews only with disregard to other people who lived there for centuries.

In Israel, Eileen asserted affinity with Palestinians as fellow Arabs who shared experiences of dispossession and displacement at the hands of Israel and Arab states. She also aimed to maintain Arab-Jewish solidarity and to shed light on the racial politics of the state of Israel, which perceived Arab Jews as racially inferior and associated them with the enemy:

> In Iraq, the government told us we are Jews and perceived us as Zionist sympathizers. In Israel, we became the enemy because we are Arabs. They thought we were inferior and called us blacks. But we always felt we are Iraqis.

This comment by Eileen exposes the racial politics and the premises of Zionism in Israel. However, Iraqi Jews were not merely bystanders in Israel. The communists among them, like Eileen, joined the Israeli Communist Party (MAKI), which critiqued state policies, included both Arabs and Jews among its members, and endorsed an international agenda based on class struggle and liberation of people from colonialism. As a non-Zionist party, MAKI did not see Hebrew as the only language in Israel and published pamphlets in different languages, including Arabic, to address issues concerning Middle Eastern Jews and Palestinians. MAKI appealed to Eileen because of its emphasis on Palestinian-Jewish solidarity. She joined the party shortly after she arrived in Israel. She participated in demonstrations against the status of Arab Jews and Palestinians in Israel, British and US support of Israel, and the tripartite aggression by France, the United Kingdom, and Israel on Egypt in 1956. Just like her political activism in Iraq, in Israel she wrote petitions, joined strikes and rallies, and educated people about the colonial project of the Israeli state. To Eileen, the struggle against colonial rule—whether it was European powers colonizing Iraq and other parts of the world or the Israeli state in Palestine—was one struggle that had regional, national, and international reach. Though Eileen felt excluded and alienated as an Israeli citizen because of her Arabness, she cultivated a form of belonging through engaging in liberation movements worldwide that spoke to her concerns and aspirations.

During the first two decades of her life in Israel, Eileen felt that she was an exile who was waiting to return to Iraq once the political circumstances changed. During our interviews, she dwelled on her yearning for Iraq and on the constant feeling of uprootedness from the land of her ancestors and heritage. Eileen was a long-distance nationalist who lived her life across borders and remained connected to Iraq despite her displacement.[55] Cultural continuity with Iraq was important to her not only for her own sake. She wanted her children to feel Iraqi and be connected to the homeland of their ancestors, and she insisted that her children learn Arabic at home and speak the Iraqi Jewish dialect with her. When her oldest son reached the age of military service, she sent him to study in France in order to avoid service in the Israeli Defense Forces and having to carry arms against Palestinians. She told me that she could not stand the idea that her children "would be trained to kill Arabs." In addition to concerns over her children serving in the army, Eileen realized that a return to Iraq was no longer possible after the Six-Day War in 1967 and after the second Ba'th coup in Iraq in 1968. The fact that the second Ba'th rule intensified the persecution of Jews who remained in Iraq closed the door for Eileen to return. Since she did not feel at home in Israel, she decided to migrate to Britain with her family. London appealed to her because the British capital was beginning to emerge as a diasporic center for Iraqis who had fled the Ba'th regime in the 1970s, including Iraqi Jews.

In London, Eileen immersed herself in the Iraqi social and political landscape. She joined the Iraqi Women's League, which was associated with the Iraqi Communist Party, to advocate for women's rights in Iraq and to draw attention to the suffering of communist Iraqi women who were persecuted under the Baʻth regime in the late 1970s. In the early 1990s, when more Iraqi refugees arrived in London and sought asylum in Britain in the aftermath of the Gulf War of 1991, Eileen became active in the Iraqi Forum, a London-based Iraqi organization dedicated to the welfare of the Iraqi community and the cultivation of an Iraqi cultural scene, to help Iraqi asylum seekers with their applications and with settling down in London. She translated for people, helped parents find schools for their children, and accompanied people to doctor's appointments. When the United States and Britain exerted pressure on the United Nations to keep the sanctions imposed on Iraq, Eileen participated in campaigns to send medicine to Iraq and to shed light on the devastating impacts of the sanctions on ordinary people. She also became active in the antiwar mobilization in 2003. Eileen believed that another war, motivated by US interests in the Middle East, would compound the suffering of the Iraqi people and would bring Iraq back under imperialism.

While these political networks in exile enabled Eileen to cultivate membership in the Iraqi community and to perform Iraqi citizenship through political activism, they also became conduits to build friendships with the Iraqi community in London in general. Eileen's house was always busy with Iraqis from all over the world. These friendships enabled her to reminisce with fellow Iraqis about the past, discuss the status quo in Iraq, and create a community of care. During our interviews, Eileen emphasized that she always felt at home when she was around Iraqis. Since return was no longer possible, the cultivation of a sense of belonging was performed through daily acts of speaking the Iraqi dialect, cooking Iraqi and Iraqi Jewish food for Iraqi friends, and engaging in political activism that aimed to draw attention to plight of Iraqis in Iraq. Moreover, the busy social life Eileen enjoyed in London allowed her to carve out an Arab Jewish identity again. Eileen found that Iraqis in London celebrated her Arab Jewishness and perceived her as a fellow Iraqi who had dedicated her life to the welfare of Iraqis.

The question of Iraqi citizenship surfaced again for Eileen in 2003, after the fall of Saddam Hussein's regime. In 2005, the Iraqi government held a parliamentary election. It gave Iraqis abroad the right to vote as long as they or their parents held an Iraqi identity card or Certificate of Citizenship. This stipulation meant that Iraqi Jews who were denaturalized in 1950 and their children could take part in the election. Eileen was elated by the election law, and she and her children went to the Iraqi embassy in London to cast their votes for candidates from the Iraqi Communist Party. Eileen shared with me her happiness at the fact that the Iraqi government finally recognized Iraqi Jews as citizens: "I was very happy. Someone at the embassy told me that I looked like a mother on her son's wedding day. This was the first time the Iraqi government recognized my identity, recognized my Iraqi citizenship. It was a big deal for me, and I cried a lot because of happiness. I also took my children to vote since their parents were Iraqis." To Eileen, the fact that she could vote on the basis of her Iraqi identity card meant the Iraqi state finally acknowledged that Iraqi Jews were still Iraqi citizens despite denaturalization and deportation. The election law conferred legal status upon them, at long last.

Eileen hoped that the election law would be the first step to regaining Iraqi citizenship. However, in 2006, the Iraqi government issued a new Iraqi Nationality Law, which came as a shock to Eileen. The law exempted Iraqi Jews from the right to regain their citizenship and assets. The new citizenship law pained Eileen, since it upheld the exclusion of Jews from the Iraqi state. She remarked that "I was very happy with the election law, and had high expectations.... Then came the Iraqi Nationality Law of 2006. I felt stripped of my Iraqi citizenship all over again."

Eileen passed away in 2014, at the age of seventy-eight. The Iraqi Forum in London published an obituary that emphasized her political role and dedication to Iraq, and the Iraqi Communist Party and the Iraqi Women's League in London held a memorial for her. The big hall in which the memorial was held was full of Iraqis and Arabs. Delegates from the Iraqi Communist Party, the Tudeh (Communist) Party of Iran, the Palestinian People's Party, the Sudanese Communist Party, the Iraqi Women's League, and the Iraqi Forum delivered eulogies to celebrate her as a fellow Iraqi and Arab who had contributed tremendously to national and regional causes and who had devoted her life to anticolonial struggle. They also remarked on her love and nostalgia for her homeland—Iraq—and her feminist stands. In her death, fellow Iraqis and Arabs recognized and celebrated her as a citizen of Iraq, even if the state no longer did.

Revisiting the Past, Reimagining the Future

The reminiscences by Iraqi Jews in these memoirs and interviews aimed to provide a corrective to Western and Israeli portrayal of Arab Jews' history in the region as one based on oppression and exclusion. Avi Shlaim's *Three Worlds* (2023) is a recent addition to the plethora of scholarly and autobiographical works that Iraqi Jews have produced over the past seven decades.

What is notable about this recent memoir is that Shlaim revisits the past in order to imagine an alternative future. As an Iraq-born professional historian of the Arab-Israeli conflict, Shlaim situates his personal story as a child of expelled Iraqi Jewish parents within a larger narrative about the modern history of the Middle East.[56] While serving as a tribute to his parents' lives in Baghdad, this memoir mobilizes a right to reclaim that is forward-looking. The majority of earlier writing and scholarship on Iraqi Jews engaged with the past as a means to challenge simplistic portrayals of the history of Iraqi Jews. Shlaim, however, approaches this vanished past to offer a hopeful note for the situation in Israel/Palestine. On the one hand, Shlaim rereads the past in order to delink Arabness from Arab nationalism and rethink it as a shared identity. Moreover, he wades into the seven-decade-old debates about the culprits behind the bombing of five Jewish institutions in Baghdad and provides new evidence that implicates Zionist emissaries in the bombings in order to scare the majority of Iraqi Jews and force them to migrate to Israel. Shlaim maintains that Zionist emissaries did not hesitate to use any means to facilitate the expulsion of Jews from Iraq. On the other hand, Shlaim perceives the vibrant social and political circles that Iraqi Jews inhabited in Iraq as a blueprint to imagine a just future in Israel/Palestine.

Shlaim opens his memoir poetically by stating that he endeavors to "reanimate a unique Jewish civilisation of the Near East which was blown away in the first half of the twentieth century by the unforgiving winds of nationalism."[57] The advent of Arab and Jewish nationalism meant that Shlaim's family belonged "to a branch of the global Jewish community that is now almost extinct. We were Arab-Jews. We lived in Baghdad and we were well-integrated into Iraqi society. We spoke Arabic at home, our social customs were Arab, our lifestyle was Arab, our cuisine was exquisitely Middle Eastern and my parents' music was an attractive blend of Arabic and Jewish."[58] Challenging the conflation between a cultural identity and a political ideology, Shlaim disengages being Arab from pan-Arabism as a nationalist dogma and redefines it as "a shared cultural heritage and language."[59] The characterization of Arabness as an inclusive and shared marker of identity was concomitant with the rejection of Zionism as a European movement in its cultural and geopolitical outlook by the majority of Iraqi Jews.[60] By emphasizing the rootedness of Iraqi Jews in Iraq and their indifference to Zionism, Shlaim maintains that "Iraq was a land of pluralism and coexistence" and that Iraqi Jews had "much more in common, linguistically and culturally, with our Iraqi compatriots than our

European co-religionists."⁶¹ Like other Iraqi Jewish writers, Shlaim reiterates that Babylon emerged as a "spiritual centre" for the Jewish diaspora and as the site where the Babylonian Talmud was written.

Shlaim offers this history of his community as a corrective to Samuel Huntington's notion of the "clash of civilizations" and the Zionist discourse on Arabs and Jews as mortal enemies.⁶² These discourses, predicated upon the idea that anti-Semitism is endemic to Arab-majority countries and Islam, mobilizes a culturalist interpretation to understand a modern political conflict. To Shlaim, the Middle East, unlike Europe, where Jews were not perceived or treated as equal citizens, did not have what is known as "the Jewish question."⁶³ Iraqi Jews did not live in ghettos or endure systemic persecution despite tensions, such as the pogrom in 1941. Ultimately, the political and social landscapes Iraqi Jews inhabited in Iraq along with fellow Iraqis did not come to an end because of "a clash of cultural or religious intolerance."⁶⁴ Rather, Shlaim argues that "the driver of our displacement was political, not religious or cultural. We became entangled in the conflict between Zionism and Arab nationalism, two rival secular ideologies. We were also caught in the crossfire of the conflict between Jews and Arabs over Palestine."⁶⁵ Quoting Edward Said, Shlaim argues that "Europe's nineteenth-century Jewish question became the twentieth-century Palestinian question."⁶⁶ In addition, the author reminds readers that Zionist leaders focused their efforts on the Jewish population in Europe until World War II, since Jews of the Middle East were seen as "inferior 'human material.'"⁶⁷ It was only in the aftermath of the Holocaust that Zionist leaders began to think of Jews of the Middle East as potential citizens in a Jewish state. As such, "the Jews of the Middle East became for the first time a vital element in the Zionist project of building a sustainable Jewish majority state in Palestine."⁶⁸ However, Israeli officials endorsed an Orientalist and racialized narrative toward Jews from the region. Here, Shlaim reiterates Ella Shohat's description of Jews from the Middle East as Zionism's "Jewish victims" and contends that "Palestinians are the main victims of the Zionist project. . . . Palestine was wiped off the map. But there was another category of victims, less well known and much less talked about: the Jews of the Arab lands. The twin currents of Arab nationalism and Zionism made it impossible for Jews and Muslims to continue to coexist peacefully in the Arab world after the birth of Israel."⁶⁹ Just as the establishment of the state of Israel led to the displacement of Palestinians, it also brought about the dispossession of Jews in Arab-majority countries at the hands of Arab politicians, but also at the hands of Zionist leaders and later at the hands of Israeli lawmakers.

Three Worlds offers a condemnation of the role Zionist emissaries played in pushing Iraqi Jews to migrate. As a historian, Shlaim approaches his memoir as an opportunity to revisit one of the most controversial episodes in the exodus of Iraqi Jews from Iraq: the bombing of five Jewish institutions in Baghdad in 1950 and 1951, including the bombing of the Mas'uda Shemtove Synagogue, which killed five people. Historians have debated for almost seven decades about the identities of the culprits. While the Iraqi nationalist press accused members of the Jewish community of orchestrating the bombings, Israel denied that Zionists could have been behind them.[70] In her book on Iraqi Jews, Orit Bashkin remarks that "again, there seems to be more circumstantial evidence that suggests Zionist involvement, but I do not think historians can provide a decisive answer at this point."[71] In the chapter titled "Baghdad Bombshell," Shlaim wades into this controversy and puts on the hat of a detective-historian who has been engrossed in this question for decades. He meticulously and suspensefully builds his case by interviewing one key witness and corroborating documents incriminating the Zionist underground movement.[72]

The story of the bombings has personal and professional significance for Shlaim. As a child of deported Iraqi Jewish parents, the accounts that he heard from his relatives who believed the Zionist underground was behind the bombing left Shlaim feeling distressed and disempowered "to think that fellow Jews might have played a part in uprooting us from our homeland." As a professional historian, the story was part of his "lifelong search for the truth of the matter."[73] Reflecting on his research and findings, Shlaim concludes that

> my correspondence with Shamil Abdul Qadir was the last stage in my quest for the truth. He left no room for doubt that the police report given to me by Yaacov Karkouli was genuine. Just the extract I have from this longer report is a serious indictment of the Zionist activists and of the methods they employed to achieve their ends, such as the payment of bribes and the forging of documents. But the most serious charge contained in the report is that Israel's emissaries turned their local Jewish followers into terrorists.[74]

Shlaim reads the role Zionist emissaries played in displacing and dispossessing Iraqi Jews as "the most shocking example" of what he calls "Cruel Zionism" that "I have encountered in my fifty years of scholarly meandering around the highways and byways of the Arab-Israeli conflict."[75] As one of Israel's new historians who challenged Israeli official history about 1948, in particular the expulsion of Palestinians, Shlaim declares that "Zionism not only turned the Palestinians into refugees; it turned Jews of the East into strangers in their own land. In 1947–1949 it was not only the land of Palestine that was partitioned but also the past. The common past of Jews and Muslims in Iraq was superseded by the new reality of the Arab-Israeli conflict."[76]

Informed by his family's fond memories about their lives in Iraq, Shlaim ends his book with brief but poignant reflections on the past. On the one hand, *Three Worlds* dismantles the Zionist discourse that Jews and Arabs "are exclusive and antagonistic ethnic categories."[77] In this framework, Zionism, as a European movement led by European Jews in order to establish a homeland for European Jews, not only "undermined the hybrid figure of the Arab-Jew" but also "deepened the divisions between Israelis and Palestinians, between Israel and the Middle East, between Judaism and Islam, between Hebrew and Arabic." To Shlaim, this rupture also entailed the erasure of "our common past, our intertwined histories and our centuries-old heritage of pluralism, religious tolerance, cosmopolitanism and co-existence."[78] On the other hand, the revisionist history Shlaim narrates is not meant to reminisce about the past nostalgically. While that past cannot be reproduced or rebuilt, it "can help us to envisage a better future." Shlaim ends his memoir by writing that "nationalism all but destroyed the identity of the Arab-Jew but perhaps it has left just enough of a remnant to warrant a little optimism about the future. One thing is certain: without reviving or reimagining the kind of religious tolerance and civilized dialogue between Jews and Arabs that prevailed in Iraq before the emergence of the State of Israel, we will not be able to move beyond today's impasse."[79] The right to reclaim in this book is predicated upon revisiting the past in order to imagine an optimistic future.

Conclusion

Through different literary and scholarly works, Iraqi Jews have reclaimed Iraq as their ancestral homeland and critiqued the misrecognition of identities and misrepresentation of history. While some Iraqi Jewish writers have reclaimed the past through narratives about shared aspirations about the future and solidarity with fellow Iraqis, others have juxtaposed the uprootedness of their community within the larger context of the loss of Palestine and the establishment of Israel and read the dispossession of Palestinians and Jews from Arab-majority countries as the product of the same historical processes brought about by the rise of Zionism, European anti-Semitism and the Holocaust, and the establishment of the state of Israel.[80] Reflecting a vanished, misrepresented, and silenced past, Ella Shohat succinctly summarizes the intertwined fate of Palestinians and Jews in the Middle when she argues that "the same historical process that dispossessed Palestinians of their property, lands, and national-political rights was linked to the dispossession of Middle Eastern and North African Jews of their property, land, and rootedness in Muslim countries."[81] Rather than a promised land, the state of Israel becomes a site of exile for Iraqi Jews and endangers a reversal of the biblical yearning for Zion. That yearning was replaced by a nostalgia for Iraq, whereby the biblical verse became "By the waters of Zion, where we sat down, and there we wept, when we remembered Babylon."[82]

THREE

THE LEGAL CONSTRUCTION OF *TABA'IYYA*

IN 1980, ON THE eve of the Iran-Iraq War, Saddam Hussein's regime waged a large-scale expulsion campaign against the so-called Iraqis of Iranian origin, or *taba'iyya iraniyya* (often referred to as *taba'iyya*). These Iraqis were mainly Shi'i Arabs and Shi'i Kurds whose families held Persian nationality under the Ottomans in order to avoid serving in the Ottoman army or paying taxes. The Iraqi government came to see them as a threat, especially with the rise of the Shi'i ulema-led religious opposition in the late 1970s and the 1979 Islamic Revolution in Iran.[1] The designation of some Iraqis as *taba'iyya* rendered two million citizens, or about 15 percent of the population, suspect and therefore vulnerable.[2] Thousands of families were stripped of their citizenship and violently expelled. For instance, Hussein's regime held families in prisons and prison camps for months before abandoning them on the border with Iran. In addition to confiscating their property and documents, the regime enacted laws that inflicted unspeakable horrors upon deported families, such as the detention of young men between the ages of 18 and 28, monetary incentives for non-*taba'iyya* husbands to divorce their *taba'iyya* wives, and sexual assault. Those who did not manage to flee the country came under pressure to collaborate with the regime.

This campaign of expulsion was not simply an arbitrary measure of an oppressive regime. Rather, the legislation authorizing the *taba'iyya*'s denaturalization in 1980 was an adaptation of the first Iraqi Nationality Law (1924) that Iraqi authorities had drafted and approved. The 1924 law undermined the notion of equal citizenship when it categorized Iraqi citizens on the basis of the citizenship they had held under Ottoman rule—namely, whether they were Ottoman or Persian citizens. In addition, this law was rooted in the question of "Persians" in Iraq. During the early days of the modern state of Iraq, the presence of Persians preoccupied British and Iraqi officials. For them, these Persians, often Shi'a of Arab descent, threatened their rule by demanding political independence and the end of the British Mandate. In short, the citizenship of *taba'iyya* speaks to the entanglement of empire, the project of state-building, decisions made by residents of Ottoman Iraq prior to the establishment of the modern state of Iraq in 1921, and political activism. The afterlives of laws made in the late nineteenth and early twentieth centuries became apparent under Hussein's regime when *taba'iyya* were depicted as a fifth column whose loyalty lay with Iran.

The first Iraqi Nationality Law and its various amendments shed light on the right to uproot and the institutionalization of difference in Iraq. This chapter focuses on how this law constituted examples of the legal constructions of citizenship and the production of Otherness. While the Iraqi Nationality Law of 1924 considered someone like King Faysal, who hailed from Mecca, to be an Iraqi citizen, it defined inhabitants who held Persian nationality as second-class citizens. In addition, the law and its amendments bring to light the haunted origins of Arab nationalism. The majority Iraqi ruling elites who assumed power under the modern state of Iraq embraced Arab nationalism and perceived Iraq as part of a greater Arab nation. However, a close reading of the Iraqi Nationality Law of 1924 ruled that an extant Ottoman nationality indubitably conferred Iraqi citizenship upon the holder. Ironically, under Saddam Hussein's regime, Ottoman subjecthood served as a guarantee of Iraqi and Arab national authenticity and loyalty. Though Iraqi officials perceived their political projects as breaking with the colonial past, they nonetheless reproduced colonial practices as the British and Ottoman legacies persisted in the postcolonial state. Under the Ba'th regime, "an authentic Iraqi" was someone whose ancestors had held Ottoman nationality, while a *taba'iyya* or an "inauthentic" Iraqi was someone whose ancestors had held Persian nationality.

This chapter offers a genealogy of the Iraqi Nationality Law of 1924 over a period of six decades. While British and Iraqi officials drafted this law as an attempt to contain a few ulemas' power, the law was reconfigured in a sinister way that engendered mass expulsion less than sixty years later. British anxieties about the political power of the ulemas and the exclusionary force of Arab nationalism together shaped this law and its implementation. The little-studied first Iraqi Nationality Law of 1924 is a primary site where colonial, national, and local discourses and practices worked to consolidate the state's right to uproot.[3] The first part of the chapter discusses the emergence of citizenship under the Ottomans as a new form of governance. The second part focuses on the legal intricacies of the Iraqi Nationality Law of 1924 and the political debates about Persian and Ottoman nationality under the modern state of Iraq. The third part examines the reinterpretation of the Iraqi Nationality Law of 1924 under the Ba'th regime, which resulted in the denaturalization of *taba'iyya* and the Ottomanization of Iraqi citizenship.

Citizenship in Ottoman Iraq

Though the Ottomans conquered the three provinces of Baghdad, Basra, and Mosul during the first half of the sixteenth century, Ottoman Iraq did not come under the control of the central government until the early nineteenth century. Following the growing threats from European countries, the "reconquest" of Iraq in 1831 reflected the Ottoman government's efforts to control outlying regions and consolidate power in the hands of Sultan Mahmud II (1808–1839).[4] The integration of Ottoman Iraq into the Porte's administrative system followed another less-obvious historical process: the migration of tribes from Arabia to Iraq and their slow conversion to Shi'ism beginning in the late eighteenth century.[5] Yitzhak Nakash argues that "Iraq's tribal map took its final shape" between 1791 and 1805, after the Wahhabis forced tribes from Arabia to Iraq. It was from these confederations "that the bulk of Iraq's Shi'i population was drawn."[6] This movement coincided with the conversion of Iraq's native tribal confederations to Shi'ism, which accelerated during the nineteenth century.[7] Several factors accounted for the rapid conversion of the tribes. These included the Wahhabi attacks on the Shi'i holy cities of Najaf and Karbala and the emergence of these cities as major market centers. Another important factor was the construction of the Hindiyya canal, which changed the Euphrates's flow, increased the fertile areas around the two holy cities, and dried up the established agricultural and commercial centers.[8] The proximity of the tribes to Najaf and Karbala enabled the Shi'i ulemas to intensify their missionary activities. According to Nakash, a major factor contributing to the conversion of both native and newly arrived tribes was the Ottoman policy of tribal settlement initiated shortly after asserting direct control in 1831.[9]

Tribal conversions to Shi'ism were an unintended consequence of this Ottoman policy. The Ottoman government perceived settlement as a way to subordinate the tribes, break their authority, and increase tax revenue and agricultural production.[10] The settlement policy, however, induced a breakdown of the tribal system and caused a crisis for the settled tribes. Conversion became a means for the tribes to "gain a new start and to rearrange their religious and social identity."[11] The spread of Shi'ism among the tribes intensified the Ottomans' anxiety over their Shi'i population in Ottoman Iraq and the influence of Persia in the country. The three provinces of Basra, Baghdad, and Mosul had been caught up in the imperial Ottoman-Persian rivalry since the sixteenth century. With the conversion of Safavid Persia to Shi'ism and the Ottoman control of Shi'i holy places in Iraq, this imperial struggle was also configured as a Sunni-Shi'i conflict.[12] A powerful Persia did not merely pose a territorial threat to the Ottoman Empire. It also brought into question both the legitimacy of the Ottoman sultan as the leader of all Muslims and the loyalty of the Shi'i population in the Ottoman Empire.

High Ottoman religious clerics issued fatwas supporting wars with Persia as well as the repression of the Shi'i population, whom they described as heretics who deserved to be killed.[13] Some of these fatwas even forbade marriages between Sunni women and Shi'i men.[14] Karen Kern argues that the prohibition of such marriages, which did not have any basis in Islamic law, shows that "domestic and geopolitical concerns" drove religious and state authorities.[15] Following a border conflict between the two imperial powers in the nineteenth century, this prohibition was emphatically reinstated. Sultan Mahmud II issued the "Supreme Mandate Concerning the Prohibition of Marriage with Iranians of 5 January 1822."[16] Couched in the traditional rhetoric of the sultan as the legitimate leader of the faithful, the mandate prohibited the marriage of Sunni women to Shi'a, Persians, heretics, people of ignorance, and people of unknown lineages.[17] It also dictated that it was incumbent upon religious clerics and the guardians of women to carry out this prohibition.[18] The increased rate of Sunni conversion to Shi'ism in Ottoman Iraq at the time further increased the government's anxiety and made the prohibition of Sunni-Shi'i marriages a more pressing issue.

This history was the background for the enactment of the Ottoman Nationality Law on January 3, 1869. This law introduced a notion of equal citizenship among all people in the Ottoman Empire, regardless of faith. Rather than religion, residence and birth became the criteria for rights and political affiliation.[19] The law specified the criteria for Ottoman citizenship (on the basis of paternal lineage and residence), the acquisition of foreign nationality, and the loss of Ottoman nationality.[20] Part of the centralizing policies of the Tanzimat reforms, the law ostensibly applied equality and universal rights and obligations to the ethnically and religiously diverse inhabitants of the empire.[21] The intent of the law, however, was to govern and control the state and society more efficiently and comprehensively under the veneer of universal conscription, civil equality, and educational and judicial reforms.[22] As such, the purpose of the law was to define who was a foreigner and who was a national subject, definitions that were crucial to the application of a universal conscription law and a better system of tax collection. Kern says the law was the "most definitive statement of Ottoman nationality . . . as well the clearest declaration about who would be included in Ottoman citizenship."[23] The notion of equal citizenship was linked to Ottoman officials' anxiety over the legitimacy of their rule as well as the loyalty of their subjects, particularly with the spread of nationalist and independence movements in the Balkans.

Ottoman officials, however, would make one exception to the 1869 Nationality Law, which was based on the Napoleonic Code. The law stated a woman marrying a non-Ottoman man would lose her Ottoman nationality and acquire the nationality of her husband. Five years later, in October 1874, the Porte passed the "Law Protecting the Prohibition of Marriage between Iranians and Ottoman Citizens." The first article upheld the prohibition of marriage between Ottoman and Iranian subjects "as in olden times"[24] and reaffirmed the duty of religious clerics to enforce this prohibition. It also decreed that if such a marriage took place, the woman and her children would remain Ottoman subjects "and liable for conscription, military tax, and all other financial obligations."[25] Alarmed by the accelerating rate of conversion to Shi'ism among inhabitants of Iraq, Ottoman officials feared that these marriages would increase the number of Shi'a in Iraq and that more Persian subjects would own land in Iraq.[26] Thus the law was imbricated in imperial rivalry and the juridical institutionalization of Sunni-Shi'i separateness.

The First Iraqi Nationality Law of 1924

During Ottoman reign (1501–1918), inhabitants of Ottoman Iraq were either Ottoman or Persian subjects. Some Shi'a acquired Persian nationality to avoid Ottoman military service and taxes. The Persian government granted these subjects citizenship in exchange for information on Ottoman affairs and the containment of Ottoman control. The British conquest of Iraq at the start of World War I and the disintegration the Ottoman Empire following the war shifted the political landscape of the country drastically. The period between the British occupation of Basra in November 1914 and the final agreement to install Faysal as the monarch in August 1921 was significant. It was characterized by a bitter conflict within the British administration between the Indian school that advocated direct rule and the Egyptian school that embraced the Arab cause and indirect rule. British promises of independence to Arabs in return for fighting against the Ottoman army during World War I and the rise of independence movements in Iraq further complicated this state of affairs. The position of the Egyptian school ultimately prevailed, and Iraq became an Arab kingdom under the British Mandate. In return for his role in the Arab revolt, the British installed Faysal as king and the defected Ottoman officers who joined him as the new state's ruling class. Two major factors led to the dominance of the Egyptian school's vision. First, President Woodrow Wilson's Fourteen Points—in particular, point 12, regarding "autonomous development" of the countries once under Ottoman rule—put an end to the old imperial policy of direct rule. Second, the outbreak of a massive revolt led by tribesmen and supported by Shi'i ulemas in 1920 exerted enormous pressure on the British to establish national rule in 1921.

The Iraq Nationality Law of 1924 and accompanying regulations of 1926 regarding the Iraqi Certificate of Citizenship as well as the acceptance or rejection of Iraqi nationality provide insights into the politics of inclusion and exclusion in this nascent nation. This law, approved by King Faysal, the prime minister, and the ministers of the interior and justice, is a combination of the articles on nationality detailed in the Treaty of Lausanne and the Ottoman Nationality Law of 1869. Though there is no direct reference to the latter in the law, the first Iraqi constitution of 1925, drafted by British officials, specifies that all laws of the modern state of Iraq would be based on Ottoman laws unless otherwise indicated.[27] In addition to the rules of paternal descent and residence specified in the Law of Ottoman Nationality, the Iraqi Nationality Law of 1924, in its inclusion of the articles of the Treaty of Lausanne, cited Ottoman nationality and habitual residence as the criteria for acquiring Iraqi nationality. The Iraq Nationality Law is more detailed than its Ottoman counterpart and consists of a preamble and four parts: Iraq Citizenship, Naturalization, Loss of Iraq Nationality, and National Status of Married Women and Minor Children.[28]

The first point on the acquisition of Iraqi nationality, based on Article 30 of the Treaty of Lausanne, states: "All persons who on the sixth day of August,

1924, were Ottoman subjects and were habitually resident in Iraq are hereby declared to have ceased to be Ottoman subjects and to have acquired Iraq nationality on that date." At first glance, this article appears to be a simple application of Article 30 in that Turkish subjects habitually resident in Iraq became Iraqi nationals. But the definition of the term "habitually resident" is significant. According to the definition in the Preamble, the category of habitual resident includes "every person who has had his usual place of residence in Iraq since the twenty-third day of August, 1921." This definition ties habitual residence to a specific date and raises questions: Why was habitual residence linked to this date in the fairly recent past? Why was there a need to set a date at all?

A 1929 British document on the Iraqi Nationality Law includes a discussion of its application and of the need to ensure that Lebanese and Syrian nationals did not acquire Iraqi nationality under the law. British officials bring up the selection of this date many times in the document. In an aside, they dismiss it as an arbitrary choice.[29] None mention that Faysal was crowned as king of Iraq on August 23, 1921. British officials could have argued that a habitual resident was any person living in Iraq on the day the country became a kingdom. Yet the only reference to a connection between Faysal's accession to the throne and the criterion for habitual residence is found in Charles A. Hooper's *The Constitutional Law of Iraq*.[30] Hooper, president of a Court of First Instance in Iraq at the time, stated that the Iraqi Nationality Law "fix[es]" the date of Faysal's assumption of power as the criterion for habitual residence, but he also dismissed this "fixing" as "incidental."[31] Indeed, it is hard to ignore the historiographical silence on this date, especially in light of the non-Iraqi origin of King Faysal, who arrived in Iraq just two months before his accession. By marking the date of "habitual residence" as August 23, 1921, this law integrated Faysal and the Ottoman officials from Arab provinces who joined him as historically rooted in the nascent nation-state.

If the application of the articles of the Treaty of Lausanne seems straightforward, with the exception of the definition of habitual residence, the appropriation of the Law of Ottoman Nationality is more ambiguous. Articles 8 and 9 of the 1924 law centered on nationality conferred on the basis of birth and/or paternal descent. Article 8 consists of two clauses. The first clause, modeled on Article 1 of the 1869 Law of Ottoman Nationality, states: "The following persons shall be deemed to be Iraq nationals: (a) Any person wherever born, whose father was at the time of that person's birth an Iraq national, and was either born in Iraq or obtained his Iraq nationality by naturalization or by virtue of Articles 3, 4, or 5 hereof." This article constitutes paternal descent as grounds to acquire Iraqi citizenship by Iraqis who are foreign-born but whose fathers held Iraqi citizenship according to Article 30 of the Treaty of Lausanne. The second clause of Article 8 deals with the eligibility of people born in Iraq to acquire Iraqi nationality. It maintains that an Iraqi national is "any person born in Iraq who has attained his majority and whose father was born in Iraq and was at the time of that person's birth ordinarily resident in Iraq." This clause is puzzling in that the legal status of the father is not mentioned. If the father is an alien, then he should fall under Article 9, which tackles naturalization. Article 9, based on Article 2 of the Law of Ottoman Nationality, asserts: "Any person born in Iraq whose father is an alien may within one year after attaining his majority, state by declaration . . . his desire to become an Iraq national." Article 9 makes clause (b) of Article 8 redundant and raises questions about its purpose.

On the surface, the redundancy and ambiguity of Article 8(b) appear unproblematic, since all the inhabitants of Iraq, regardless of previous status, are considered to be Iraqi nationals. The interpretation of Article 8(b), however, is situated in the question of differential inclusion in the nation. It distinguishes between Iraqis on the basis of the nationality held under the Ottomans. In essence, clause (b) refers to inhabitants whose fathers held Persian nationality. The eligibility of a person born in Iraq whose father was a Persian national to acquire Iraqi nationality is thus contingent upon double birth, of the person and the person's father inside Iraq. Examined from this angle, Article 8(b) and Article 9 define two different groups—namely, aliens and inhabitants who held Persian nationality.

This differential categorization in the Iraqi Nationality Law found its application in the guidelines issued in 1926 by the Office of the Under-Secretary of State for Foreign Affairs.[32] These instructions consist of application forms for an Iraqi passport and Iraqi Certificate of Citizenship. The rules of the Iraqi Certificate of Citizenship, which is an identification document, state that a person who became an Iraqi national under Articles 3 and 8 and was willing to acquire the nationality certificate could do so by filling out Form 3(a), titled "Declaration to Be Made by Applicant for a Certificate of Iraqian Nationality." The first item in this form asks for the article in the Iraqi Nationality Law under which the applicant acquired Iraqi citizenship. The applicant had to specify whether it was Article 3, Article 8(a), or Article 8(b).[33] Moreover, these different categories were indicated by the letter following the number of the Iraqi Certificate of Citizenship. The letter C (or *jim* in Arabic) referred to the acquisition of nationality under Articles 3 and 8(a). In other words, the letter C signified that this person or his ancestors held Ottoman citizenship under the Ottomans. The letter B, by contrast, signaled that a person was granted Iraqi citizenship under Article 8(b)—namely, the person and/or his father held the Persian citizenship. Not only did this system of classification instate unequal citizenship, but it also institutionalized difference by meting out differential legal statuses. Since children inherited the letter on their father's Iraqi Certificate of Citizenship, this law and its applications set the grounds for future discrimination.

A close reading of the Iraqi Nationality Law, in the absence of documents on its drafting, reveals a great deal about the politics of exclusion. The purpose of the Iraqi Nationality Law was not merely to identify outsiders and noncitizens but also, and more importantly, to define which inhabitants "belonged" to the nation, based on the Arab-nationalist imaginings of Iraqi statesmen. If Article 3 and the definition of habitual residence aimed to deem King Faysal legally equal to the rest of the inhabitants of Iraq, Article 8(b) assigned an inferior legal status to a portion of the population that held Persian nationality.

Indeed, the new Iraqi ruling elites' attempts to define Iraqiness and Arabness were a source of controversy at the time. A year prior to the law's enactment, British officials deported Shaykh Mahdi al-Khalisi to Persia for his opposition to the Anglo-Iraqi Treaty of 1922. The treaty did not differ in essence from the Mandate and did not grant Iraq complete independence. Many Iraqi statesmen and nationalists opposed it.[34] It was the Shi'i ulemas, however, who brought the situation to a standstill by issuing a fatwa against both the treaty and participating in the election of the first Constituent Assembly that was to ratify it. Khalisi was from an established Arab family that had acquired Persian nationality to avoid Ottoman military service.[35] He and other prominent ulemas were banished "on the basis of a decree that invested the government with the power to deport 'aliens' for political offences, although the principal men of religion involved were Arabs and not Persians."[36] None other than King Faysal signed the decree, which was met with dissent and opposition. Faysal's own origins and "foreignness" became a source of debate. A petition signed by four hundred figures bitingly stated, "If the King pretends that the ulema are 'aliens,' then this epithet must be applied also to him because he is a Hijazi by origin and his Prime Minister—'Abd-ul-Muhsin as-Sa'dun—

although a Muntafiqi [from the Muntafaq region in Iraq] is a Hijazi.... Moreover, all the King's suite are aliens."³⁷

A close reading of archival documents show that the purpose of this law was in part to assimilate and include Persian subjects. British and Iraqi officials did not savor the fact that there were Persian consular officers in many Iraqi towns and cities, and they were intent on weakening Persian influence in Iraq. The law was one of many similar measures that the Iraqi government implemented in an attempt to terminate the privileges granted to Persian nationals under the Ottomans.³⁸ Yitzhak Nakash argues, "Under this law, Persians were automatically considered Iraqi nationals unless they themselves renounced it by a fixed date, which was extended twice until it was set for January 1928."³⁹ The Persian government condemned the law on the grounds that it would turn Persians in Iraq into Iraqi citizens, since they did not have the time to comprehend its consequences. But the Iraqi government was successful in its efforts. The number of people designated Persians dwindled under monarchical rule; most either left Iraq or took on Iraqi nationality.⁴⁰ As such, the Iraqi Nationality Law of 1924 was a means of including those holding Persian nationality, rather than excluding them. The law's intention to include subjects under monarchical rule is best evidenced by the fact that it was not used to deport any Shi'i ulemas. The banishment of Shaykh Mahdi al-Khalisi and other ulemas took place before the law's enactment in 1924. The issue at stake was the nature of this inclusion. Through the assignment of different letters to indicate the article in the nationality law under which a person acquired Iraqi nationality, the Iraqi Certificate of Citizenship set and institutionalized a legal distinction with devastating implications in the future.

This differential inclusion and the position of subjects holding Persian nationality became an instrument of both British colonial and Iraqi national governmentality. The early years of British rule were characterized by anxiety over the influence of the Shi'i ulemas over the Shi'i population. The power that the ulemas wielded became clear in their role instigating and leading the tribes during the 1920 revolt. Realizing the challenge the Shi'i ulemas could pose to their interests, British officials were determined to weaken their influence. The fact that most of the ulemas were not in fact Ottoman nationals was the justification for their exclusion from decision-making. British officials in Iraq saw them as "aliens, Persians, who owed neither loyalty nor commitment to Iraq."⁴¹ As Toby Dodge argues, experiences in India and Orientalist understandings of Iraq deeply influenced British policy.⁴² British officials understood Iraqi society in terms of the rural/urban binary and ethnic and religious groups, and they perceived Islam in general and Shi'ism in particular as conservative and opposed to progress.[43] The citizenship law's differential inclusion of subjects holding Persian nationality was a means of curbing the influence of the "Persians." As such, the anxiety over the presence of Persians—most of whom were Arabs—in Iraq was rooted in the imperial struggle over power as well as the British officials' Orientalist views of Iraq.

Nationalist elites echoed British perceptions of the Persians. The new ruling class came to power with the support of the British, who were concerned with establishing a state in which their interests were protected.[44] This preoccupation led the British to rely on groups and individuals who would carry out their plans. The ex-Ottoman officers who joined Faysal during World War I, as well as the notables associated with Ottoman rule, emerged as the new ruling class. These elites aimed to consolidate their status and preserve their power. They were also largely acculturated in the Ottoman discourse on the Shi'a. When Civil Administrator Percy Cox suggested having a Shi'i minister in the new government, so as to preempt accusations of discrimination, he met with fierce opposition from the prime minister and other ministers.[45] As such, there was continuity between Ottoman and British rule in terms of laws and practices (such as the Iraqi Nationality Law and the underrepresentation of the Shi'a) as well as the constitution of the new ruling elites.

The Arab nationalist ideology that these new elites championed was couched in suspicion about the loyalty and origin of subjects holding Persian nationality.[46] Sati' al-Husri's memoirs of his early years at the Ministry of Education throw in relief the question of citizenship and national identity.[47] Al-Husri was an influential ideologue of Arab nationalism and an Ottoman Syrian-born former government official. He came to Iraq with King Faysal to establish a modern educational system and assumed the position of director at the Ministry of Education. The shifting boundaries of who is an Iraqi are powerfully illustrated by al-Husri's clash with the prominent Iraqi poet Muhammad al-Jawahiri, who held Persian nationality.[48] The details of this confrontation, which took place in 1927, would become iconic of al-Husri's opposition to the Shi'a and provide a glimpse of the highly contested contours and borders of the "Arab" at this moment in Iraqi history.

In a chapter in the first volume of his memoir, titled "Iranian Teachers Who Made Trouble," al-Husri stated that the minister of education,[49] in his inability to differentiate between Shi'i "Iranians" and Shi'i Iraqis, asked him to appoint al-Jawahiri as an Arabic teacher.[50] In his meeting with al-Jawahiri, who came from an Arab family, al-Husri first asked about his nationality. Al-Jawahiri, no stranger to provocation, said that he was "Iranian" and that he still had relatives in "Iran." Al-Husri refused his application, arguing that non-Iraqis could not be appointed. Al-Jawahiri retorted that Syrians and Lebanese had been appointed as teachers. To al-Husri's surprise, just a few days after their confrontation, al-Jawahiri applied for and acquired Iraqi nationality. During his first week on the job, al-Jawahiri published a poem ridiculing the corrupt Iraqi ruling class and expressing longing for "Persia." Al-Husri showed the poem to the famous Iraqi poet Ma'ruf al-Risafi, who told him that the poem smacked of *shu'ubiyya*.

The term *shu'ubiyya* originally referred to a literary movement under the Abbasids, which celebrated the cultural achievements of non-Arab Muslims and regarded the Arab literary tradition as unsophisticated.[51] In the Iraqi state's early days, the term gained currency and Iraqi officials used it to cast doubt on the Arabness of the Shi'a.[52] Al-Husri subsequently fired al-Jawahiri, which triggered a long correspondence between him and 'Abd al-Mahdi al-Muntafaqi, then minister of education. Al-Husri repeated al-Risafi's complaint about the poem's *shu'ubiyya* and argued that al-Jawahiri was not truly Iraqi and that he had acquired Iraqi nationality out of convenience. He went on to argue that education in Iraq had suffered because of "Iraq-born Persians." The minister affirmed al-Jawahiri's authenticity as an Iraqi; the poet's family had lived in Iraq for a century and a half, he argued. In his version of the encounter, al-Jawahiri sneered at al-Husri, remarking that he was a newcomer in Iraq who needed a translator because he was new to the Arabic language.[53]

This affair testifies to the question of contrasting visions of the nation, but it also reveals the intricacies of Iraqi citizenship. Al-Husri perceived Iraq as part of a larger Arab nation. The presence of Others—namely Jews, the Kurds, Assyrians, and Shi'is—threatened that nation. Although hiring Syrian and Lebanese teachers was not problematic for al-Husri, the employment of a native of Iraq raised fears. Al-Husri used *shu'ubiyya* as shorthand to express the fear of and the anxiety about the Others within. Rather than taking al-Jawahiri's biting critique of the Iraqi government and praise of "Persia's beauty" as the sarcastic political critique it was, al-Husri read it as a transparent sign of national treachery. The al-Jawahiri/al-Husri affair also sheds light on the active amnesia that nationalism necessitates. Al-Husri actively forgot that the inhabitants of Iraq had been either Ottoman or Persian subjects only a decade earlier and did not become Iraqi citizens until the passage of the Iraqi Nationality Law of 1924 and that he himself had acquired Iraqi nationality only recently. In this web of active forgetting, Ottoman nationality emerges as not only normative but also deeply intertwined in the definition of the Arab Iraqi national. While both Ottoman and Persian nationalities were "foreign" in the context of the emerging nation-state, elites like al-Husri nativized Ottoman nationality.

The Iraqi Nationality Law was one mechanism through which the modern state of Iraq constructed and reconstructed legal and social categories. This construction entailed destruction in that it severed subjectivities and identities from their complex and contingent political, historical, and social realities. Ethnic, linguistic, and religious affiliations thus became legal markers. Subjects who held Persian nationality and/or had familial and religious networks in Persia became "aliens." National elites, who were part of the Ottoman establishment, were Iraqis and Arabs. The Iraqi Nationality Law introduced a tiered citizenship system, which could be discerned in the two types of identification that Iraqis have held since 1930: the Identity Card and the Iraqi Certificate of Citizenship. The Identity Card contains only personal information: gender, date and place of birth, marital status, religion, occupation, and physical characteristics, including blood type, height, deformities, and color of skin, eyes, and hair. The Identity Card also states that a person is an Iraqi. The Iraqi Certificate of Citizenship, by contrast, classifies people on the basis of the nationality they held under the Ottomans. Those whose fathers or grandfathers held Persian nationality had the letter B marked on their Certificate of Citizenship.

The Iraqi monarchy under British tutelage never used the Iraqi Nationality Law to deport Shi'i Iraqis. As discussed above, the expulsion of the ulemas in 1923 occurred before the enactment of the law. This is one indication among many that the threat the Shi'i religious establishment posed to the Iraqi government had receded in this period. Indeed, Iraqi and British officials at the time were instead concerned about the influence of secular parties, like the Iraqi Communist Party. During this period of monarchal rule, the Iraqi Nationality Law of 1924 remained valid and was further amended to enable ruling elites to deport Assyrians, Jews, and communists. Under the Ba'th regime, the amended Iraqi Nationality Law of 1963, which remained valid until 1990, retained the definitions and articles of the original law.[54] Hussein's regime used the law to denaturalize thousands of *taba'iyya*. The expulsion campaign in the early 1980s thus raises the questions: How could differential inclusion turn into exclusion? How was a law enacted to include all inhabitants reconfigured in the early 1980s?

The Nationality Law Under Saddam Hussein

The Ba'th Party's ascent to rule in 1968 was marked by drastic changes in the political structures of the country. The new ruling class consisted mainly of Ba'th army officers, who hailed from certain clans and families from the northwest. Ahmad Hasan al-Bakr was one of the main officers behind the 1968 coup and became president, prime minister, chairman of the Revolutionary Command Council, and secretary-general of the Ba'th Party. Shortly after assuming all these positions, he began eliminating allies and rivals alike and promoting his kinsmen, most notably Saddam Hussein. The Ba'th Party became a means to wield power while Tikriti officers came to dominate the army.[55] Political rivals and dissidents were arrested and harassed. The government increasingly feared the Shi'a and the Kurds as groups who posed a serious threat to its rule and legitimacy. In 1979, an already powerful Hussein seized power and became president of Iraq. His reign started with a cold-blooded purge of the Ba'th Party, the liquidation of the ICP, the persecution of the Shi'i opposition and Kurdish movements, and the elimination of anyone who was perceived to present a threat.

From its early days, the Ba'th regime had a strained relationship with the Shi'i religious establishment. Ahmed Hasan al-Bakr attempted to co-opt the ulemas in Iraq's territorial dispute with Iran in 1970s. Distrustful of the regime's socialist agenda and Sunni army officers, the ulemas refused to lend their support to the regime or to condemn the shah.[56] Al-Bakr unleashed a campaign of harassment against them and their supporters. Intent on breaking "the Iranian threat," al-Bakr ordered Iranian religious students expelled, the endowment of Kufa University in Najaf confiscated, and twenty thousand individuals "allegedly of Iranian descent" banished to Iran in 1969.[57] With the rapid deterioration of Iranian-Iraqi relations, the expulsion campaign continued. In September 1971, the government deported around forty thousand Shi'i Kurds to Iran.[58] When Iran occupied the Persian Gulf islands of the Tunbs and Abu Musa, which the British had bequeathed to the United Arab Emirates in November 1971, the Iraqi government expelled sixty thousand "Iranians" the same month.[59] It is unclear if these deportees were "Iranians," Iraqis who held

Iranian nationality, or *taba'iyya*. There were around twenty-three thousand people in Iraq carrying Iranian passports in 1968.[60] Most of the deportees were Iraqis who held Iranian nationality because their (grand)parents had maintained it after the passage of the Iraqi Nationality Law of 1924 and were later denied Iraqi nationality.[61]

On the eve of the Iran-Iraq War in 1980, Hussein's regime waged a campaign of mass deportation of *taba'iyya*. These Iraqis were Shi'i Arabs and Kurds who had the letter B on their Iraqi Certificate of Citizenship. This campaign started amid a confluence of events in 1979: the rise of Hussein to power and his quelling of opposition, the Islamic Revolution in Iran, and the increasing activism of Iraqi Shi'i parties. The rising militancy of the latter since the mid-1970s particularly alarmed the regime. In 1977, spontaneous demonstrations in Najaf and Karbala during 'Ashura (the annual commemoration of the murder of Prophet Muhammad's grandsons in Iraq in the seventh century) posed a serious threat to the government's stability.[62] Encouraged by the popular uprisings in Iran in the summer of 1979, militant underground parties clashed with the security forces throughout that period. When the major Shi'i parties—al-Da'wa Party, Jund al-Imam (Islam's Soldiers), and Munazzamat al-'Amal al-Islami (Islamic Task Organization)—endorsed armed resistance later that year, the government retaliated with extensive arrests and executions.[63] In March 1980, the regime issued a decree "making membership in al-Da'wa punishable by death."[64] The Islamic Task Organization made an attempt on the life of Tariq 'Aziz, a close associate of Hussein and then deputy prime minister, prompting an escalation of regime violence. The government summarily executed Muhammad Baqir al-Sadr, a founder of al-Da'wa Party and a prominent scholar who believed the ulemas had a role to play in politics, and his sister Bint al-Huda.[65] An expulsion campaign of *taba'iyya* immediately followed. Over forty thousand people were deported to Iran that year alone.[66] In the early 1980s, at least forty thousand more Iraqis and as many as four hundred thousand were expelled.

The campaign against *taba'iyya* was rooted in the regime's anti-Iranian rhetoric, which intensified during the Iran-Iraq War. Eric Davis argues that during the war, "the state's emphasis on the *al-Shu'ubiya* movement not only became more prominent, but the interpretation of the movement underwent a metamorphosis."[67] As mentioned above, *shu'ubiyya* was a term used to refer to anti-Arab sentiments. In 1962, 'Abd al-'Aziz al-Duri, a prominent Iraqi historian, published a book on *shu'ubiyya*. Ostensibly concerned with the decline of the Abbasid Empire, the book aimed to disparage the communists and leftists in their conflict with the pan-Arabists. Al-Duri argues that *al-shu'ubiyya* movement—which he defined as constituting a literary, religious, and cultural attack on Arab society—had assumed different forms throughout history. The real danger to Arab communities, he argued, was more internal than external.[68] Davis asserts that al-Duri's emphasis on the so-called Persian hatred of Arabs and Islam meant that Shi'i Iraqis who identified with their Iranian coreligionists became suspects "based strictly on a state of mind, namely their adherence to a purported historical memory that rejects Arabism."[69] Al-Duri's book was reprinted in second and third editions in 1980 and 1981 with the outbreak of the Iran-Iraq War. *Shu'ubiyya* came to define Iraqi-Iranian relations more generally. It expressed a teleology that narrated Persian animosity toward Arabs and territorial ambitions in Iraq that had originated in Babylonian times.[70] In this framework, Saddam Hussein's regime defined *taba'iyya* as agents of Iran, suspect in terms of both their loyalty to Iraq and their "authentic" Arab origin.[71]

Saddam Hussein delivered an example of this teleological narrative in an interview with the journalist 'Uthman al-'Umayri from *al-Sharq al-Awsat*, an Arabic newspaper published in London, just after the war with Iran had ended. In response to a question on the fate of *taba'iyya* who were eager to return to Iraq, Hussein elaborated:

> One of the factors that encouraged the Iranian regime's aggression against Iraq was the presence of a considerable Iranian community in Iraq. Some of them kept Iranian nationality. Others were naturalized but they remained loyal to Iran. This is one factor that encouraged [the Iranian regime to attack Iraq]. It thought it could occupy Iraq within weeks if not days, and then it could overtake all of the Arab homeland. This is a fact, not divination.... When the showdown intensifies and taking up arms becomes necessary, it is natural that a state's sensitivity toward its internal security and internal front is heightened. When we find someone who has lived on Iraq's riches and is driven by his original background or lineage to strike Iraq, it is our duty to send him back to his "uncles" and not allow him to gnaw at Iraq's body through his double loyalty or, say, through his loyalty to Iran and opposition to Iraq.... Our national security will remain the main measure of who we allow to return and who we don't allow to return, but also the main measure of who we will keep in Iraq, who is of Iranian origin, or who we don't allow to stay in Iraq.[72]

In this *shuʿubiyya* framework, the Iran-Iraq War is not portrayed as a political conflict over territory in a regionally and internationally charged context. Hussein conveniently ignored the fact that it was Iraq that first attacked Iran, presenting the latter as the aggressor threatening all Arab countries. According to him, the Iranian regime relied on the Iranian community to attain its goals. Not only does Hussein's comment cast doubt upon the loyalty of these Iraqis, but it portrays them as the enemy within waiting for an opportunity to attack Iraq. This ideological stance links citizenship, loyalty, and national security. Hussein emphasized that a person of Iranian origin who acted against the security of Iraq and who betrayed attachment to their older roots would be stripped of Iraqi nationality.[73]

A month after the beginning of deportation, the Revolutionary Command Council issued Resolution 666 of 1980, which "stripped Iraqis of foreign origin of their citizenship if they are found to be disloyal to the country, the people, and the [1968] Revolution's superior social and nationalistic goals."[74] This decree did not simply define Iraqis based on their origin, but it also gave the government the power to decide who was loyal to the regime. On the one hand, this resolution tied the question of national loyalty to loyalty to the regime and rendered dissident political views tantamount to national treason. On the other hand, an "Iraqi of foreign origin" implies another category—namely, Iraqis who are of "native" origin. Since all the inhabitants of Ottoman Iraq either held Ottoman nationality (*tabaʿiyya ʿuthmaniyya*) or Iranian nationality (*tabaʿiyya iraniyya*), it follows that all Iraqis were, ultimately, of foreign origin. In other words, all the inhabitants of Ottoman Iraq were *tabaʿiyya*. In singling out the *tabaʿiyya iraniyya* as foreign, the regime anchored indigenous Iraqiness within Ottoman nationality and embedded it in the shifting meanings of the term *tabaʿiyya*. Under Hussein's rule, the term *tabaʿiyya* came to mean "Iraqis of Iranian origin." The attribute *iraniyya* was often dropped. From a generic term that meant nationality or subjecthood/nationality, *tabaʿiyya* became synonymous with Iranian nationality, reflecting the degree to which Ottoman nationality became the basis of Iraqi authenticity.

Under Hussein's regime, the distinction between "authentic" (*asli*) and "inauthentic" (*ghayr asli*) Iraqi became widespread. In announcements for government jobs, for instance, it was stated that the applicants and both of their parents should be "authentic" Iraqis. An "authentic" Iraqi held an Iraqi Nationality Certificate with the letter C. The Iraqi nationality of such a person was marked as "Ottoman." An "inauthentic" Iraqi, on the other hand, had the letter B, a *taba'iyya* nationality. Sha'ban and Babakhan have argued, mistakenly, that the terms *authentic* and *inauthentic* appeared in different documents, such as the constitution, the Iraqi Nationality Law of 1924, and the Iraqi Certificate of Citizenship since monarchal rule. In fact, the terms do not appear in any of these documents. Similarly, they are not mentioned in any public state documents enacted under the Ba'th regime. Even the use of the term *Ottoman* in official documents is rare. Though the term *Ottoman* was often used in job announcements and among Iraqis in conversations about eligibility for jobs and academic disciplines, it did not appear in official publications. One document where the term appears is the Interim Constitution of 1964. Article 41 states:

> The President of the Republic shall be an Iraqi of Iraqi parents from a family domiciled in Iraq since at least 1900 AD, and which at that time held Ottoman nationality. He shall be a Muslim who observes religious rites, must not be less than forty years old, must be enjoying his civil and political rights, and must not be married to a foreigner. An Arab woman of Arab parents and grandparents will be considered an Iraqi for this purpose.[75]

In addition, the Interim Constitution of 1968 establishes Ottoman citizenship as the criteria for certain rights and positions. For instance, Article 26 states that "an Iraqi citizenship is defined by law and cannot be stripped of an Iraqi whose family lived in Iraq before August 6, 1924, held the Ottoman citizenship, and chose the Iraqi citizenship afterwards."[76] In the section on the armed forces, the constitution dictates that "a person's family should have been living in Iraq since 1900 and should have held Ottoman citizenship." Interestingly, this interim constitution does not have any reference to the citizenship held by the families of the president and the ministers. Likewise, the Interim Constitution of 1970 does not include specific criteria regarding these positions either.[77]

Given that the inhabitants of Ottoman Iraq were either Ottoman or Persian subjects prior to 1921, the condition of holding Ottoman citizenship indicates that people who carried Persian citizenship (and their children) could not occupy these positions. Apart from the question of access to some state jobs and occupations, this distinction reveals the haunted origin of authenticity. Authenticity became associated with Ottomanness, and inauthenticity with Persianness. Being Ottoman emerged as normative and indigenous whereas being Persian indicated foreignness. While Arabness and Persianness became mutually exclusive, Arabness and Ottomanness were not antithetical in this framework. By defining authenticity in relation to Ottomanness, Hussein's regime, like al-Husri several decades before, located the authenticity of the Arab nation in a non-Arab nationality. In its fear of the Other within and its efforts to cast doubt upon this Other's Arab origin, the regime alienated the very core of the nation that it sought to protect. If the Arab nationalist discourse celebrated authenticity and the glorious Arab past and rendered the loyalty of non-Sunni and non-Arab Iraqis suspect, the Iraqi Nationality Law and its amendments cast Ottoman rule as the source of Arab authenticity in Iraq.[78]

The denaturalization directives were accompanied by the confiscation of the deportees' property and assets and followed by legislation that fragmented families—in particular, laws that granted monetary rewards to Iraqi men if they divorced their *taba'iyya* wives and that detained young men between the ages of 18 and 28. Moreover, Iraqi deportees reported many instances of young women being subjected to rape and sexual assault during the deportation campaign, which will be discussed in chapter 5. Like the mass expulsion of Iraqi Jews in 1950, Iraqis of Iranian origin became stateless and penniless. As a mechanism of collective punishment, the policies of denaturalization aimed to exact as much pain and harm upon a whole community as possible.

Conclusion

The differential inclusion of the inhabitants of Iraq embedded in the Iraqi Nationality Law of 1924 and in the Iraqi Certificate of Citizenship in particular had a long historical legacy. The mass expulsions of *taba'iyya* in the 1980s were based on the reconfiguration of that law. While the Iraqi Nationality Law of 1924 was ambiguous on the question of differential national inclusion, the Iraqi Certificate of Citizenship meted out different legal statuses to Iraqi citizens depending on the nationality they or their fathers had held under Ottoman rule. By institutionalizing difference through differential inclusion, the 1924 law left the door open for reinterpretation in future political contexts. The reconfiguration of the law and the classification of citizenship under Hussein's regime transfigured differential inclusion into exclusion. By assigning a different legal status to the inhabitants who held Persian nationality, the Iraqi Nationality Law of 1924 became a means of exclusion from the Iraqi state decades later in that it defined the parameters of legal belonging. Not only did this law perceive people in terms of essentialist categories, such as ethnicity and sect, it also entailed the severance of social markers from their wider historical and political contexts. Although the Iraqi Nationality Law of 1924 would have severe repercussions less than sixty later, in terms of engendering all-encompassing conditions of dispossession for Iraqis whose ancestors held Persian citizenship, it, especially under Hussein's reign, constituted Ottoman citizenship as inviolable and guaranteed since Iraqis whose ancestors opted for the Ottoman citizenship were not targeted.

FOUR

HAUNTED HOMES

THIRTY YEARS AFTER the expulsion of Iraqi Jews in 1950–1951 under the country's monarchical rule, *taba'iyya* were subjected to a massive expulsion campaign in 1980–1985 under Saddam Hussein's regime. On the eve of the Iran-Iraq War (1980–1988), the Iraqi regime denaturalized and deported thousands of Shi'i Arabs and Shi'i Kurds to Iran after confiscating their property and documents under the pretext that they were of Iranian origin. Like Iraqi Jews who arrived in Israel and confronted Zionist and anti-Arab sentiments, Iraqi deportees who arrived in Iran had to deal with Persian nationalism and anti-Arab sentiments. While Hussein's regime perceived them as Iranians, the Iranian regime considered them as Arabs who did not belong in Iran, even though they shared Iran's Shi'i belief system. Even the Kurds among them were called "Arabs" in Iran. Penniless and stateless, Iraqi deportees had to grapple with the inability to start again in a hostile country, facing discrimination while trying to find work or go to school. Like Iraqi Jews whose identities became disarticulated in the nexus of nationalist ideologies, *taba'iyya* faced mutually exclusive binaries that rendered unintelligible their complex sense of belonging, as well as the entangled family and historical connections between Iran and Iraq. Though *taba'iyya* affiliated with Iraq, their regional connections coupled with national and imperial politics rendered them conditional and precarious citizens under Saddam Hussein's regime.

To understand the flexible citizenship and subjectivity of *taba'iyya*, this chapter focuses on *Qismat*, a historical novel written in Arabic. The novel deals with the question of haunting and displacement in Iraq throughout the twentieth and early twenty-first centuries. The author, Hawra al-Nadawi, conducted archival research and interviews with Iraqis in Iran and Iraq in order to document their history of expulsion and denaturalization.[1] Born to Arab and Kurdish parents and brought up in Denmark, when her family fled Iraq in 1991 after years of imprisonment, al-Nadawi grew up listening to her grandmother's stories about deportation and about family members who were stripped of their Iraqi citizenship.[2] To my knowledge, this novel is the only literary work that focuses on the experiences of *taba'iyya*.

The novel centers on a woman named Qismat (which means "fate" or "lot" in Arabic), who kills herself, her two young children, and her unborn child by drowning in the Tigris. The ghost of Qismat haunts surviving family members in Iraq and in exile over several decades, as the novel explores the legacy of deportation in the modern state of Iraq. The first part, covering the period between 1950 and 1975 with references to the nineteenth century, opens with Qismat's suicide in 1950 and gestures to the expulsion of Iraqi Jews while narrating the histories of familial migration from Iran to Iraq and of gender and patriarchal relations in the 1950s. The second part, covering the period between 1980 and 2009, is about the experience of deportation to Iran and the fragmentation of the family, whose members end up in Iran, Canada, Norway, Russia, and Syria. This section is marked by narratives of alienation, misrecognition, legal precarity, and deprivation that descendants of Mulla Ghulam (Qismat's father, whose grandfather migrated from a border town in Iran to Baghdad in 1873) experienced in Iran and Iraq. The third part opens in 2004, when one deported family member travels from Iran to Iraq after the fall of Saddam Hussein's regime in 2003 in order to reclaim the property he lost when he was deported, but he ends up dying of a heart attack during an explosion in Baghdad. The novel ends by returning to 1950, and the reader gets a glimpse of what pushed Qismat to kill herself and her children.

In *Qismat*, the right to reclaim—in particular the homeland and the past—is expressed through haunting. As the ghost of Qismat keeps appearing to living family members at different historical conjunctures, it foreshadows the loss of the homeland and intergenerational trauma. Avery Gordon defines haunting as "a constituent element of modern life. It is neither premodern nor individual psychosis; it is a generalizable social phenomenon of great import. To study social life one must confront the ghostly aspects of it."[3] Moreover, she argues that "to be haunted is to be tied to historical and social effects."[4] This linkage between haunting and modernity means that "haunting is one way in which abusive systems of power make themselves known and their impacts felt in everyday life," and it "is an animated state in which a repressed or unresolved social violence is making itself known, sometimes very directly, sometimes more obliquely."⁵ The emergence of the modern state of Iraq after the fall of the Ottoman Empire was marked by violence, as communities were stripped of their nationality and property, becoming excluded and effectively statelessness. As such, haunting speaks to the legacy of unresolved violence that has received little attention or acknowledgment. In the case of *taba'iyya* whose experiences and stories remain silenced and undocumented in the Iraqi national narrative, haunting becomes a venue to reckon with that repressed history and lay bare the impact of oppressive structures of power on individuals. In this framework, haunting serves as a mediation that "describes the process that links an institution and an individual, a social structure and a subject, and history and a biography. In haunting, organized forces and systemic structures that appear removed from us make their impact felt in everyday life."⁶ Haunting is not about a return to the past but "a reckoning with its repression in the present."⁷

In addition to being the first literary work written by an Iraqi author whose family was subject to denaturalization and deportation, *Qismat* can be read a historical text that documents the experiences of generations of families who moved back and forth between Iraq and Iran. As an autobiographical archive that chronicles the lived realities of five generations between 1873 and 2009, the novel offers an account of the ways political and social transformations in Iraq between the end of the nineteenth century and the early twenty-first century opened avenues for social mobility and the cultivation of an Iraqi subjectivity but ultimately engendered displacement and dispossession. Through an intergenerational account of family members who were designated as *taba'iyya* under the modern state of Iraq, al-Nadawi showcases the entanglement of individual lives with national politics and imperial interests over almost a century and a half. The opening of the novel with the suicide of Qismat in 1950 points to a pivotal moment in the modern history of Iraq. Around seventy years prior to 1950, people who resided along the Iran-Iraq border saw opportunities for a prosperous life in Iraq. And thirty years after 1950, the descendants of these Iraqi citizens became exiles in different parts of the world and experienced death upon returning to Iraq for a visit in 2005. In this narrative, displacement, exile, broken dreams, violence, and death emerge as qismat—or the lot—of *taba'iyya* in particular and of other Iraqi communities in general.

In short, al-Nadawi employs a multigenerational narrative to address different instances of social and political violence in Iraq under monarchical rule, Saddam Hussein's reign, and post-Saddam Iraq. While the first part of the novel focuses on patriarchal injustices and the deportation of Iraqi Jews, and the second part explores the disarticulation of identity upon denaturalization and expulsion, the third part deals with the rampant violence after 2003, which renders Iraq a death trap. Through the themes of haunting and displacement, *Qismat* is a rumination on repressed violence, citizenship and belonging, intergenerational trauma, and the failure of the project of modernity in Iraq. The ghost of Qismat, while tying different histories and lived realities together through haunting, invites the readers and the protagonists to grapple with the idealized but unjust past as well as the unruly and dystopic present.

Omens of Modernity

The first part of *Qismat* offers a social and political reading of modernity in Iraq, from 1950 to 1970. In the novel, modernity in Iraq emerges as a fraught gendered and political project. While the story opens with Qismat's family mourning her and her children's deaths, it ends with a conversation between Qismat and Perka, a soothsayer who could foretell an ominous future for their community—namely, Shi'i Kurds. Qismat's suicide, which brought shame upon the family and raised recurring questions about her mental health, speaks to the social changes in the country related to patriarchy and the status of women, the legacy of the expulsion of Jews from the country, and the uncertain future the country faced in 1950. One can read the figure of Qismat as a condemnation of patriarchal structures and lack of attention to mental health problems in the country at the time. But the story and suicide of Qismat could also symbolize a country that had destroyed its children (both Iraqi Jews and *taba'iyya*) through displacement and violence. Qismat could stand for the nation and its fate. Indeed, the women in the novel—Qismat's sisters, who dominate the first half of the narrative—are tasked with reproducing a patriarchal system as well as the community and nation. Qismat interrupted this process when she decided to end her life and the lives of future generations.

In the mid-twentieth century, Iraq stood at a crossroads. Modernist sensibilities spread among the young generation, who were involved in anticolonial struggle against the British and the monarchy. As young people joined progressive parties to demand political independence, social justice, and gender equality, ruling elites attempted to repress many of these forms of expression, though they still encouraged women's access to education and work. The future of the country was an open question. Would Iraq be an inclusive and democratic country, or would it resort to repression and exclusion? Would the wave of modernity bring about genuine change or fail as a social and political project in the nascent state? The answer the novel presents suggests that the events in 1950, when Qismat committed suicide and killed her children, foretold a bleak future. The year 1950 is significant: it is when the Iraqi state denaturalized and expelled Iraqi Jews. However, Iraqis who came of age at the time and took part in anticolonial demonstrations and the vibrant literary scene perceived the 1940s and 1950s as a golden age.[8] Hence, the dominant narrative among progressive and leftist Iraqis about social and political vibrancy is marked by haunted silence about the fate of Iraqi Jews. The opening of the novel in 1950 pays tribute to that absence and the history of expulsion and foreshadows how a similar fate of displacement and silence awaits another community, *taba'iyya*. In this framework, the project of modernity in Iraq becomes haunted and fractured by that silenced and unacknowledged political violence, and Qismat, as a gendered symbol of the nation-state, represents the motherland that killed not only its children but also itself.

The opening of the novel is haunted by this absence of former Jewish residents. The narrator explains that al-Dahana, an old neighborhood in Baghdad, was originally inhabited by Jewish and Christian families. While Jewish families were deported, some of the Christian families moved to new neighborhoods. Shi'i Kurds as well as Arab families from outside Baghdad began to reside in this old, mixed neighborhood later on. Through the narrator, the reader realizes that this neighborhood is haunted on two levels. First, the narrator explains that Iraqi Jews brought ghosts into the neighborhood because they buried their dead in their houses in order to remain close to them.[9] Second, the neighborhood was haunted by the expulsion of its original Iraqi Jewish residents. This instance of mass displacement was foreboding, in that such a fate could befall other minority groups. This fear was expressed by Qaim, Qismat's aunt, who was unsettled by Qismat's ghost haunting the house. Qaim asks the soothsayer Perka to come to the house and conduct rituals to appease Qismat's ghost. Perka tells Qaim not to worry about Qismat's ghost, who is harmless, but to fear the unknown. Naively, Qaim thought that Iraqi Jews were expelled because they lived with the ghosts of the dead, and she says, "How can I not worry about her ghost? Haven't you seen what happened to our Jewish neighbors who lived with their dead ghosts? Don't you remember how they were tortured and subjected to pogroms, and then expelled and deported? Wherever they went, ruin followed them."[10] Ironically, it is Perka who tries to dissuade Qaim from this faulty logic about the deportation of Jews, to emphasize that the ghosts of the dead are harmless, and to assert that one cannot change fate, as it is predestined.

The novel also dwells on questions around gender, patriarchy, and the status of women. While this part of the novel narrates the expulsion of Jews and the history of the family's migration to Iraq, it mainly revolves around Mulla Ghulam's daughters, who were all married off at a very young age (as young as twelve in the case of Qismat) to tough older men. Though education of women in Iraq in the 1950s became more common, Mulla Ghulam's daughters did not benefit from this modernist shift in gender relations, unlike their brothers, who went to school. While the political project of modernity was doomed to fail, as far as Iraqi Shi'i Kurds were concerned, the gendered project of modernity bypassed younger women, who were perceived by their families as a burden and were expected to get married and have children as soon as possible. Moreover, these young women saw it as their duty to uphold a patriarchal system and to reproduce the family and the community.

Hence, the first part of the novel is a condemnation of the patriarchal system in Iraq, which expected women to be mainly mothers and housewives. Qismat's suicide could be read as a social commentary on patriarchy and mental health in the country. The narrator mentions that Mulla Ghulam was concerned about Qismat's excessive naivety and mental health. Qismat had mood swings. Sometimes she was overly joyous and cheerful, while at other times she was depressed and gloomy. Her father thought that Qismat was "mentally deranged." To deal with this situation, he promised Qismat in marriage to the twenty-five-year-old Hussein when she was nine, though the marriage did not take place until she was twelve. He reasoned that marriage would protect Qismat's honor and that having children would force her to grow up and behave properly. Everyone's lack of attention to and understanding of Qismat's mental health led to her death. Qismat's sisters did not fare better, in that they were all married off at a very young age as well. The reader cannot help thinking about the prospects Mulla Ghulam's daughters would have had if they had gone to school, since patriarchal values about women's status were transforming at the time. The women in the novel, just as in the nation, were at a crossroads: either they could be required to marry at a young age, or they could join other young Iraqi women in seeking education and equality. In the end, they seem to be victims on two levels: the state failed to see them as full Iraqi citizens, and their families failed to provide them with the new opportunities that were becoming available to women in the mid-twentieth century. As women, Qismat and her sisters were rendered politically and socially precarious subjects who could not have a say about citizenship or marriage, though they were at the center of reproducing the family, community, and nation. In the novel, it is telling that the CIA-backed Baʻth coup took place in 1963 but the women were not aware of the event or its repercussions, as the men did not think about sharing the news of the coup with them since they viewed them as in charge of daily life and children strictly.

The first part of the novel aims to document a vanishing world. It is a world where Iraqi Jews are no longer part of Iraqi society. It is also a world where gender relations and particularly the status of women are transforming. It is a world where ruling elites aim to build a modern state but cannot embrace all the citizens of Iraq. It is a world where Mulla Ghulam's family seeks new opportunities in Iraq but does not think of extending these opportunities to their daughters. The present in 1950 was a promising but fraught moment: the Iraqi state and Mulla Ghulam's family could have taken different directions but did not. Though the 1950s are celebrated by Iraqi leftists and progressives as a time of optimism, it was a decade that foretold a bleak future. Just as the Iraqi state sacrificed Iraqi Jews when it refused to see them as Iraqi citizens, Mulla Ghulam sacrificed Qismat in order not to deal with her mental health. Despite the literary, social, and political vibrancy during that decade, the silences and erasures were ominous. Politically, Qismat's suicide can be read as Qismat seeing the future (through Perka, who forewarned her of a terrible future) and taking agency by killing herself and her children in order to avoid deportation, destitution, family separation, tragic deaths, and pain. While the old world was vanishing, the future was stillborn. That the state could expel a whole community of Iraqi citizens with no major protests from the population opened the door for future expulsions. That this history of expulsion was erased amid romanticization of the 1950s foreshadowed future silences. Both the nation and the father failed at protecting their children. That the future was going to be grim is indicated by the fact that the first section ends in 1975, shortly after the first wave of the deportation, which began in 1970 and reached a climax in 1980–1985. By then, the old house of Mulla Ghulam, in al-Dahana, which had been built by Iraqi Jews in the nineteenth century, was completely haunted by many ghosts, including the ghosts of Qismat and former tenants.

These ghosts haunted the present in order to alert the inhabitants of unresolved social and political violence and of the repression of the past.

Narratives of Alienation and Misrecognition

The second part of the novel starts in 1980, when the massive wave of expulsions began, and it ends in 2009, delineating the lives that some Iraqi deportees had built in Iran. This section marks a shift in gender and generational representation. While the first part is recounted by a narrator and focuses on the lives of Mulla Ghulam's daughters, the second part is narrated by three grandsons of Mulla Ghulam, who are scattered in Iran, Syria, and Sweden. Through first-person narratives, these three men attempt to make sense of their experiences of displacement, to build a future in a place that is not marked by trauma and exclusion, and to document daily struggles in exile and in Iraq. This section aims to bring the personal and the political together by showing how cataclysmic events—such as deportation, statelessness, loss of assets and careers, and alienation—are accompanied by daily struggles over taken-for-granted things, such as one's name, language, clothes, and food. The loss of a homeland translates into the loss of all rights and individuality, as well as family. The denial of nationality also entails existing in a permanent state of liminality, a condition of statelessness, where a person is no longer perceived as an Iraqi citizen but also is not accepted as an Iranian citizen—a betwixt-and-between status. The right to reclaim in this novel endeavors to document these ruptures and to show the ways *taba'iyya* navigated this uncharted territory and still aimed to build a semblance of a coherent life through either trying to build roots in Iran or to migrate to a Western country in order to start again.

While the first part of the novel traces the roots Mulla Ghulam's family established in Iraq, the second part examines the conditions of uprootedness for those descendants who were deported, as well as the political uncertainty for those who stayed in Iraq. The narratives by two cousins, Louay and Salar, who are Qismat's nephews, represent parallel worlds that were forcibly separated by borders. Louay was deported to Iran with his family but managed to be smuggled to Sweden thirteen years later. Salar stayed in Iraq with his family when Iraqi authorities did not deport them; he tried to leave Iraq in the 1990s to escape oppression and a foreclosed future, but he decided that exile was not for him. This section opens with an exchange between the two cousins, who have managed to get in touch for the first time after the family had been fragmented in 1980. The fact that Louay is in Sweden and Salar is in Damascus means they can write to each other for the first time. Iraqi deportees in Iran were completely cut off from their families in Iraq during the Iran-Iraq War. The narratives of these two men reflect the alienation and misrecognition they confronted in Iran and Iraq and what daily life looked like in the aftermath of deportation.

For this generation of Mulla Ghulam's grandchildren, Iraq is the homeland they know and are attached to. They take for granted that they are Iraqi citizens and cultivate an Iraqi subjectivity. However, Saddam Hussein's authoritarian rule and inability to see Iraqis who held Persian citizenship before the establishment of the modern state of Iraq as Iraqi citizens engendered conditions of precarity and misrecognition. These cousins, who ended up in different parts of the world and speak different languages, are haunted by the loss of homeland and questions of belonging. Moreover, the ghost of Qismat appears to each of them while they are in exile and in Iraq. As a symbol of the lost motherland, Qismat provides familiarity and emphasizes the inability to let go of one's homeland. While Louay can no longer visit Iraq, the ghost of Qismat becomes a bridge to Iraq. She is the homeland that refuses to disappear despite exclusionary nationalistic ideologies. Just as Qismat haunted the living in the first part to indicate unresolved violence and the failed project of modernity, she haunts the living in exile in order to keep them connected to Iraq.

In the absence of literary and academic work on *taba'iyya*, the second part of *Qismat* provides a meditation on the concept of home, the construction of identity, and the conditions of rupture as experienced by the young men who were subjected to deportation. Louay grew up in Iraq in a middle-class neighborhood after his father, Majeed, became a successful businessman once he migrated from Iran to Iraq in the early 1950s. Louay was only thirteen years old when his family was deported, an event that transformed the family, politically and socially. Politically, the family became stateless and lost all the wealth the father had built in Iraq over thirty years. The Iraqi authorities put the family in a camp before ordering them to walk to Iran in an area that was filled with land mines. The family finally makes it to Illam, a Shi'i Kurdish town in Iran on the border with Iraq from which Majeed hailed. Stateless and destitute, Louay and his siblings experience a world turned upside down overnight and have to live in a place where the smallest things in life can no longer be taken for granted. Louay reflects that his family is one of the fortunate ones:

his father has managed to get Iranian citizenship and start a business with money his wife had smuggled out of Iraq. Despite his ability to start again in Iran, Louay's father becomes a cruel and stingy man, never acknowledging his wife's role in enabling the family to start again in Iran. He also becomes an Iranian nationalist who wants his family to forget about Iraq. Socially, Louay feels out of place in Iran. He cannot get used to the food in Illam, which he finds to be bland and fatty. He also had to wear old Kurdish clothes when the family first arrived in Iran, a far cry from the modern and fashionable clothes he wore in Iraq. Moreover, people in Illam were aggravated by his father's quick success and bad manners, ridiculed the children's broken accents, and called them Arabs. This environment in Iran left Louay and others of his generation who had only known Iraq and identified as Iraqis feeling socially and politically alienated.

Louay becomes haunted by the loss of home. He reflects: "In our case, the original home for our tribe did lie in an Iranian territory, but I still cannot understand what it means that we are Iranian since we are really Kurds. So if we are not Iraqi citizens though we lived all our life there, what indicates we are Iranian since we never saw Iran before we were thrown on the borders on a cold winter day."[11] Louay's life after arriving in Iran becomes uncertain. Denaturalization meant the loss of control over even the most basic things. He asks, "Why is there someone else who decides for me the shape and soul of my country? How could he have the authority that gave him the right to strip me of my country just because a [great] grandfather I do not know happened to be born in a remote geographic place?"[12] To Louay, the demarcation of borders between Iraq and Iran is a random process that enables ruling elites to exclude certain citizens according to their nationalistic ideologies. However, Louay insists on asserting an Iraqi identity when he claims that "I'm the homeland walking on feet holding the body of a thin teenager who is thirteen years old, and whose name is Louay Majeed al-Sayegh. . . . I'm that homeland but they did insist on ignoring me and rejecting me the day they took us away from our house with only the clothes on us to a party headquarters in some unknown place outside Baghdad."[13] For Louay, his sense of rootedness in Iraq has been negated by the ruling elites.

Louay not only finds himself stripped of his Iraqi nationality, but he is also stripped of his Arabic name. Upon arrival in Iran, his father decides to give all his children Persian names. He changes Louay's name from Louay Majeed al-Sayegh to Ameed Kaka Zadah. This new name, which Louay could never get used to even after years of living in Iran, became "like a big prison in which we were thrown."[14] Overnight, this new name erased his identity, past, and years he had spent in Iraq.[15] Moreover, the fact that Majeed didn't give his children the chance to choose their names shocked Louay: "At the time, I could not understand how my father could think of these new names so fast once he renounced the idea of Iraq and transformed himself into a real Iranian citizen, whose sons' names have deep Iranian nationalistic connotations."[16] While the Iraqi state stripped Louay of his nationality and homeland, his father stripped him of his name and destroyed his hope of ever returning to Iraq, remarking that return was impossible. He addresses his father:

> We are Iraqis. We had a big house in one of the most beautiful neighborhoods in Baghdad. Our house, Dad! The house you made so much effort in order to buy. The house you put so much time into to make neat and elegant.... You supervised the garden, and paid special attention to the two palm trees. I even remember you saying proudly while looking at them that you would plant more palm trees. You said palm trees bestow upon the house a true Iraqi characteristic. So why are you surrendering now without showing any resistance as if it was normal to build a big life only to walk away from it so easily.[17]

The political and familial alienation means that Louay constantly feels uprooted: "With every day, the ugly feeling of uprootedness and the sense of futility grew deeper inside me. How could this mountainous village with its beautiful nature and pure air, which could be a wonderful place for recreation, represent the nightmare of deportation and absolute cruelty."[18] In Iran, Louay finds himself obsessing over small things that remind him of his previous life in Iraq and his present situation in Iran. A small task, like buying bread for his mother, becomes a moment of alienation when he has to ask the baker, in a poor Persian accent, for ten flatbreads, and the baker ridicules him, saying, "You Arabs eat a lot."[19] Moreover, deportation meant that the family had left Iraq without taking any personal belongings. Without photos that documented memories in Iraq, Louay feels that he and his family "were uprooted from everything in order to experience a new birth, where we cannot recall the memories of our previous lives."[20] To combat this feeling of uprootedness and the complete transformation of life in Iran, Louay clings to the memory of the last family picture in Baghdad, taken a few months before they were deported on his brother's birthday, which shows the affluent life they had in

Iraq. Louay compares himself and his brothers in the picture to the Beatles, saying they looked elegant along with his parents. The memory of this picture becomes both a refuge in exile, since it connects him to the beautiful past, and a reminder of that lost past. This picture stands in stark contrast to a family picture that was taken two years after their arrival in Iran, where they are wearing old, shabby clothes and trying to force smiles. While the memory of the picture in Iraq depicts a beautiful past, the picture in Iran represents the harsh reality and the loss of status in Iran and aggravates the feeling of uprootedness.

This experience of uprootedness causes time to become less yielding and less promising for Louay.[21] In the aftermath of catastrophes, David Scott remarks that "the present seems stricken with immobility and pain and ruin,"[22] and the self becomes "paralyzed by nostalgia for the past."[23] Louay experiences the present in Iran as an impasse and feels that his life stopped in Iraq: "My heart is still the heart of a thirteen-year-old boy who was forced to live a life that is not his. I'm still that student in middle school in Palestine Street. In Iran, I did what I had done in Iraq for years. I kept listening to ABBA and Bee Gees through the cassettes I exchanged with Iranian students."[24] As Louay is stricken by nostalgia for the past in Iraq, he feels that the present has become stunted. He remarks that growing up has become a slow process of aging: it entails growing up in years but does not lead to any meaningful growth in terms of flourishing as a human being. This feeling of aging but not flourishing, of years passing without any meaning, and of inhabiting the present but living in the past conveys the sense that his life has become "a stupid joke."[25] In his determination to keep his attachment to Iraq, Louay clings to past memories as a way to cultivate an Iraqi subjectivity. But nostalgia can be dangerous because it can plunge a person into melancholia. Louay affirms, "I remained subsisting on the crumbs of memories, which I forgot sometimes, only to be slapped by them again. Then, I paid attention to the fact that life was passing by quickly without having the opportunity to go back to Iraq. Every time, I confronted this reality, I felt lethargic and spent days in my room."[26] The disjointed present exacerbates the feelings of helpless and hopelessness.

Once, while Louay was taking a walk in the mountains, he came across a grave with an incomplete Quranic verse from al-'Asr: "By the passage of time, surely humanity . . ." Louay completes the verse in his head: "is in grave loss." He feels that the missing part of the verse reflects his life: "'Is in grave loss.' It is me! I'm that losing half, the rejected half. Half a dream, and half a truth.

Half a man who hasn't entered adulthood yet. Half Iraqi that no one takes his Iraqiness seriously. Half a human being, and whatever is left of him is in grave loss. I'm half the verse that was engraved on a forgotten and old grave at the edge of a mountain overlooking a deep valley."²⁷ This realization that his life is always missing something makes Louay decide to flee to Sweden in 1993 in order to start a new life. Upon landing in Sweden, national misrecognition becomes clear during his interview with a Swedish official. Louay's story as an Iraqi citizen who was deported to Iran and lived there for thirteen years does not fit with widely accepted asylum narratives in Europe. When Louay tells the Swedish authority that he is an Iraqi, they bring him an Egyptian translator, but he cannot communicate with him because he does not understand the Egyptian dialect and his classical Arabic is not good. While the use of the Arabic language becomes an occasion for confusion, his Arabic and Persian names compound the ambiguity. After failing to communicate with the Egyptian translator, the Swedish official brings in an Iranian translator, who tells Louay to stick to the narrative that he is an Iraqi who was deported to Iran and to deny that he holds Iranian nationality and that he is a Kurd, since these factors would complicate his case. While processing his case, the Swedish official asks Louay which name he would like to use, and he insists on using the name Louay Majeed al-Sayegh, feeling grateful for the humanity the Swedish authorities are showing him. To Louay, it is ironic that he can assert his Iraqi identity only in a country like Sweden. While his expulsion from Iraq erased his Iraqi subjectivity, his voluntary relocation to Sweden enables him to reclaim his name and Iraqiness.

While Louay's narrative depicts life in exile in Iran and his attempts to have a different future in Sweden, the account by his cousin, Salar, examines the lives of *taba'iyya* who stayed in Iraq. Salar's story depicts what life would have looked like for Louay and his family had they stayed in Iraq under Saddam Hussein, who drove the country into two wars and sanctions. Salar tells the reader how his family prepared to be deported after the expulsion of Mulla Ghulam and his family and Majeed and Mariam's family, waiting in constant anxiety until 1985, when the campaign of deportation came to an end. During this long wait, the family had fragmented, as some members had fled to Canada, Russia, and Norway rather than staying and awaiting their fates. Those who stayed in Iraq lost contact with deported family members. For instance, Salar's family had no idea whether his grandparents, aunts, and cousins made it safely to Iran.²⁸ Moreover, for years, his mother did not know that her parents had died a few years after arriving in Iran. Salar reflects on his mother's mourning: "My mother did not have the chance to mourn them freshly as the news was often uncertain and muddled, and reached us after months or sometimes years. The path of mourning for my mother was destined to be ongoing."[29] Deportation uprooted families, scattering them all over the world and breaking lines of communication. Indeed, Salar fleetingly comments that the neighborhood in Baghdad where his family had lived had transformed after its original inhabitants had been expelled and were replaced by new inhabitants settled by the Iraqi regime. The neighborhood acquired the taste of exile and pain though his family still lived there. This sense of internal exile, of feeling like a stranger in their own neighborhood, pushed the family to move to a different neighborhood.

In addition to his reflection on the fate of his extended family, Salar provides an account of life in Iraq, which he finds boring, alienating, and purposeless. He intentionally fails at the university in order to repeat the academic year so that he can avoid serving in the Iraqi army during the Iran-Iraq War. Young men could avoid or delay military service in Iraq only if they were students, so failing examinations on purpose was a common practice during Saddam Hussein's regime. Wandering in the old neighborhoods in Baghdad and frequenting brothels, Salar "made friends with young men who were caught up between the kilns of wars and the fires of families, among other depressing situations. To break the monotony of these days, which were suffocated with tedium and powerlessness, I cultivated cursed talents that would keep me preoccupied."[30] Since nothing positive is happening in his life, Salar starts sculpting naked figures out of soap and taking electronic appliances apart and putting them back together. In 1993, Salar goes to Damascus with the idea that he might go to Europe. For the first time, he gets in touch with Louay, who urges him to come to Sweden and offers to put him in touch with his smuggler. However, Salar decides that exile is not for him and goes back to Iraq without providing any explanation to Louay, who is heartbroken by the decision. Salar shares his reasoning with the reader: "How could I tell him [Louay] . . . that I'm empty inside with nothing but a mass of complexes and psychological pains. . . . There is no place in Sweden for people like me. That beautiful country and those serene cities do not go along with my nature because I'm a creature of this deformed homeland."[31] A second-class citizen in a country embroiled in war and chaos, Salar is suspended in time, with no past to cling to or a future to look forward to. Salar is alienated from his country and from himself.

On his way home after arriving back in Baghdad, Salar sees Qismat's ghost:

> I had a glimpse of her . . . as if she were resurrected from the Tigris, where she drowned. She was hiding among people but then she appeared in her glaring red dress, which I recognized from an old picture my mother kept, and I was sure it was her relying on my instinct. Oh, you faithful death, you did not change her features at all, but kept her youth and beauty unlike life, which changed most of us and stripped us of a lot, leaving us merely lifeless and joyless shadows while we were at the peak of our precious youth.[32]

For Salar, the meaning of life and death has flipped: death has become associated with youth and beauty, while life brings about old age and a negation of its essence. Salar seems to imply that the dead fare better in Iraq than the living in that it brings peace and serenity while life entails symbolic death and an impasse. Salar notices that Iraqi people around him all look exhausted because of the hard life they lead, "which left its cruel stamps on their tired forehead."[33] Taken by his aunt's spectacular beauty and elegance, Salar gives her a salutation, while she looks at him and smiles at him. That the figure of a dead person who escaped a bleak future by suicide can convey joy and youth speaks volumes about the status quo in Iraq. While Qismat found peace in death, the living have to inhabit a stunted past, present, and future. One could argue that Qismat haunted the inhabitants of al-Dahana in the 1950s to remind them of the failed project of modernity and the expelled inhabitants—namely, Iraqi Jews. Yet one could also say that Qismat haunted the younger generation as a way to give them support during a bleak time. Either way, the younger generation was doubly haunted: they were haunted by past events that shaped their future, and they were haunted by the silenced and unresolved violence of the present. This silenced past had tragic repercussions in the present in that the conditions of dispossession continued for decades without any effort to acknowledge or pay tribute to them.

Iraq as an Open Wound

The last section of the novel deals with the situation in Iraq after the fall of Saddam Hussein's regime when Louay and his father, Majeed, decide to go back to Iraq in order to reapply for their Iraqi citizenship and reclaim assets that had been confiscated upon deportation in 1980. This visit to Iraq in 2004 becomes a sort of family reunion, as family members still in Iraq are reconnected with deported relatives after twenty-four years. Although Majeed is focused mainly on his lost wealth, to the disappointment of everyone around him, who thought the main purpose of his visit was to reconnect with relatives and friends, Louay takes the opportunity to reflect on his relationship to Iraq and his family, whom he had left when he was thirteen years old. Since deportation, Louay had dreamed about visiting Iraq; however, return is accompanied by disenchantment.

> Louay almost felt regret when he looked upon the devastation that befell the country, and wished, for a second, if Baghdad stayed in his heart the way he remembered it when he was deported as a child. His head was filled with scenarios about the meeting that would reunite him with his family and country. When these scenarios took place, they did not meet any of his expectations or dreams since they [the family] met him for the first time in complete darkness. When he saw life as it really was, it pained him to see faces that aged before their time. Finally, he took solace by convincing himself that he has to be content that he has a new life that could make up for what he lost, and that he has to accept things as they are!³⁴

Louay realizes that the Iraq he fondly remembered and yearned for no longer existed. Rather than a joyful reunion, Louay meets his relatives in a darkness that reflects the devastation of the country because of frequent power outages; he sees people who are exhausted by violence and sanctions. Moreover, Louay's desires do not always make sense to those who had stayed in Iraq. For instance, Louay expresses to Salar his desire to regain his Iraqi citizenship, but Salar does not understand why, because Louay's Swedish citizenship allows him to travel freely—even to Israel—which he could not do with Iraqi citizenship. Unable to explain, Louay changes the topic by asking Salar why the family moved from the old neighborhood, implying that his relatives had let go of his grandfather's house too easily. Salar has to explain that the move was necessary for their survival, because they wanted to avoid government surveillance and because the makeup of neighborhood had changed drastically when some of the inhabitants were deported and new inhabitants loyal to the regime moved in. Whereas Louay attempts to assert an Iraqi subjectivity by reclaiming his Iraqi citizenship and to cling to the memories of his past by holding onto his grandfather's house, Salar is the voice of reality, reminding Louay that an Iraqi citizenship is useless and that surviving under an authoritarian regime means letting go of fond memories. The two cousins inhabit different worlds: one of them is invested in reclaiming citizenship of which he had been stripped, while the other perceives such a symbolic gesture as meaningless in a country that has destroyed its children and erased their history. In the face of Salar's cold logic that he can go anywhere in the world with his Swedish citizenship, Louay cannot articulate to his cousin why he still clings to the identity of his childhood.

Salar ends the conversation by commenting that if Louay misses the ghosts in the old house, he should not worry, since they all came with them to the new neighborhood. This comment opens a space for the two cousins to talk about Qismat, and Louay remarks that Qismat followed them to Iran as well. However, the two cousins, though they were happy to see Qismat during moments of crisis, are not charitable to her during this conversation. Salar describes her as ungrateful and impious, while Louay compares her to a curse. Qismat emerges as a contradictory figure for the cousins. While she can be a link to Iraq and the past, she also haunts the family and draws attention to unresolved violence. It is telling that it is Louay who thinks of his aunt as a curse, since she stands for the motherland that destroyed its children but refused to disappear. Louay is at once haunted by the aunt who killed herself and by the country that stripped him of his nationality. This relationship to his homeland and aunt becomes fraught during the visit to Iraq in that Louay is attached deeply to a place that destroyed him and his family. The love for the homeland is accompanied by the pain of betrayal. Iraq becomes a haunted place for the silenced violence it visited upon its children. However, Salar ends the conversation about Qismat by saluting her: "Frankly, I cannot but salute her for her insolence and recklessness in facing this cursed life! As if she gave life the middle finger and said, 'Fuck you, it is not an honor to live this life. I'll take my loved ones with me.'"[35] Salar reads Qismat's decision to kill herself and her children as a rejection of her wretched life and as an effort to spare her children a bleak future.

The next day, Louay, Majeed, and Salar go to different ministries to inquire about reclaiming property and nationality.[36] After a visit to the municipality, the three stop to drink tea at Al-Wathba Square. Soon after they arrive, an explosion shakes the area. Although the three are shielded from the blast, Majeed dies of a heart attack from the shock. Instead of regaining his lost property and nationality, Majeed loses his life, and instead of reclaiming his nationality, Louay loses his father, even though they were never on good terms after the deportation. Louay has to stay in Iraq for three weeks instead of one, as he had planned. He has to wait for his family to come from Iran to bury his father in Najaf. As soon the burial is over, Louay flies back to Sweden. Upon landing in Sweden, Louay sighs with relief that "this journey of suffering [has come] to an end. His journey was supposed to last for one week, but was extended for three long and exhausting weeks, during which he had to confront his past and part of his future in a rough and strange way. The most shocking thing was surviving a certain death with his cousin Salar. . . . Louay had been in Baghdad for twenty-four hours when he had to make the quick decision to bury his father in Najaf, and to inform his family of the father's death."[37] He could not even enjoy being in Iraq for a day without facing death and losing a family member. His desire to reacquire his Iraqi citizenship dissipates, and he decides to go back to Sweden, where his only real future lies, as soon as possible. Iraq can only remain an open wound.

While most of the novel focuses on the lives of Qismat's relatives who were haunted by her ghost, the reader gets to hear Qismat's perspective for the first time in the last chapter. As a ghost, Qismat merely appeared to the living but did not communicate with them. However, al-Nadawi transfers the reader to a conversation between Qismat and Perka, just a few days before her suicide, during one of her depressive episodes. Qismat passes a haunted house in the neighborhood, where she sees the shadow of a woman, and, curious about the woman, she attempts to go inside the house. However, Perka appears before her and prevents her from entering the house. Perka, the soothsayer, tells Qismat two omens: first, that she will live a long and quiet life, that she will have many grandchildren, and that her husband will become a successful merchant; and second, that a bleak future awaits the county in fifty-five years, around 2005. Perka says, "I even see this place very clearly after long years. I see a young man's deformed corpse thrown in that corner fifty-five years from now. This young man will be killed because of clashes with the residents of another neighborhood, another ethnic group, or another sect. I'm not sure but it is something like that. He'll be killed because of his different identity anyway!"[38] While Perka can see the civil war that will grip Iraq after the fall of Saddam Hussein's regime, Qismat becomes curious about whether she will be in a different country or dead in fifty-five years. Perka informs her that a significant part of their community will not be in Iraq by that time. After a short pause, he adds, "You're one of them. You'll be one of those who leave this country years before all the atrocities that will take place. The fate that is awaiting our community is worse and dark."[39] When Qismat asks about the fate of her children, Perka says that she cannot take his words seriously.

For the next two days, Qismat is tormented by the haunted house and Perka's words, in addition to her manic-depressive moods. In the end, she decides to drown herself with her two young children and unborn baby in the Tigris.

As she walks toward her death, she hears a voice replete with hope: "We'll survive. We'll survive."⁴⁰ To Qismat, death represents hope in that it spares her and her children a future filled with pain, tragedy, and loss. In light of the deportation campaign between 1980 and 1985 and the violence following the US invasion in 2003, Qismat and her children would not have fared well. Like Louay and his family, she could have been deported to Iran and forced to live away from her family and country. Or like Salar and his family, she could have stayed in Iraq but lived under an authoritarian regime that dragged the country into three wars and sanctions. In the end, she or her children could have died in an explosion like Majeed fifty-four years later. Through Perka, Qismat can see the future. Given her sick soul, as the narrator describes it, she might have thought that she did not have the strength to deal with these tragedies or to see her children torn between countries and die due to violence. Qismat's tragic death by suicide at the age of nineteen eliminated the tragic future that awaited her. One can say that she decided to exercise some agency by choosing to exit life altogether and to come back as a ghost to haunt the living. As a silent ghost, she beckoned to unresolved and silenced violence, represented by the expulsion of Iraqi Jews and by the deportation of *taba'iyya*. That these events could happen in the first place with no protest or acknowledgment paved the way for future violence, displacements, and silences. Qismat haunted the living over generations to remind them of a history of loss and lingering trouble.

Conclusion

The ghost of Qismat in this historical novel is an allegory for a country haunted by violence, repressed memories, and erasures. Qismat, as a ghost, is a social figure that attempts to draw attention to social and political structures that have affected certain Iraqi communities but whose legacies remain silenced. Qismat haunts the living throughout the decades in order to draw attention to the plight of expelled communities and the precarity of women. As a woman who was married off at a young age and was left on her own to deal with her mental health issues, Qismat shows the cruelty of a patriarchal society. As a symbol of the motherland that killed itself and its children, she sheds light on the deportation of Iraqi citizens who felt a deep attachment to Iraq. Moreover, as someone who could see the future, she forewarns of later deportations and of the consolidation of patriarchal values during times of crises. In addition, *Qismat* is a meditation on the notions of belonging and citizenship from the perspective of Iraqi citizens who were rendered expendable and deportable by ruling elites. The deported protagonists in this novel occupy a betwixt-and-between status and have to grapple with alienation and misrecognition. The right to reclaim challenges official discourses that perceived Iraqis whose ancestors held Persian citizenship as the Other and brings about an alternative reading of the history of modern Iraq that draws attention to the expulsion of Iraqi Jews. A repressed past, wherein a whole community was expelled, becomes a harbinger for another repressed future, when another community was deported and silenced. At the end of the novel, even the fond memories of the past have to be destroyed upon an encounter with the homeland in the present. Just as Qismat haunted the living, Iraq itself becomes a ghost haunting the living.

FIVE

GENDER RUPTURES

SHORTLY AFTER THE ENACTMENT of the law that stripped *taba'iyya* of their citizenship in 1980, the minister of the interior issued guidelines regarding the implementation of the law, which included an article that exempted young men between the ages of 18 and 28 from deportation and ordered their detention until further notice.[1] Almost a year later, the Iraqi Revolutionary Command Council, headed by Saddam Hussein, signed a law that gave money to any Iraqi man who divorced his *taba'iyya* wife. These laws were accompanied by the sexual assault and rape of women by state officials in charge of carrying out the deportation orders. Though I could not find any directives or laws that called for sexual violence, the practice was widespread enough that it was common to hear stories about rape when I lived in Iraq in the early 1980s and when I started my research among the Iraqi diaspora in London two decades later.

The gendered forms of cruelty unleashed during the campaign to expel *taba'iyya* show how the Iraqi regime perceived the body as a gendered site of governance and violence. While *taba'iyya* women's bodies were violated, young *taba'iyya* men's bodies were eliminated for fear that they might fight against Iraq during the Iran-Iraq War if deported to Iran. Recent scholarship has examined how the state—whether through neoliberal reforms, education, military service, police brutality and surveillance, sexual and gender violence, or failure to deal with toxic waste—perceives bodies as sites of intervention in order to debilitate and govern.[2] In the case of Iraq, the bodies of both men and women emerged as arenas for the state to assert its sovereignty through its capacity to determine not only who was disposable and who was not but also who was violable and who was not.³ The very precarity of citizenship as a right for individual Iraqis translated into the state's unfettered right to detain, disappear, and kill young men; to violate young women; and to break up marriage contracts. As stateless and denaturalized individuals who were presented as a fifth column collaborating with Iran against the Iraqi state, young Iraqi men and women lost the right to bodily integrity, life, and family relations.

Whereas *taba'iyya* women experienced sexual violence while they and their families went through an all-encompassing campaign of dispossession, families of detained young men had to spend two decades wondering about their fate, only to learn after the fall of Saddam Hussein's regime in 2003 that they had been killed and buried in mass graves. The inability to find closure was exacerbated by rumors that these young men had died under torture or had become guinea pigs for the regime to carry out chemical experiments. These different forms of gender-based violence invited different responses from Iraqi deportees. While my Iraqi interlocutors in London mourned disappeared young men as martyred heroes, they were either silent on cases of divorce or equivocating when talking about sexual violence. Though Iraqi deportees perceived sexual assault as state-perpetuated violence against women whose purpose was to inflict as much pain as possible upon denaturalized families, they still mobilized the language of women's honor (*sharaf*) when reflecting on the silence surrounding this topic. Divorced and violated Iraqi women came to signify dishonor and disgrace rather than being acknowledged as victims of sexual violence. Although I heard stories about specific young men, knew their names, and saw their pictures, I was left with only hints about faceless and nameless women who had been divorced by their husbands or subjected to sexual violence.

This chapter examines the ways that Saddam Hussein's regime perceived both *taba'iyya* men and women as national threats and devised different laws to govern and discipline them and their bodies, employing violence to shatter families and exacerbate the loss of citizenship and expulsion to Iran. While part of this chapter examines these gendered laws and measures, it also discusses the question of researching and writing about gender-based violence. The first part of the chapter offers an account of my decades-long attempt to find an Iraqi woman who was divorced by her husband. The second section revolves around the regime's suspicion of *taba'iyya* women, which relates back to some of the concerns that Ottoman officials had about Iranian women marrying Ottoman men. While offering an archival reading of specific laws, it also discusses unwritten practices—namely, sexual violence against women. The third part employs archival and ethnographic material to reflect on the disappearance of young men and the inability of their families to mourn or find closure. In this story, the right to kill and disappear exercised by Saddam Hussein's regime translated into denial of the human need to have a body and a cause of death in order to be able to mourn, perform required rituals of burial and commemoration, and move on by finding closure.

Pursuing an Archive of Silence and Disavowal

Writing this book has been a source of anxiety and doubt ever since I envisioned it as a viable project. The challenge I faced was to find a *taba'iyya* woman whose husband had accepted the generous monetary reward offered by Saddam Hussein's regime. Since gender-based violence was an integral part of citizenship laws and experiences of expulsion in Iraq, I could not figure out how I could publish a book that had such a glaring gap. Since I began my ethnographic research on my first book in 2006, I have been asking Iraqi deportees I met in the United Kingdom if they or their friends and families knew of any women who were divorced. The answer I always heard was negative. When I finally turned to this project around 2019, after I finished my first book, I intensified my efforts to try to find at least one divorced woman. I asked Iraqi friends—both those who themselves were *taba'iyya* and those who had friends who were *taba'iyya*—in the United States, the United Kingdom, Jordan, and Iraq if they knew anyone. To my disappointment, all these incessant inquiries yielded nothing. I thought if a wall of silence has been built around the question of divorce, then how could I even ask about sexual violence or write a book on citizenship having failed to cover the question of gender adequately? Moreover, if violence against women was shrouded in silence, how could I respect this desire to save face and respect privacy while trying to document the magnitude of violence some *taba'iyya* families faced, as well as the entanglement of citizenship practices, gender, and patriarchal norms? The only leads I had were the divorce directive issued by the Iraqi Revolutionary Command Council in 1981 and a quick mention of a *taba'iyya* woman divorced by her husband in Zahra Ali's *Women and Gender in Iraq*.[4]

As I read through my fieldnotes and listened to interviews, I realized that this silence about divorce was concomitant with a discourse of disavowal about sexual violence. When I interviewed *taba'iyya* Iraqis in London who had been deported to Iran in the 1980s but managed to seek asylum in the United

Kingdom years later, I heard references to rape and sexual assault. While reflecting on the hardships of deportation, such as crossing the Iran-Iraq border in winter on foot through areas filled with landmines during the Iran-Iraq War, Iraqi deportees often promptly mentioned that they had heard stories of young women who were sexually assaulted by Iraqi officials in charge of overseeing the deportation, usually in deportation camps or on the way to the border. My interlocutors often added that these Iraqi women resorted to one of two options to "protect their family's honor:" they died of suicide or they married a relative or the first man who proposed to them as soon as they arrived in Iran. That my interlocutors employed the language of honor, rather than sexual violation or bodily integrity, explains the reluctance to share personal stories, since they perceived acts of sexual and gender violence as tainting not only the woman's honor but also her family's honor. Interestingly, my interlocutors invoked the Arabic phrase used in Iraq when a woman's reputation is in question but she still manages to find a husband: *ustur ʿaleha*. The word *ustur* comes from the verb *satara*, which literally means "to cover, to hide, to screen." When used in colloquial Iraqi in the phrase *ustur ʿaleha*, the word connotes that a man carried out a magnanimous act by marrying a woman whose reputation was in question because of her own behavior or something outside her control. Not only did Iraqi women who were defined by the state as *tabaʿiyya*, and hence deportable and violable, have to endure sexual trauma, but they also had to confront patriarchal norms about women's honor and try to restore their family's reputation, either through death or marriage.

The discourse of honor was accompanied by a discourse of disavowal. The majority of Iraqi deportees I interviewed or talked to brought up the issue of sexual violence of their own accord while reflecting on the horrors that Saddam Hussein's regime had inflicted on their community. However, they all were quick to comment that they were lucky because the young women in their families did not meet such a fate. This discourse of disavowal seems to be constituted in a deep-seated desire to acknowledge that rape and sexual assault were integral to the regime's deportation campaign, as well as in a need to preempt any suspicion that the listener might have regarding the speaker's family. What has been striking to me about this move is that it attempts to hint at sexual violence but, at the same time, deny and disavow it at the personal level. I talked to many Iraqi deportees in different places in the world over almost two decades and yet I always heard the same narrative. Were all the people I talked to so lucky indeed? Or were they trying to make sure I knew about this horror but distance themselves from it in order to protect their loved ones or to avoid reliving traumatic memories? Had some of the *taba'iyya* women, who were middle-aged by the time I met them, experienced sexual violence when they were deported, and is this why they alluded to it? Was it only shame and patriarchal values that prevented them from sharing their stories, given that many Iraqi men and women I met during my research were candid about graphic details of torture and atrocities they witnessed? Since many of the *taba'iyya* women have young brothers who disappeared, did they think that their sexual trauma paled in comparison to the unknown and horrific fate that the young men faced, and hence, the focus of the story should be the young men, rather than them?

Thinking of gender-based violence in terms of silences and disavowals enabled me to look for traces and hints and forego my obsession with direct evidence. In her research on the aftermath of mass violence, Yael Navaro asks about the feasibility of research when witnesses are exterminated or are unable to bear witness and when regimes tamper with "material remains."[5] She problematizes anthropological methodologies that assume "the availability, presence, and accessibility of 'evidence.'"[6] Rather, Navaro proposes "a negative methodological practice" and invites the anthropologist to "locate her-/himself not in the anticipation of the presence of evidence about mass atrocity, but in the political domain of spaces where these events have been glossed over or misappropriated and where access to evidence continues to be limited, complicated, or denied."[7] With the mass denaturalization and deportation of *taba'iyya*, I had to work with traces of gender-based violence, since its experiences were erased not because of the death of witnesses but because of the societal perception of rape and sexual assault as unspeakable acts that bring shame upon a family. Such silencing makes the anthropological search for evidence through interviews with victims impossible. Disavowal constitutes a technique to equivocate—to reference something but also to deny it as a personal experience. Rather than repression, Iraqi deportees framed the unspeakable as an act that took place "out there" but not "here." Disavowal invokes the presence of violence but the absence of evidence. As an ephemeral archive of horrors that comes to life during the moment of narration, disavowal seeks to document without implicating the speaker and/or their relatives as victims of sexual violence. Disavowal utters the unspeakable without the specter of shame, stigma, and social death.

As I was thinking about these issues, COVID-19 brought the whole world to a standstill. Writing became a therapeutic distraction for me from all the uncertainty and my phobia of illness. Finishing this book consumed all my attention as I was on sabbatical during the first few months of lockdown. As I made progress with the rest of the book, I began to get anxious about absences and inaccessibility of evidence again. As vaccines became available and the prospect of doing research reemerged as a possibility, I decided to reach out to more friends to ask if they knew any *tabaʿiyya* woman who had been divorced by her husband and to conduct archival research at the Hoover Institution, where parts of the Baʿth Party's archives ended up after they were stolen and smuggled to the United States following the US invasion of Iraq in 2003. As far as ethnographic research was concerned, I sought the help of a close Iraqi friend in London, who has a wide network of Iraqi friends and acquaintances all over the world and who opened many doors for me when I did my fieldwork for my first book. This was a Hail Mary on my part, since I thought if all the Iraqi deportees I knew and had met did not know anyone, how could this friend who was not *tabaʿiyya* know anyone. To my utter shock, this friend called me one day to share some mixed and unexpected news. She informed me that she had recently met an Iraqi woman whose family held Ottoman nationality but whose husband was *tabaʿiyya*. The twist in this story was that the husband was deported along with his parents and siblings, but his wife, Sahar, was not, since she had Ottoman citizenship. When she came under pressure from Saddam Hussein's regime to divorce her husband and marry a Baʿth member instead, Sahar fled to Iran with her young children to join her husband. The bad news was that Sahar was hesitant to talk to me.

I immediately got in touch with Sahar on WhatsApp, and we exchanged a few voice messages in June 2022. Sahar, like all Iraqis I met in the United Kingdom during my research, was suspicious and wanted to know why I was asking questions about *tabaʿiyya* divorced women. I told her about my research and my efforts to document what *tabaʿiyya* went through, given the scant scholarship on the topic. I tried to reassure her about confidentiality and anonymity in anthropological writing, but she told me to contact her again in a few weeks, as she had just returned from a long and exhausting trip overseas. A few weeks later, my friend told me that Sahar had to have heart surgery and that an interview would be difficult at the time. In July 2023, during a trip to London, my friend got in touch with Sahar, and she agreed to give me an interview. I met Sahar in a mall in West London shortly after that. Just like all my Iraqi interlocutors that I interviewed over the years, Sahar wanted to know my story—in particular, information related to my parents and my research. Once I told her that every member of my immediate family had died in

Iraq because of Saddam Hussein's persecution, she shared her story with me openly. In the interview, which I will discuss in the next section, Sahar, who had spent decades in Iran, shed light on the relationships between politics, gender, and violence.

The archival research at the Hoover Institution did not yield much information. Though I suspected that might be the case before I began, I still wanted to make sure I did not overlook any resource I had access to. I hoped to get a sense of the scale of the phenomena of divorce and disappearing by finding some lists about or references to husbands who had received monetary rewards after they divorced their *taba'iyya* wives and to young men who had perished under unknown circumstances. The Boxfiles Database from the Ba'th Regional Command Collection contained limited and short documents about deportation and citizenship. What was striking about the documents in this database was the fact that the directives were written in non-incriminating and matter-of-fact language. These visits to the archives left me with two impressions. The first is related to the number of ministries and departments that were involved in the process of deportation—namely, the Ministry of the Interior, the Iraqi Revolutionary Command Council, the Bureau of Citizenship and Personal Affairs, the Public Security Directorate, the Iraqi Intelligence Service (Mukhabarat), the Council of the Presidency (Diwan al-Ri'sa), and various local and regional branches of the Ba'th Party. Noticeably, the parliament and the police were not part of the communication or legislation processes. The second impression is that the database I looked at was not like the Stasi archive, with exhaustive reports and details about people, laws, procedures, or processes.

Despite the lack of archival evidence as well as the reluctance among Iraqi deportees to share experiences of sexual and gender violence openly, my interview with Sahar provided insights into the ways Saddam Hussein's regime sought to inflict pain and injury upon Iraqi deportees through family separation, disappearance of young men, and sexual violence. Moreover, it aimed to undermine family relations by bribing one spouse to betray the other. The denaturalization and deportation of *taba'iyya*, as such, speaks to the relationship between gender, governmentality, and violence. Interestingly, *taba'iyya* men and women were both subject to different forms of gender-based violence: while the young men had to be exterminated, women had to endure sexual violence and betrayal from their husbands.

The Right to Violate

Gender-based violence speaks to issues related to citizenship laws and gender, as well as the body and debility. Regarding citizenship rights, Iraqi women, like many women all over the world at different times, were subject to marital denaturalization if they married a foreign man.[8] For instance, the Iraqi Nationality Law of 1924 defined married women as minors, alongside underage children and "crazy" (*majnoon*) and "imbecile" (*ma'touh*) individuals. Moreover, it dictated that an Iraqi woman marrying a foreigner would lose her Iraqi citizenship but could reclaim it within three years after divorce or the death of her husband.[9] Marital denaturalization was retained in subsequent amendments to the law in later decades.[10] As such, the law of 1980, which provided monetary incentives for husbands to divorce *taba'iyya* wives, aimed to override the legal dependency of wives on their husbands regarding citizenship rights and rendered married women subject to their husband's beneficence, since these women were not included in the deportation orders. The reality some *taba'iyya* women confronted was that their husbands could decide to stay married to them and, hence, spare them expulsion, or they could face divorce, deportation, and separation from their children, who would stay in Iraq, since they inherited the father's citizenship. Rather than national symbols of tradition, authenticity, and motherhood, *taba'iyya* women emerged as threats to the state and had their husbands coaxed by Saddam Hussein's regime to uphold its campaign of denaturalization and deportation.

In 1980, the Iraqi Revolutionary Command Council issued Resolution 474. This directive stated that "an Iraqi husband who is married to a woman of the *taba'iyya iraniyya* will be rewarded 4,000 Iraqi dinars if he is a man of arms and 2,500 Iraqi dinars if he is a civilian when he divorces his wife or when she is deported."[11] If the Ottomans were concerned about marriages between Ottoman (Sunni) women and Persian (Shi'i) men, the Iraqi regime saw women who were *taba'iyya* as the threat. In this decree, a *taba'iyya* wife imperiled her husband's loyalty, and, in turn, the nation's strength and sovereignty. Husbands emerged as symbols of the nation, while *taba'iyya* wives represented the interests and culture of the Other. No longer limited to women, national integrity was located in men's national struggle against the enemy within. Indeed, the rules for holding certain army ranks and state positions, such as president, stipulated that the applicant's parents and spouse must hold Ottoman nationality. Though the Iraqi regime did not ban such marriages outright, it attempted to control them. For instance, a secret Ba'th memorandum stipulated that a party member could not marry before the Ba'th Party Secretariat granted permission, after investigating and determining the Arabness of the family of the applicant's betrothed. A member whose marriage permit was denied but insisted on marrying this Other would be expelled from the party.[12]

Sahar's life story shows the ways that citizenship for Iraqi men and women was differently forged in the crucible of the state's written and unwritten policies, patriarchal norms, and gender relations. The denaturalization of *taba'iyya* became an exercise in undermining family relations when both *taba'iyya* young men and *taba'iyya* women married to Iraqi men with Ottoman citizenship emerged as national threats. Whereas young men were physically eliminated through disappearance and death, *taba'iyya* women were subject to gender violence when the regime granted their husbands monetary incentives to divorce them. Moreover, Sahar's life experience speaks to unwritten practices that took place during the deportation campaign—namely, sexual violence against young *taba'iyya* women, as well as pressure on Iraqi women whose family held Ottoman nationality to divorce their *taba'iyya* husbands. The accusations of foreignness leveled by the regime rendered both *taba'iyya* men and women disposable and violable through different gendered legislation and unwritten laws. Sahar's narrative speaks to the different forms of violence and precarity that her in-laws and Iraqi deportees she met in Iran endured.

Sahar was born in the early 1950s. Her family identified as Arab and historically held Ottoman citizenship. At the age of fourteen, Sahar was married off to her husband, who was a Shi'i Kurd whose ancestors held Persian nationality under the Ottomans. Though her husband had a university degree, he could not secure a job in the state apparatus because he was *taba'iyya*, so he worked as a merchant with an uncle. Sahar, who had her first child when she was only fifteen, described her life in her in-laws' household as "peaceful and joyful." Though her in-laws were staunchly secular and Sahar had come from a religious family, they accepted her as she was, though they often teased her about her religious beliefs.

In early 1980, Sahar's life was upended when her in-laws and their relatives—around thirty households—were deported to Iran, along with her husband, because they hailed from Iran and had lived on the Iran-Iraq border generations ago. Though Sahar's father-in-law and husband had been born in Iraq, lived all their lives in Baghdad, and identified as Iraqis, they were not spared deportation. Moreover, both the immediate and extended family faced multiple forms of violence and tragedy. For instance, one of her husband's uncles, who was a successful merchant in Shorja, was executed by Hussein's regime under the pretext that he belonged to the Da'wa (Call) Party. In addition, this uncle's five sons were later detained and disappeared when their mother and one sister were deported to Iran. Shortly after arriving in Iran, their mother passed away and their sister was married off to a deported relative.

Sahar's immediate family also faced adversity during the deportation campaign. As an Iraqi citizen whose ancestors had held Ottoman nationality, Sahar did not lose her citizenship or face deportation. When the police came to the house to deport her husband, Sahar insisted on going and taking their children with him. The family was transferred to Headquarters No. 3, where denaturalized families awaited deportation. While some families were deported immediately, others waited for months. When Sahar got to the detention camp with her family, she was advised by an officer, whom she described as decent, to go back to Baghdad with her children when it was their turn to be deported. The officer told her stories about sexual violence against young and beautiful women and encouraged her to assert that she held Ottoman citizenship. Scared for her daughters and herself, Sahar managed to convince the officials in charge of deportation to let her and her children go back to her parents in Baghdad, while her husband was deported to Iran. While she was living in Baghdad and trying to find a way to join her husband and in-laws in Iran, Iraqi officials contacted Sahar. They informed her that they could dissolve her marriage to her husband, grant her 3,000 Iraqi dinars if she agreed to the divorce, and marry her off to one of "the national heroes," a member of the Ba'th Party. As part of this arrangement, the officials told Sahar that "her Magi and Persian" children would be deported to Iran since they were *taba'iyya iraniyya*.

After this encounter, Sahar became determined to find a way to flee Iraq with her children. However, reaching Iran proved to be a lengthy and expensive ordeal. Sahar had an Iraqi passport, and securing an Iranian visa as the Iran-Iraq War raged was no easy feat. She sold her jewelry in order to finance trips between three countries in the region in the hope that an Iranian embassy in one of them would grant her and her children a visa. Finally, during one trip, Sahar met a young Iraqi man who informed her that he could secure a visa if she was willing to pay bribes. To her tremendous surprise, this young man kept his promise, and Sahar and her children got an Iranian visa and flew to Tehran, where they reunited with her husband. But reuniting with him was painful. Not only did Sahar learn that her father-in-law had died a year earlier, but she was also heartbroken when her children could not recognize their father, because he had aged significantly during the previous two years. While reuniting with her husband was a relief, Sahar faced the harsh reality that the majority of deported Iraqi families endured in Iran. As the Iran-Iraq War brought devastation to Iranian border and major cities, Iranian neighbors perceived Sahar and her family as Arabs whose homeland was bombing their country. Moreover, the Iranian government did not allow deported Iraqis to attend Persian schools, buy a house, or work legally. Sahar and her husband sent their children to an Iraqi school established by Iraqi Shi'i scholars who wielded some influence in Iran because of their family lineage or scholarly standing. A few years later, Sahar and her husband married off their daughter to an Iraqi relative who lived in Europe, while her eldest son managed a way out of the legal, educational, and professional impasse he faced in Iran by seeking asylum in Australia.

In Iran, Sahar worked at an Iraqi political organization with religious leanings, first as a volunteer and then as a paid employee. The job involved providing support to Iraqi families whose breadwinners had been killed by Saddam Hussein's regime. In addition to helping families of martyrs, the organization also looked after deported families. There, Sahar met many Iraqi *taba'iyya* women whose husbands had divorced for the monetary reward offered by the regime. She also came across young women who had been raped or sexually assaulted upon deportation. Like other stories I heard from Iraqi deportees, Sahar reiterated that some of these young women had been married off to deported relatives who agreed to do the honorable thing by marrying a woman whose honor had been defiled (*ustur 'aleha*), while other women died by suicide, especially if they got pregnant. Though I did not ask her if she could put me in touch with women who had experienced sexual violence, Sahar also stressed that none of these women would be willing to talk about what had happened. Interestingly, Sahar commented that she shared incidents of sexual and gender violence with me so that I could write about them as part of the brutalities inflicted upon families by Saddam Hussein's regime, even though I could not have access to these women. Reflecting the perception of rape, sexual assault, and divorce as social taboos by the majority of Iraqis, Sahar wanted to me to document the atrocities without the possibility that these women would lose face in front of me or anyone else.

In 2002, Sahar left Iran on her own to try to reach Britain and apply for asylum. She and her husband thought she would have a better chance of getting asylum alone and then applying for family reunion later. After her application was approved, Sahar managed to bring the rest of her family to London. However, life in the United Kingdom was not easy either, despite the social benefits and services provided by the British government to refugees. Sahar's husband died in 2006, and she had to work to provide for her children and to pay some of the debt she had incurred covering the legal expenses for her asylum case. In order to sustain her family, Sahar made and sold Iraqi food and used some of the jewelry she had smuggled out of Iraq as a way to meet emergency expenses. However, despite all the challenges, Sahar was happy to be settled in London. After 2003, she visited Iraq but did not want to live there again because, in her words, "people in Iraq have changed a lot. Everything is fake. People are rotten because of injustices." In addition, Sahar was a warm, social, and friendly person who managed to build a wide network of Iraqi women friends; they provided support to each other during difficult times and socialized together in their houses or cafés in shopping centers in London. The fact that London was a major center for Iraqis in Europe enabled Sahar, like the majority of Iraqis in the British capital, to enjoy an Iraqi life in diaspora.

My conversation with Sahar shows how Saddam Hussein's regime mobilized patriarchal norms and the legal apparatus to further inflict injury upon deported families. Indeed, citizenship for Iraqi women became entangled in the cauldron of the state and patriarchy. On the one hand, the directive that offered husbands a monetary reward if they divorced their *taba'iyya* wives endowed husbands with the power to decide if their wives remained Iraqi citizens and could continue to live in Iraq or would be deported. Since Saddam Hussein's regime categorized *taba'iyya* wives as a national threat, it perceived husbands as the appropriate agents to defend the nation through divorce. *Taba'iyya* women were doubly dispossessed in this case, first by the state through legislation that defined them as foreigners, and second by their husbands, who retained the power to act upon the state's laws. In this instance, the state attempted to coax husbands to uphold its deportation campaign but did not overrule their power, since the ultimate decision about divorce remained with husbands. On the other hand, not only did the unwritten practice of incentivizing Iraqi women whose ancestors held Ottoman citizenship to divorce their *taba'iyya* husbands aim to bypass these men's prerogative to exercise their right to end a marriage, but it revealed the ways the state posited itself as the ultimate patriarch—or the father of the nation—who could annul marriages when the husbands were deemed the internal enemy. Finally, the state, personified in the figures of officials in charge of deportation, employed sexual violence against young women in order to inflict injury, since sexual assault not only engendered psychological and physical trauma but also transgressed many social taboos: the violation of women, the failure of their male relatives to protect them, and the loss of honor and reputation for the whole family.[13]

Patriarchal norms around divorce and sexual assault among Iraqi deportees meant that these women were considered dishonored victims who brought shame upon the family. As such, any accounts of what they had been through had to be silenced and erased, though references to their plight abounded in conversations about deportation. As long as the unspeakable remained an abstract act that referred to faceless and nameless women, it could be hinted at. Unlike the archive of silence that surrounds women's experience with gender and sexual violence, *taba'iyya* young men between the ages of eighteen and twenty-eight who were detained by the regime and later disappeared emerged as celebrated martyrs in their families' narratives.

The Right to Disappear

During the deportation campaign, *taba'iyya* women were not the only victims of gender-based violence. Saddam Hussein's regime defined young *taba'iyya* men as a threat to the nation as well. On April 10, 1980, the minister of the interior, Sa'adoun Shakir Hamadi, sent a confidential directive to the governors of Iraqi provinces, the Bureau of Police, the Public Security Directorate, the Bureau of Border Control, and the Bureau of Citizenship and Personal Affairs. Directive 3884 states that the enclosed instructions about the implementation of deportation orders aim to clarify any confusion and rectify any mistakes. Signed by the minister of the interior, Article 3, which lists the people exempt from deportation, dictates that "young men between the ages of 18 and 28 included in the deportation directive will be exempt from deportation, and will be kept in detention centers in their provinces until further notice."[14] The fate of these disappeared young men became a source of agony for their families, who did not know how or when their loved ones died, and where they were buried. This lack of knowledge about the cause of death was aggravated by rumors in Iran and Iraq that these young men were deployed to the frontlines during the Iran-Iraq War to serve as human shields, that they died under torture, or that they were subject to chemical experiments as Saddam Hussein's regime developed its arsenal of chemical weapons. In addition, the fact that these young men had no known graves or death certificates meant that their families could not perform any burial and mourning rituals. In this case, the right to disappear emerged as retribution technologies whose purpose was to inflict lifelong injury and harm upon deported Iraqis.

I heard many stories about disappeared young men from my interlocutors who had been deported to Iran and managed to relocate to London. Sulaf's narrative reflects the anguish and multiple traumas deported Iraqis endured. I met Sulaf at an event about mass graves and the disappeared in Iraq organized by an Iraqi Muslim organization in London in 2006. Unlike many Iraqi interlocutors who were initially hesitant to talk to me, Sulaf was welcoming and enthusiastic to share her story. After a few inquiries about my family and my research, she invited me to visit her at her apartment so that she could tell me about the disappearance of her brothers when her family was deported in the early 1980s. In addition, Sulaf shared that her brothers' unknown fate had engendered a lifelong commitment to find out what had happened to them and to draw attention to the atrocities that Saddam Hussein's regime perpetuated. She also informed me that our conversation was part of her efforts to make people in the West aware of this erased violence, and she urged me to write about her and her brothers in my book. Sulaf lived in a modest apartment in West London that the council had provided to her family—her husband and their four children—upon applying for asylum in the early 1990s. The window sills in the living room had pictures of her three disappeared brothers with black ribbons around each frame with artificial flowers between them. As soon as we walked into the living room, Sulaf stepped toward the pictures and told me each brother's name, school grade and college level, passion or hobby, and age upon disappearance. Moreover, she always referred to her brothers and other disappeared young men as martyrs who died young at the hand of an authoritarian regime and who would go to heaven on Judgment Day.

Sulaf hails from an Arab Shi'i family that lived for generations in the holy city of Najaf. Under Ottoman rule, her ancestors acquired Persian citizenship in order to avoid military service in the Ottoman army and having to pay taxes to Istanbul. Sulaf's father was a successful merchant who provided an affluent life for his family. On April 7, 1980, he, along with around eight hundred influential and wealthy Shi'i merchants, was summoned to the Chamber of Commerce in Baghdad, which informed the merchants that they needed to have their trade licenses renewed and should bring all the documents they had—such as identity cards, certificates of citizenship, property deeds, and commerce licenses. Upon arrival at the Chamber of Commerce, state officials ordered the merchants to hand over all their documents and get in buses parked outside the building. The merchants were not allowed to call their families and had no idea where they were heading. After hours on the road, the buses reached the border, and the state agents told the merchants to get out and walk across to Iran. This was the start of the deportation campaign against *taba'iyya*. The families of these merchants waited anxiously for them to return from the meeting, not knowing what had happened to them. Bit by bit, rumors of the deportation began to circulate. It was not long before these merchants' families faced the same fate.[15]

The disappearance of Sulaf's father was a source of tremendous anxiety for the family. For three months, they had no idea about his whereabouts despite their frequent inquiries at different state institutions, such as the Public Security Directorate and Ba'th Party branches in Najaf and Baghdad. They finally heard on Iranian radio that Iraqi merchants had been deported to Iran. At that time, Sulaf's mother tried to leave the country legally with Sulaf, who was seventeen years old, and her three sons. However, the officials at the Bureau of Passports informed them that they were banned from leaving the country and that their house was under surveillance since they were *taba'iyya*. On New Year's Day in 1981, five men in military uniform came to the house and ordered them to accompany them to the Public Security Directorate in Najaf. Shortly afterward, Sulaf and her mother, who were separated from the three sons, were transferred to a different prison in Najaf, where they spent three months. After moving to another prison in the south of the country, Sulaf and her mother were finally transferred to a prison in Baghdad, where they spent six months. During this time, Sulaf and her mom had no idea what happened to the boys and had no contact with Sulaf's father in Iran. In addition to the uncertainty about the fate of their family members, Sulaf and her mother were living in abysmal conditions. The food was always inedible and insufficient, and the hygiene standards were dreadful. At one point, Sulaf and her mother had to share a small room with sixty-five other women. One day, following a year spent in different prisons and detention centers, they were asked to get into a pickup truck, which drove them to the border with Iran. From there, they had to walk for three days in the cold and amid minefields until they reached Iran. Upon arrival in Iran, Sulaf and her mother still didn't know where the brothers were. They had expected to be reunited with the boys at some point during the journey to Iran. When they finally reunited with Sulaf's father in a refugee camp set up by the Iranian government for Iraqi deportees, he collapsed when he did not see his young sons. Rather than bringing a sense of relief, the reunion confirmed the family's suspicion that the sons had disappeared.

Deportation and the disappearance of her brothers transformed Sulaf in two important ways. On the one hand, she became more pious. Not only did Sulaf think that Saddam Hussein's regime had targeted her family because they were Shi'i Muslims, but she also found solace in religion to help cope with the disappearance of her brothers. She began to read extensively about Sayyida Zainab, Prophet Muhammad's granddaughter and the sister of Imam Hussein. In the story of Ashura, Sayyida Zainab figures as a model of strong and outspoken Muslim womanhood. Ashura commemorates the martyrdom of the Prophet's grandson Imam Hussein in the seventh century in Karbala, in what is now Iraq. After the men's martyrdom, the women and children were taken as captives to Yazid, the caliph of the Umayyad Dynasty, in Damascus. Sayyida Zainab showed tremendous courage and leadership after the murder of her brothers by challenging Yazid's authority and by narrating the events in Karbala for posterity. Sulaf read her family's ordeals through this religious lens. Just as Yazid was an unjust ruler and usurper of the Muslim caliphate who went as far as murdering Prophet Muhammad's grandson in order to stay in power, Saddam Hussein emerged as an unjust ruler who persecuted Shi'i Iraqis. Rather than despair, Sulaf decided that she should cultivate fortitude in the face of calamities, reasoning that if Sayyida Zainab was capable of that, then she should be able to do the same. Devout Shi'i Iraqis I met in London believed that the calamity that Sayyida Zainab had endured was unrivaled in history, and it was incumbent upon them to live up to her standard of strength and defiance in the face of unspeakable tragedies.

On the other hand, Sulaf became more politically active in order to find answers about her brothers' disappearance, taking inspiration from Sayyida Zainab again. Just as Sayyida Zainab was an outspoken and fearless sister who dedicated her life to her murdered brothers' cause, Sulaf decided to devote her life to uncovering her brothers' fate and speaking up against injustices. Sulaf describes herself as a *mujahida*, a woman who embarks upon *jihad* for a just and noble cause. Although the Arabic term has multiple connotations, including armed resistance, it also refers to personal struggles, whether to cultivate virtuous qualities or to solve structural problems, such as inequality and poverty.[16] For Sulaf, *jihad* has entailed a lifelong and painstaking pursuit of the truth about her brothers, which has required tenacity and patience (*sabur*). In Iran, Sulaf became involved in fundraising in order to help less fortunate Iraqi deportees, especially women who had been subjected to sexual violence or families whose young men had disappeared. After spending a few years in Iran, Sulaf and her parents moved to Damascus in order to be closer to Iraq and in an Arabic-speaking country. There, she managed to establish contacts with wealthy families from the Persian Gulf in order to solicit donations and to set up a permanent charity fair in collaboration with a Muslim organization. Following the Gulf War of 1991 and the failure of the uprising against Saddam Hussein's regime in the north and south, Sulaf, who was married by then, decided to seek asylum in the United Kingdom. Once she arrived in London, she religiously took part in the weekly sit-ins organized by Iraqi Shi'i activists in order to shed light on their disappeared family members and to urge the British government to take up their case.

For more than two decades, Sulaf tirelessly worked to draw attention to disappeared Iraqis and to find any information about her brothers, but with no success. In 2003, two months after the fall of Saddam Hussein's regime in the aftermath the US invasion, she went back to Iraq. Sulaf's incessant efforts yielded the following bits of information: Her brothers, who had been detained on the first day of 1981, had been transferred to the Abu Ghraib Prison in Baghdad and then to Nugrat al-Salman prison in the south. They had been killed by the regime in 1987, and the minister of the interior, who issued Directive 3884, signed their death sentences. However, Sulaf had no idea how they died, where they were buried, or what had happened to them between 1981 and 1987. Eventually, she discovered that her brothers were buried in mass graves, but had no clue which ones. Sulaf became one of countless Iraqis who rushed to the mass graves that were discovered all over the country in 2003 in the hope of finding any information about disappeared loved ones.

After dwelling on her decades of political mobilization and activism, Sulaf shared with me the emotional toll of this pursuit and lack of knowledge:

> It has been unbearable to go on living while not knowing what happened to my brothers. Even though it was not safe to visit Iraq in 2003, I went after two months of the fall of the regime because I was desperate to find answers. Deep inside, I always hoped they could still be alive. I thought maybe they are forgotten in some prison. I just needed to know. This is why I went to Iraq immediately after the fall of the regime in 2003. I have been tormented all these decades about their fate. Once a young man who was

fifteen years old when he was deported with his family asserted to me that he saw Ba'th officials bury his elder brothers alive in front of his family. Another Iraqi deportee I met in London told me that his cousin, who worked as an ophthalmologist at Abu Ghraib Prison, informed him that the regime gouged and sold the detained young men's eyes. I also heard rumors from other Iraqis that these young men were used as guinea pigs in chemical labs or human shields on the battlefield. When I hear these stories, I keep imagining worst-case scenario. Despite all my efforts, I still don't have a grave to visit, or a specific date to commemorate their death, or a cause of death.

Sulaf's remarks about the anguish she lived with show that Saddam Hussein's regime did not only exercise its right to kill and disappear. It also denied the families of disappeared men the right to mourn by conducting a proper funeral and having a grave. In this framework, the right to disappear robbed families of a basic human need: the ability to find closure and to perform death rituals.[17] Moreover, my conversation with Sulaf brought up two issues that other Iraqi deportees shared with me over the years. The unspeakable horrors that Saddam Hussein's regime visited upon millions of Iraqis led to the perception that some Iraqis suffered more than others. For instance, Iraqis whose family members were disappeared saw death—and specific knowledge about how a life was lost—as a mercy and blessing. This hierarchy of suffering is predicated upon the idea that certain tragedies are more horrific than others, and that some forms of agony haunt the living for the rest of their lives. The ability to find closure and to mourn is read as a privilege: having answers means that a person can find solace and not be endlessly tormented about the fate of loved ones. Moreover, Sulaf's remarks reveal the different survival mechanisms people developed to deal with cruel and unbearable reality. Sulaf maintained that her Shi'i faith—in particular, the tragedy of Karbala—gave her tremendous strength. She found solace in the fact that it was God who "imparted patience and perseverance upon her" in order to endure this ordeal and that Imam Hussein's stand against injustices constitutes an ongoing revolution on oppression to this date.

Ultimately, Sulaf managed to find some peace of mind. While in Iraq in 2003, she paid a visit to Imam Hussein's shrine in Karbala shortly after she discovered that her brothers had been killed in 1987. Describing herself as "hysterical" after stepping into the shrine, Sulaf implored Imam Hussein that she wanted "to see her brothers in a dream." After this trip to Iraq, she went to Iran to visit a cousin who had remained in Iran after deportation. One day, as Sulaf went to the basement to sleep, she glimpsed one of her disappeared brothers: "I could see him clearly. He was wearing a white *dishdasha* [gown]. When I saw him, I got petrified. I pulled the blanket over my head, and fell asleep." Sulaf did not want to share the dream with her cousin, fearing that her cousin might believe the basement was haunted. However, upon returning to London, she told a close friend who had also lost her brothers in mass graves about seeing her brother. That night, Sulaf had a dream: "I saw a door open, and my brother came in and said: 'I'm back. Don't freak out.' I hugged him just like I did before we were deported. He told me it took him an hour to get here, and he asked me not to be scared." At this point, Sulaf woke up and decided to call the religious scholar at the mosque she frequented to ask him about the dream. The scholar informed her that the dream meant that her brothers had been living with her the whole time and that they were telling her that they were all right. The scholar's interpretation of the dream was the solace that Sulaf had been looking for over the decades: that her brothers were no longer suffering. Not only did this conversation provide some comfort, but it also enabled her to trust that the dream was a message from her brothers asking her to no longer be tormented about their fate. Rather than absolute closure, Sulaf found contentment.

The disappearance of young men during the deportation campaign became an open wound for their families, who had to live with unknowability, and many of them embarked on decades-long searches for the truth and efforts to draw regional and international attention to their plight. While women who endured sexual violence or were divorced by their husbands were faceless and nameless victims, disappeared young men emerged as real human beings, with names, hobbies, and hopes. Sulaf talked at length about her brothers, about their academic interests and pursuits, about their goofy and sweet personalities, about their love for soccer, and about their fondness for her as the only girl and youngest child in the family. The gender-based violence mobilized by Saddam Hussein's regime against both men and women during the deportation campaign has been commemorated differently by Iraqi deportees. Having to confront double jeopardy from the state and society, deported Iraqi women who experienced sexual and gender violence had to be silenced and erased as individual human beings so that their honor and reputation and that of their families would not become a topic of gossip, disgrace, or shame. By contrast, disappeared young men were always celebrated as martyrs whose lives and ambitions were cut short by a brutal regime. The entanglement of the state, patriarchy, and gender has had further repercussions for the politics of commemoration. Deported Iraqi women who experienced gender-based violence were spoken of in broad and abstract terms by their families and friends in order to protect their anonymity, whereas disappeared young men were eulogized as individuals with dreams and families who spent their lives to find the truth about their fate. Interestingly, unknowability and anonymity played out differently in cases of gender-based violence: knowing about what had happened to women necessitated a politics of silence and disavowal in order to protect their honor while not knowing what had happened to young men prompted activism and speaking out.

Conclusion

The process of denaturalization and deportation always involves different forms of precarity, such as statelessness, poverty, loss of careers and assets, and prejudices in host countries. In the case of *taba'iyya*, Saddam Hussein's regime resorted to gender-based violence to compound deported Iraqis' distress and trauma. Sexual and gender violence did not only unleash unspeakable horrors upon individual victims and their families, but it also shaped the politics of remembrance and the perception of suffering. When I lived in Iraq (until I left in 1997) and when I conducted research among Iraqis in London over two decades since 2006, I always heard Iraqis idealizing and romanticizing the monarchy as a time when morality contained oppression. Given the scale of Saddam Hussein's oppression, the monarchical past was reimagined as "the good old days" when people looked forward to the future and experienced vibrant political, social, and literary lives. Comparing the scale of violence under the monarchy to that during Saddam Hussein's rule, Iraqis came to believe that the elites who ruled Iraq until the fall of the monarchy in 1958 showed respect and restraint toward political dissidents. Not only did this nostalgia for the past erase the abject poverty under which the majority of Iraqis had lived, but it has also worked to dismiss, minimize, and silence the violence many Iraqi communities endured under the monarchy, including the massacre against the Assyrians in 1933, the many military campaigns against the Kurds, the denaturalization and deportation of Iraqi Jews and other Iraqis, imprisonment and execution of political dissidents, censorship, closures of newspapers critical of the monarchy and the British, use of force against protesters, and dismissal from jobs, among others. The fact that Iraqi Jews were allowed to leave Iraq without experiencing physical attacks was perceived by Iraqis who were deported in the early 1980s as an example of the monarchy's moderation and tolerance.

In addition, the romanticization of the past has been concomitant with a sensibility that there is a hierarchy of suffering. Many Iraqi deportees I met over the years, like Sulaf and Sahar, believed that some Iraqis suffered more than others, that some suffering paled in comparison to others, and that "the more you suffer, the more you're an Iraqi." Interestingly, the conviction that some communities have a monopoly on suffering has been couched in religious terms for some deported Iraqis. When I first started my research in London in 2006, I often heard devout Iraqi Shi'is—whether they had been deported, had family members killed or disappeared in the 1980s and 1990s, or had witnessed horrific sectarian violence as the US occupation thrust the country into a civil war and a proxy regional conflict—employ the term "Shi'i persecution" (*mathloumiyyat al-Shia*) to convey their perception that their religious community has lived through unrivaled suffering since the murder of Prophet Muhammad's grandson in Karbala. In this framework, the brutality of Saddam Hussein's regime and the spiraling violence after 2003 became part and parcel of a longer history of persecution that dates back to the seventh century. Tragically, this narrative has engendered deep divisions among different Iraqi groups—such as the communists, Assyrians, and Kurds, among others—who all believed their community suffered unspeakable injustices and oppression under the modern state of Iraq. Predicated upon the idea that some suffering is more legitimate than others, this narrative of the Shi'i persecution eventually reinforced a sectarian discourse that emerged among Iraqi exiles in London. The vilifying rhetoric mobilized by Saddam Hussein's regime against *taba'iyya* as well as the numerous horrors that took place during the deportation campaign eventually reconfigured political imagination and the notion of the self, in that some Iraqi deportees read their persecution as situated in deep-seated hatred of the Shi'is as Shi'is, rather than being part of a systematic campaign of horror that touched any Iraqi whose loyalty to the regime became suspect.

CONCLUSION

THE GHOSTS OF IRAQ

SINCE THE FORMATION OF the modern state of Iraq in 1921, British and Iraqi officials utilized citizenship laws and directives to denaturalize and deport Iraqis whose political aspirations, hybrid identities, and transregional networks rendered them "political undesirables." Rather than an unconditional right, Iraqi citizenship emerged as a precarious privilege closely linked to the ruling elites' nationalistic visions, geopolitical concerns, and efforts to discipline the population. The mass expulsion of Iraqi Jews in 1950–1951 and *tabaʿiyya* in the early 1980s throws into relief the fact that citizenship can serve as a platform to mete out collective punishment through the rhetoric of treason, foreignness, and national security in order to justify denaturalization and deportation. While authoritarian and liberal governments have resorted to denaturalization during political crises in order to get rid of certain individuals, the history of deportation in Iraq shows how ruling elites—under both monarchical and republican regimes—employed and reinterpreted laws to render whole communities legally vulnerable and, hence, deportable. As denaturalized citizens, Iraqi Jews and *tabaʿiyya* lost the right to have rights. Iraqi citizens who were stripped of their citizenship confronted political, legal, economic, cultural, and social precarity and experienced racism and discrimination in the countries to which they were deported. Statelessness was accompanied by the loss of careers and assets, the confiscation of documents, gender-based violence, ruptures of friendship and social networks, family separation, psychological scars, and even death.

After the fall of Saddam Hussein's regime in 2003, following the US invasion, the Iraqi government issued a new Iraqi Nationality Law in 2006.[1] While this law broke new ground in terms of gender reforms, the right to hold dual citizenship, and a clear path to naturalization, it did not constitute a break regarding denaturalized Iraqis' rights to reclaim their Iraqi citizenship. The law dictates that Iraqis who were stripped of their Iraqi citizenship for political, racial, and sectarian reasons have the right to reclaim it. It also grants the children of denaturalized citizens the right to reclaim Iraqi nationality. However, the law exempts Iraqi Jews and their children from the right to reapply for Iraqi citizenship. Moreover, the legal exclusion of Iraqi Jews and their children was concomitant with linguistic and historical erasures. The law does not mention Iraqi Jews by name; rather it states that Iraqis "whose citizenship disappeared" (*zalat*) according to Law 1 of 1950 and Law 12 of 1951 were exempt from reclaiming their citizenship. Rather than using the term *Iraqi Jews*, the law alludes to them through denaturalization legislation. While the law rendered the term *Iraqi Jews* unutterable, it also employs a curious wording to describe Iraqi Jews' loss of citizenship—namely, the verb *zala*, though it uses the word *asqatat*, which translates as "a person was stripped of their citizenship by an authority," in reference to other cases of denaturalization. The verb *zala* in Arabic means "to disappear, recede, evaporate, go, or pass away." Although the literal English translation makes the sentence sound grammatically incoherent or conceptually incomprehensible, the Arabic rendition of it implies that something natural has taken place. In this framework, Iraqi Jews were not stripped of their citizenship by the state but somehow saw their citizenship just disappear or go away, as if the loss of citizenship was a natural occurrence, rather than a legal decision.[2]

However, the Iraqi Nationality Law of 2006 contains contradictions that could serve as grounds for legal action by Iraqi Jews and their descendants. On the one hand, Article 2 postulates that "an Iraqi citizen is someone who acquired Iraqi citizenship according to the Iraqi Nationality Law of 1924, Number 42." Moreover, Article 3 defines an Iraqi as "someone who was born to an Iraqi father or Iraqi mother." According to the former article, all Iraqi Jews who acquired Iraqi citizenship after the establishment of the modern state of Iraq in 1921 are Iraqis. According to the latter clause, Iraqi Jews born after 1924 to one Iraqi parent are considered to be Iraqis. Tellingly, the two articles in this law that exempt Iraqi Jews and their children from the right to reclaim their citizenship and property employ the term *Iraqis* to refer to them. While these two articles avoid using the word *Jews* and use the 1950 denaturalization law to allude to Iraqi Jews, they still admit that expelled Iraqi Jews are Iraqis.

Ironically, as the law forecloses the possibility for Iraqi Jews to reacquire their citizenship and fails to even mention Iraqi Jews, it inadvertently acknowledges that Iraqi Jews are Iraqis. In effect, this law affirms the Iraqiness of Iraqi Jews but disavows and erases their Jewishness. The Jewishness of Iraqi Jews is conveyed only through the dates and numbers of denaturalization laws.

The reasons provided for enacting this law pose another contradiction and grounds for challenge. The last four lines of the law read: "The purpose of the law is to unify all rulings related to Iraqi citizenship, to annul clauses that strip any Iraqi who acquired a foreign citizenship of Iraqi citizenship, to enable the Iraqi who was stripped of his citizenship arbitrarily to regain it, and to connect the Iraqi in any part of the world to his homeland and to encourage him to feel a sense of belonging to the soil of Iraq even though he acquired another citizenship." According to this rationale, Iraqi Jews have the right to reclaim their Iraqi citizenship. In fact, the word used in Arabic to describe loss of citizenship—*ta'suf*—can serve as grounds for Iraqi Jews to challenge this law. Though *ta'suf* is often translated as "arbitrary," the English translation does not quite convey the Arabic meaning. In English, *arbitrary* connotes something random, inconsistent, or offhand. However, in Arabic, *ta'suf* connotes that something unjust, forceful, or oppressive has been carried out by the authorities.

While the Iraqi Nationality Law of 2006 upholds the exclusion of Iraqi Jews from the legal and national realms, the great majority of *taba'iyya* confronted tremendous bureaucratic hurdles in order to reclaim their citizenship after 2003. My conversations with Iraqis who had been deported to Iran but had relocated to London about the procedure to reacquire their Iraqi citizenship revealed that deported Iraqis who occupied powerful positions within the state managed to reclaim their citizenship and property easily, while denaturalized Iraqis who had no such connections had to pay bribes, endure humiliation, and navigate a bureaucratic maze. UK-based deported Iraqis often conveyed that even though the Iraqi Nationality Law of 2006 looked good on paper, it did not mete out equal treatment to all Iraqis who were denaturalized and deported under Saddam Hussein's regime in the early 1980s, since it benefited only deported Iraqis who assumed power after 2003 and their cliques who served their sectarian agenda. In short, Iraqi deportees in London read the Iraqi Nationality Law of 2006 and its bureaucratic measures as confirming the sectarian nature of post-Saddam Iraq and as constituting Iraqi citizenship for denaturalized Iraqis as a conditional privilege that they could claim only through nepotism and sectarian politics. In this framework, the Iraqi Nationality Law of 2006 foreclosed the possibility of regaining Iraqi citizenship for Iraqi Jews, and the implementation of the law rendered Iraqi citizenship elusive for *tabaʿiyya*, rather than a guaranteed right.

The story of uprootedness and reclamation I narrate in this book has been informed by encounters, reflections, and happenings that are personal, political, and academic all at once. These multiple registers include growing up in Iraq and seeing our neighbors deported and co-opted by Saddam Hussein's regime; listening to my mother's memories about the past and explanation of the tiered citizenship systems; having a grandfather who was stripped of his Iraqi citizenship; attending schools in Baghdad that instilled the regime's ideological education while having that same vilifying curricula debunked by my mother at home; deciding to do a doctoral degree in anthropology and conduct fieldwork in Iran with Iraqi deportees; having to change the location of my research after the election of Mahmoud Ahmadinejad as president of Iran in 2005; choosing London as a site of fieldwork; meeting Iraqis from different religious, ethnic, political, and class backgrounds (including Iraqi Jews); listening to narratives of displacement and exile brought about by flight or expulsion; navigating a deeply divided Iraqi diasporic scene in London along sectarian and ethnic lines but coming across enclaves that cherished an inclusive vision of Iraq at the same time; getting stuck in the United States once securing a US visa as an Iraqi became extremely difficult after the US occupation in 2003 and using my research funds to conduct further archival research on Iraqi citizenship laws and amendments in the Library of Congress since I could not travel abroad to do follow-up research for almost eight years; and reading scholarly literature on citizenship and colonial rule. The confluences of these personal experiences, archival and ethnographic research, and political events have shaped the legal and autobiographical archives included in this book and have engendered insights about the nature of the Iraqi state as well as the possibilities that the condition of diaspora could bring about.

A close reading of the evolvement of citizenship directives in Iraq has made me realize that the loss of Iraqi citizenship through denaturalization legislation is not marginal but integral to the history of the modern state of Iraq in the twentieth and twenty-first centuries. Interestingly, the tendency among most Iraqis I know and have met over the decades to idealize the monarchical reign as the time of high hopes, when people inhabited vibrant political and cultural spaces and imagined utopian futures, and as a time when ruling elites exercised restraint and showed respect in dealing with political opponents has been predicated upon silences, erasures, and dismissals.[3] The history of deportation under the monarchy is often erased in these nostalgic narratives. If the topic comes up, my Iraqi interlocutors (and Iraqis I knew when I lived in Iraq) employed two techniques to justify this silence. On the one hand, they perceived instances of deportation under the monarchy as unconnected, singular, or instigated by the actions of the denaturalized citizens or some unruly politicians. Accordingly, Assyrians' demands for independence and collaboration with the British are thought of as the cause of deportation of the Assyrian patriarch and the Simele Massacre; Iraqi Jews are seen as victims of a deal between the Zionist underground movement and corrupt Iraqi politicians or as scapegoats for the displacement of Palestinians during the Nakba; and the deportation of communists is viewed as being brought about by Iraqi and British officials' anxiety over leftist politics in the country. Furthermore, a good number of Iraqis I interviewed even took these cases of denaturalization as proof of the tolerance of the monarchy. They argued that the absence of sexual violence was a testament to the "good old days" in comparison with the expulsion of *taba'iyya* thirty years later. Finally, Iraqis in London often dismiss the expulsion campaign under Saddam Hussein's reign as the arbitrary action of a ruthless and unscrupulous tyrant.

The tendency to romanticize the monarchical regime and to forget its abuses in light of the rise of Saddam Hussein to power is understandable given the atrocities that touched almost all Iraqis throughout his reign, whether because of his oppression, wars, or sanctions. However, this inclination to idealize some imagined past has meant that the different instances of denaturalization and deportation in Iraq throughout the twentieth century have been understood as singular events that are separate from each other. The Iraqi Nationality Law of 1924 and the various amendments lay bare the fact that the different cases of denaturalization and expulsion make up a connected story and a consistent strategy. The legal documents show that the denaturalization orders built upon each other and that the monarchical rule and the republican reign under the Ba'th Party reproduced the same rhetoric of foreignness and treason and employed citizenship as a tool of governmentality. Here, denaturalization and deportation emerge as a structure that was first put in place by the British but was endorsed and utilized by Iraqi officials not only to inflict punishment upon certain individuals and communities but also to rewrite the history of different Iraqi groups in a reductionist, ahistorical, and simplistic way.[4] Ultimately, denaturalization and deportation have not been random measures but rather systematic strategies of rule and discipline at the very heart of the modern state of Iraq.

Nevertheless, the foreclosure of citizenship as a legal status and Iraq as a homeland to inhabit does not eliminate the right to reclaim through diasporic networks. Along with expulsion, the modern history of Iraq has been dotted by instances of flight, which have accelerated greatly over the past five decades.[5] Iraqis who were members of religious and ethnic groups—such as Chaldeans, Armenians, Assyrians, Kurds, and Turkomans—left Iraq in the first half of the twentieth century, given their discomfort with the Arab nature of the Iraqi state. Following the fall of the monarchy in 1958, elite urban Arab families associated with the monarchy relocated abroad. The reign of terror ushered in by Saddam Hussein after he became president in 1979 led to the displacement of thousands of Iraqis either through flight or deportation. The first mass exodus from Iraq took place in the late 1970s, as Saddam Hussein began to consolidate his power and eliminate political dissidents, whether Ba'th Party members, communists, Kurds, or underground Shi'i groups. The early 1990s saw the flight of a number of Iraqis from the country following failed uprisings against Saddam Hussein's regime and harsh UN-imposed economic sanctions (1990–2003). Finally, the US invasion of Iraq in 2003 initiated more waves of displacement. The institutionalization of a sectarian quota system, rampant violence carried out by the US military and local and regional groups (Iraqi militias, al-Qaeda, and the Islamic State), the spread of corruption, environmental collapse, and the dismantlement of the state through neoliberal reforms forced many Iraqis to flee the country in the hope of finding a better and safer future somewhere else.[6]

The emergence of Iraqi diasporic communities worldwide over the past decades has opened a space for Iraqi exiles to maintain friendships and networks of solidarity they established before displacement, forge new connections with fellow Iraqis they never met in Iraq, revive political alliances, and cultivate an inclusive Iraqi identity. Edward Said provides an insightful reading of nationalism and exile. He asserts that nationalism "is an assertion of belonging in and to a place, a people, a heritage. It affirms the home created by a community of language, culture, and customs; and, by so doing, it fends off exile, fights to prevent its ravages."[7] While nationalism entails rootedness and continuity, exile is predicated upon discontinuity and severance from one's roots, land, and past.[8] Here, Said does not approach nationalism as an exclusive political ideology promoted by a nation-state but as an expression of cultural affinity and a feeling of being at home. Nationalism, in this context, connotes a shared place and a sense of community with fellow citizens who embrace and cultivate similar political views and cultural sensibilities. By contrast, exile is often seen as a negative status of existence, defined solely by ruptures, uprootedness, alienation, and discrimination. However, exile can be productive and generative alongside divisions over national imagination, the past, indigeneity, and violence. New configurations of subjectivity—based on political, emotional, and cultural belonging—can become possible in diasporic centers. Since the mid-twentieth century, more and more people are on the move in the world, whether voluntarily or involuntarily. In the case of Iraqi exiles, diasporic sites—in particular, in Western countries where Iraqis from different backgrounds reside—enabled some of them to construct diverse Iraqi enclaves defined by shared cultural and political sensibilities and predicated upon undermining simplistic binaries.

A good number of Iraqi Jews and *taba'iyya* fled Iraq as soon as the expulsion campaign started and settled in neighboring countries, the United Kingdom, Europe, or North America. Some of those who were expelled to Israel and Iran left for Western countries after enduring decades of discrimination and exclusion. Some members in these two communities, along with other Iraqi communities in diaspora, worked to build Iraqi enclaves within a diasporic context defined by multiple forms of trauma and political disenchantment and within the imperial context of cultivating these Iraqi connections in the very bellies of colonial and imperial beasts—namely, the United Kingdom and the United States—that played major roles in shaping the political landscape of Iraq for decades and embraced Orientalist discourses about its population. Despite the ironies and contradictions of diasporic life, some Iraqis—including Iraqi Jews and *taba'iyya*—worked to reclaim an inclusive Iraqi community. In this framework, the right to reclaim has not been limited to reminiscences about the past or literary and scholarly productions. It also involves inhabiting and constructing a lived reality in diaspora, informed by past experiences of coexistence and a shared sense of belonging. In her reflection on the expulsion of Iraqi Jews and on the concept of the Arab Jew, Ella Shohat remarks that "these traumatic displacements have shaped new national and ethnic/racial identities where officially stamped classifications did not necessarily correspond to cultural affiliation and political identifications. Emotional belonging has existed in tension with identity cards and travel documents such as passports and *laissez-passers*, or with the lack of such papers altogether."[9] Though Iraqi ruling elites under different regimes foreclosed the possibility of citizenship for Iraqi Jews and *taba'iyya* as whole communities, cultural affinity, a sense of rootedness in Iraq, and emotional belonging negated the state's practices of vilification and exclusion.

These reflections on diaspora and emotional belonging are not meant to romanticize exile or displacement or to suggest that diasporic centers in the West are sites of liberation. After all, Iraqis in London are deeply divided over political ideologies, sectarian and ethnic differences, the interpretation of the past, hierarchies of suffering, and class sensibilities. These divisions and disagreements have caused the breakdown of long-term friendships, as I often heard over the years when I was doing fieldwork in London. In addition, the great majority of Iraqi exiles have had to endure discrimination, racism, and downward mobility after they were forced to leave Iraq. Rather, this optimistic note is informed by my interactions with some Iraqis in London. For instance, I met Iraqi Jews for the first time in my life in the United Kingdom. Their warmth and generosity toward me as a fellow Iraqi as well as their love for Iraq have always been refreshing amid the tragic news from Iraq after 2003. In addition, one of my long-term interlocutors who became a close friend was deported from Iraq with her family. Her honesty about her life, her tenacity to lead a path she believes in despite social pressures and Orientalist stereotypes, and her acceptance of me—she is a devout Muslim while I'm irreligious—have been a source of admiration and a confirmation that different friendships can evolve in diaspora. These two examples are among the many heartwarming interactions I have had with some Iraqis in London over the years.

Growing up in Iraq under Saddam Hussein's reign, I never had close friends, given the way the regime attempted to co-opt even schoolchildren to inform on their friends' parents. My relationship with other students remained surface level. Though some students managed to share their honest political opinions and rumors of repression with each other, I was too petrified to take any risk given the political pressure my parents lived through. Fieldwork with Iraqis in London was the first time in my life I could have conversations with Iraqis without censoring myself and could have friends without worrying that they could harm me or my family. Living among the

Iraqi diasporic community during my fieldwork and subsequent visits unexpectedly provided an opportunity for me to develop friendships with fellow Iraqis. Likewise, my friendship with some Iraqi scholars in the United States has engendered a sense of solidarity and tenderness as we have navigated stereotypes about Iraq and Iraqis and produced work to critique militarism, imperialism, and Orientalism. Writing this book, itself a tribute to the relationships I have cultivated with fellow Iraqis in exile, has made me think that diaspora can work in strange ways: you can feel like you lost your homeland through uprootedness, violence, and oppression but then discover that there are Iraqi enclaves where you can feel deep affiliation—a sense of familiarity, ease, solidarity, and shared experiences and outlooks.

Since I began thinking about doing archival and ethnographic research about *taba'iyya* for my doctoral degree back in 2002, I have been thinking of my childhood neighbors, especially their two daughters, frequently. Sometimes they haunted my thoughts as I sat down to write. After the end of primary school, our friendship began to fizzle out as we moved to different middle schools. As the Gulf War of 1991 was about to end and the uprisings against Saddam Hussein's regime in the south and north were spreading, the mother of the two daughters paid my mother a visit. I vividly remember that visit. We sat in the dark living room lit by candles, since power outages happened often as a result of bombings of power plants. The mother apologized for writing reports about my mother to the regime and explained that she was forced to do so once she and her daughters were spared deportation. Of course, her co-optation was an open secret in the neighborhood and was never a cause of breakdown of neighborly relations. She often visited us in the 1980s, and her conversation with my mother revolved around mundane details, like the end-of-the-year examinations or recipes. During that visit in early 1991, my mother reassured our neighbor that she completely understood and harbored no ill feelings. However, Saddam Hussein managed to stay in power, and that visit seemed to have broken a taboo: it was meant as an acknowledgment of the role our neighbor was pushed into and as an apology and a gesture to turn a new page on a painful era in Iraq's history. That Saddam Hussein's regime survived the war and rebellion meant that our neighbor would have to resume her role as an informant. After that visit, our relationship with the mother and daughters became limited to superficial greetings in the streets. Rather than constituting a closure, the apology divulged a public secret that was supposed to remain unspoken, though known by everyone.

I do not know what happened to this family. I have no idea if they are still in Iraq or fled at some point, like many Iraqis, or if they are dead or alive, since I lost contact with everyone I knew in our neighborhood in Baghdad. I do not even know their last name, so I can't search for them on the internet or social media. Under Saddam Hussein, the use of last names was banned in order not to show that his family controlled the government, so everyone used their father's and grandfather's name instead. As I finish writing this book, I wish I could have a conversation with any member of this family. Having done all this research, I wonder what the experience of deportation was like for them: Did they end up in deportation camps on the borders? What were the living conditions? How did Iraqi officials in charge of deportation bring up the issue of serving as an informant in exchange for staying in Iraq? Did they witness or experience instances of sexual violence? What did they think at that time? Did they think they were lucky in comparison to other deportees, since they did not have brothers who would have been detained and disappeared? And how would they reflect on that episode? Did life get worse for them during the US invasion, like the majority of Iraqis? Do they remember the 1980s nostalgically as a time when oppression and murder took place behind closed doors, unlike the public scenes of spectacular violence after 2003 that were circulated time and again on news networks and social media, and when there was a functioning state despite all its shortcomings?

The last question always makes me ponder on the politics of remembering and forgetting among Iraqis. During my follow-up research trips to London after 2016, not only did I hear nostalgic stories about the monarchy, but I increasingly came across many Iraqis who remembered the 1980 nostalgically as "the good old days" in comparison to the debilitating sanctions imposed by the United Nations after Iraq invaded Kuwait in 1990, the increased oppression of Saddam Hussein after the defeat and isolation of Iraq after the Gulf War of 1991, the total collapse of the country after the US invasion, and the horrific violence committed by the US military, Iraqi militias, and fundamentalist groups. Most of these Iraqis lost family members and friends under Saddam Hussein's regime, so their nostalgia is not the product of privilege or ignorance. That the status quo in Iraq has gone from bad to worse under the US occupation has reconfigured the way Iraqis from different generations reimagine the past. The nostalgic yearning for an idealized past—which was intolerable for some people when it was experienced as the present—has been concomitant with forgetting. Some non-Jewish Iraqis in London even told me that Iraqi Jews "got away" when they were deported, since they were spared more horrors had they stayed in Iraq. Remembrance and nostalgia have operated in a paradoxical manner among Iraqi exiles: not only do certain periods get glorified as the golden age, but the very violence of that time was hailed a sign of restraint and respect, and, in the process, was brushed off, silenced, erased, and forgotten.

NOTES

Preface
1. The father lived and worked abroad in order to avoid being conscripted in the Iraq army during the Iran-Iraq War.
2. Babakhan (2002, 198–99).
3. Bashkin, *New Babylonians* (2012, 2).
4. Shiblak (2005, 45–50).

Introduction
1. Coutin (2016).
2. Weil (2013); Naguib (2020); Heckman (2021); and Boum and Berber (2023).
3. Weil (2013, 2).
4. Ibid.
5. Ibid., 1.
6. For instance, Naguib (2020); Whewell (2019); Hack (2015); Zimudzi (2007); Louro (2018); Delnore(2015); and Weil (2017).
7. The State Department illegally revoked W. E. B. Du Bois's passport in 1952 in order to prevent him from leaving the United States and attending a peace conference in Canada. While the Supreme Court restored passport rights for "suspected communists" in 1958, the State Department refused to renew his passport while abroad, which amounted to the annulment of his citizenship. For more details, see Andrew Lanham, "When W. E. B. Du Bois Was 'Un-American,'" *Boston Review*, January 13, 2017, https://www.bostonreview.net/articles/when-civil-rights-were-un-american/. The dissident Russian writer Aleksandr Solzhenitsyn was stripped of his citizenship in 1974 and deported to West Germany by the Soviet Union after being charged with treason. Likewise, Milan Kundera was stripped of his Czech citizenship by the Czechoslovakian Communist regime in 1979 because of his political views.
8. https://www.amnestyusa.org/press-releases/bahrain-alarming-spike-in-expulsion-of-citizens-arbitrarily-stripped-of-their-nationality/.

9. Hunter and Reece (2020).
10. https://www.bbc.com/news/world-middle-east-64654634.
11. https://www.theguardian.com/world/2023/feb/16/ortega-regime-strips-nicaraguans-citizenship.
12. https://www.gov.uk/government/publications/nationality-and-borders-bill-deprivation-of-citizenship-factsheet/nationality-and-borders-bill-deprivation-of-citizenship-factsheet.
13. Diane Taylor, "Hundreds Stripped of British Citizenship in Last 15 Years, Study Finds," *The Guardian*, January 22, 2022.
14. Maya Foa, "Judges Have Refused to Save Shamima Begum," *The Guardian*, August 8, 2024, https://www.theguardian.com/commentisfree/article/2024/aug/08/judges-shamima-begum-uk-ministers-home-secretary-keir-starmer-government.
15. Zoe Williams, "The Shamima Begum Ruling Proves It: Some UK Citizens Are Less Equal Than Others," *The Guardian*, February 23, 2024, https://www.theguardian.com/commentisfree/2024/feb/23/shamima-begum-british-citizens-foreign-born-parent-court-appeal. France has very similar rules to Britain. See https://www.service-public.fr/particuliers/vosdroits/F32827?lang=en; and https://schengen.news/france-revokes-citizenship-for-4-citizens/.
16. Lawrance and Stevens (2017).
17. Babo (2017); Price (2017); and Stock (2017).
18. Coutin (2016, 4).
19. DeGooyer et al. (2020, 2).
20. Ibid., 2.
21. Ibid., 8.
22. Sluglett (2007, 52 and 222–25).
23. Ibid., 50.
24. Batatu (1978, 326).
25. I discuss this case in detail in chapter 3.
26. Unfortunately, the archives did not include documents about discussions of this law. Given that Iraq was de facto ruled by the British, it is extremely possible that British colonial officials were involved in the enactment of this law.
27. It was through this provision that my grandfather managed to acquire the Iraqi citizenship. To my knowledge, he was the only foreign-born individual who was not part of the ruling elites to acquire the Iraqi nationality according to this provision.
28. I discuss the implications of this distinctions in more detail in chapter 3.
29. Law no. 62, issued on August 15, 1933.
30. Donabed (2015, 118–22).
31. Benjamen (2022, 16–17).
32. Another Assyrian deported from Iraq because of his political activism is Pyotr Vasili. In 1934, Vasili, an Assyrian whose parents hailed from Amadiyya in northern Iraq and emigrated to Tiflis (Georgia) during the Ottoman reign, was banished from Iraq. Vasili was a communist revolutionary who became active in south Iraq. It is not clear from the studies that discuss him whether he acquired the Iraqi citizenship and

whether his banishment in 1934 was in connection to Law 62 of 1933. See Benjamen (2022, 30–31); and Batatu (1978, 404–10).

33. *Al-Waqa'i' al-'Iraqiyya*, October 9, 1954.

34. Law 17, 1954, published in *Al-Waqa'i' al-'Iraqiyya* on September 1, 1954.

35. Sha'ban (2002, 66).

36. *Al-Waqa'i' al-'Iraqiyya*, January 20, 1960.

37. *Al-Waqa'i' al-'Iraqiyya*, March 31, 1963; and June 25, 1963.

38. Muhammad Hussein al-Najafi, *Tariq al-Shaab*, February 7, 2022, https://www.tareeqashaab.com/index.php/newspaper-articles/3163-51-87-7-2022. Alda Benjamen also mentions that Daud al-Saigh, another communist, was stripped of his nationality in 1963 (2022, 46) and discusses the case of another Assyrian communist, Aprim Barkhu, whose Iraqi nationality and the prospects of deportation became a contentious issue in 1963–1965 during his trial and appeals (2022, 71–76).

39. In the late 1960s to the early 1970s, the Ba'th regime expelled nearly 40,000 Iraqis of Iranian origin under the pretext that they were "Iranian threats" to Iraq. According to Sha'ban, the Iraqi authorities expelled around 70,000 Faili Kurds (2002, 91). When I did fieldwork in London, Iraqi interlocutors told me that those who had been deported between 1969 and 1971 did not hold the Iraqi citizenship though the majority of them had been living in Iraq for generations. Their parents and grandparents simply opted to keep their Persian citizenship after 1924 even though they identified as Iraqis. Sha'ban seems to corroborate this impression when he mentions that the Shi'i Kurds who were deported in the late 1960s and early 1970s had hoped to have their citizenship status settled and to acquire the Iraqi citizenship after the fall of the monarchy in 1958 (2002, 91).

40. Tripp (2007, 207–14). See also Abdul-Jabar (2003, 225); and Allawi (2007, 31).

41. *Al-Waqa'i' al-'Iraqiyya*, May 26, 1980.

42. *Al-Waqa'i' al-'Iraqiyya*, April 27, 1981.

43. Jayal (2013, 2).

44. Thomas (2011, 60).

45. Ibid., 7.

46. Bashkin (2009, 104).

47. Ibid., 89.

48. Beinin (2004, xiv).

49. Under Ottoman rule, Iraqi Shi'is were caught up in the struggle between the Ottoman Empire, which was Sunni, and Persia, which was Shi'i. With the decline of the Ottoman Empire and loss of land by the end of the nineteenth century, Sultan Abdulhamid II began to stress the unity of his Muslim subjects and to appoint Arab subjects to important positions in the government. Moreover, he felt the need to have an educational system that would bring uniformity among his people in order to guarantee their loyalty to the state (Deringil 1991, 346–47). While these measures resulted in the creation of Arab cadres, which later became the ruling elites in Arab states (including Iraq), they did not have an impact on Shi'i inhabitants of Iraq.

50. For more details about my engagement with the concept of storytelling and

living archives, see Saleh (2021, 31–33; and 2022).

51. Behrouzan (2018, 132). Here Behrouzan analyzes the 1980s generation in Iran, but her framing applies to the experience of Iraqi Jews and *taba'iyya* as well.

52. Ibid., 133.

Chapter 1

Portions of chapter 1 are developed from Zainab Saleh, "The Denationalization of Iraqi Jews: The Legal and Rhetorical Production of Otherness," *Palestine/Israel Review* 1, no. 2 (2024): 392–420.

1. Baskhin, *New Babylonians* (2012, 103).
2. Ibid., 117–18.
3. Ibid., 13–14.
4. Petryna and Follis (2015).
5. Ibid., 403.
6. Vora (2013, 5 and 15).
7. Bashkin (2009).
8. Bashkin (2017, 6).
9. Bashkin ("Colonized Semites," 2021); Shenhav (2002); Shohat (1988; 2006; 2020); and Zamkanei (2016).
10. For a detailed discussion of these events, see Bashkin (*New Babylonians*, 2012, 100–40); Moreh and Yehuda (2010); and Yehuda (2017).
11. Qazaz (2013). In his introduction to this collection, Qazaz remarks that "the excerpts in this anthology deal with political, social, economic, and security issues and matters that had tremendous impact" on the Iraqi Jewish community (18). While his wording conveys the impression that these excerpts do not represent a comprehensive reproduction of all the articles on Iraqi Jews, he maintains that the political repression against communist and leftist elements in Iraq after the failure of the popular protests against the Anglo-Iraqi Treaty in 1948 was concomitant with the spread of ultranationalist propaganda and anti-Jewish rhetoric. Qazaz notes that *Al-Yaqdha* and *al-Nahda* began to publish articles that promoted anti-Jewish hatred while leftist newspapers as well as the Iraqi government remained silent and did not challenge these vilifying writings (30). In lieu of doing archival research on Iraqi newspapers housed in libraries all over the world, I have relied on this underutilized anthology to gain insights into the anti-Jewish rhetoric in the ultranationalist press for two reasons. First, this book does not purport to provide an exhaustive reading of the portrayal of Iraqi Jews in all Iraqi newspapers. Second, I am interested in these incendiary articles given that the ideas expressed in them were incorporated in Abdul Razzaq al-Hasani's *Ta'rikh al-Wizarat al-Iraqiyah* (1955).
12. Al-Safwani 1949, quoted in Qazaz (2013, 176).
13. Ibid.
14. *Al-Yaqdha* 1949, quoted in Qazaz (2013, 177).
15. Firhad, *Al-Nahda* 1949, quoted in Qazaz (2013, 181).
16. *Al-Yaqdha* 1949, quoted in Qazaz (2013, 200–201).

17. Dawoud 1949, quoted in Qazaz (2013, 213).
18. *Al-Yaqdha* 1949, quoted in Qazaz (2013, 255–66).
19. Bashkin (*New Babylonians,* 2012, 197).
20. Ibid., 197.
21. Ibid., 187–88.
22. Shlaim (2023, 156).
23. Ibid., 120.
24. Bashkin (*New Babylonians,* 2012, 191).
25. All the laws employ the masculine pronoun when referring to an individual. It is similar to the use of *he* or *man* in English, before the addition of *she* and *they*. I decided to stick to this literal translation throughout this book.
26. *Al-Waqa'i' al-'Iraqiyya,* March 2, 1950.
27. *Al-Waqa'i' al-'Iraqiyya,* August 15, 1933.
28. Shlaim (2023, 121).
29. Ibid., 121–22.
30. Ibid., 123.
31. Ibid., 125.
32. Bashkin (*New Babylonians,* 2012, 191).
33. Shlaim (2023, 127).
34. Bashkin (*New Babylonians,* 2012, 192).
35. Ibid., 192.
36. *Al-Waqa'i' al-'Iraqiyya,* March 10, 1951.
37. *Al-Waqa'i' al-'Iraqiyya,* March 22, 1951.
38. Shlaim (2023, 127–28).
39. Ibid., 128.
40. Ibid., 128.
41. Ibid., 128.
42. Bashkin (*New Babylonians,* 2012, 192).
43. al-Hasani (1955, vol 8, 158).
44. Ibid., 158–59.
45. Ibid., 208–11.
46. Ibid., 209.
47. A point raised by one of the external reviewers, which I also heard from Iraqis in London, is that Iraqi Jews were not "expelled" in 1950 since they were "invited to register" to leave Iraq though they faced persecution and threats. The purpose of this section—which dwells upon anti-Jewish articles in ultranationalist newspapers, the denaturalization decree and its title and justification, the invocation of the 1933 decree, the consequences of the change of government in Iraq, and the confiscation of the properties of anyone who registered to leave—is to emphasize that Iraqi authorities stripped Iraqi Jews of their Iraqi citizenship. As such, the "choice" Iraqi Jews made by registering to give up their citizenship does not really entail a freely made decision given that they confronted anti-Jewish rhetoric and discrimination and that they could not foresee the implications of this decision once Nuri Al-Said became the

prime minister again. Moreover, Iraqi Jews employ the term *tasqit*, which literally means stripping a person of their citizenship, in order to bring home how they have understood and articulated their experiences.

48. Bashkin (*New Babylonians*, 2012, 230).
49. *Al-Waqa'i' al-'Iraqiyya*, January 20, 1960.
50. *Al-Waqa'i' al-'Iraqiyya*, March 31, 1963.
51. *Al-Waqa'i' al-'Iraqiyya*, June 25, 1963.
52. *Al-Jimhuriyya* 1967, quoted in Qazaz (2013, 488).
53. *Al-Jimhuriyya* 1967, quoted in Qazaz (2013, 489 and 490).
54. *Al-Jimhuriyya* 1967, quoted in Qazaz (2013, 494).
55. *Al-Jimhuriyya* 1968, quoted in Qazaz (2013, 496).
56. *Tapu* is an Ottoman word that refers to deeds.
57. *Al-Waqa'i' al-'Iraqiyya*, March 3, 1968.
58. Bashkin (*New Babylonians*, 2012, 230).
59. *Al-Jimhuriyya* 1969, quoted in Qazaz (2013, 510).
60. Bashkin (*New Babylonians*, 2012, 230).

Chapter 2

Portions of chapter 2 are developed from Zainab Saleh, "Precarious Citizens: Iraqi Jews and the Politics of Belonging," *Political and Legal Anthropology Review* 44, no. 1 (2021): 107–22.

1. Bashkin (*New Babylonians*, 2012, 2). For a detailed discussion about the different articulations of *Arab Jew* in Iraq, and the rejection of Zionism by the majority of Iraqi Jews, see Baskhin (*New Babylonians*, 2012, 1–14).
2. Ibid., 3.
3. Shohat (2017, 77).
4. The question of belonging for Iraqi Jews, like other Iraqis, transformed over time. Under the Ottomans, Jewish residents in Ottoman Iraq identified as Ottoman subjects. With the rise of nationalism following World War I, they began to identify as Iraqi citizens. See Bashkin (*New Babylonians*, 2012, 4). For a detailed history of the daily experiences Jews shared with Christians and Muslims under the Ottomans, see Sharkey (2017).
5. During my fieldwork in London between 2006 and 2008 and between 2016 and 2024, Iraqi Jews I met there always affirmed that they were Babylonian Jews, who lived in Iraq for millennia.
6. Bashkin (*New Babylonians*, 2012, 4–5).
7. Shohat (2017, 4).
8. Quoted in May (2020, 46).
9. Ibid., 43.
10. Bashkin (2017, 6).
11. Shohat (1988, 1–2).
12. Shohat (2017).
13. Shlaim (2023, 301).

14. Beinin (2004, xv).
15. Ibid., xiv.
16. Ibid., xiv.
17. Rejwan (2004, 97).
18. Ibid., 98.
19. Ibid., 99.
20. Ibid., 99.
21. Ibid., 106.
22. Ibid., 107.
23. Ibid., 100.
24. Ibid., 100–101.
25. Ibid., 101.
26. Ibid., 139.
27. Ibid., 139.
28. Ibid., 140.
29. Ibid., 140.
30. Ibid., 144.
31. Ibid., 145.
32. Somekh (2007, 7).
33. Ibid., 7.
34. Ibid., 10.
35. Ibid., 12
36. Ibid., 13.
37. Ibid., 70.
38. Ibid., 71.
39. Ibid., 77.
40. Ibid., 78.
41. Ibid., 162–64.
42. Ibid., 164.
43. Ibid., 164–65.
44. Ibid., 167.
45. Ibid., 165.
46. Ibid., 167.
47. Ibid., 91.
48. Ginat (2011); Heckman (2021); and Sternfeld (2020).
49. Bashkin, (n.d., 2).
50. Ibid., 2.
51. Bashkin (*New Babylonians*, 2012, 94).
52. Bashkin (n.d., 5).
53. Pursley (2019).
54. Saleh, *Return to Ruin* (2021).
55. Schiller and Fouron (2001, 3–4).
56. Shlaim (2023, 6–7).

57. Ibid., 7.
58. Ibid., 7–8.
59. Ibid., 8.
60. Ibid., 9.
61. Ibid., 8.
62. Ibid., 12.
63. Ibid., 13.
64. Ibid., 14.
65. Ibid., 14.
66. Ibid., 13.
67. Ibid., 14.
68. Ibid., 15.
69. Ibid., 15.
70. Bashkin (*New Babylonians,* 2012, 207–8).
71. Ibid., 208.
72. Shlaim (2023, 148).
73. Ibid., 149.
74. Ibid., 149.
75. Ibid., 151.
76. Ibid., 296.
77. Ibid., 301.
78. Ibid., 301.
79. Ibid., 301.
80. Shohat (1992, 5).
81. Ibid., 5.
82. Shohat (2006, 226).

Chapter 3

Portions of chapter 3 are developed from Zaïnab Saleh, "On Iraqi Nationality: Law, Citizenship, and Exclusion," *Arab Studies Journal* 21, no. 1 (2013): 48–78.

1. Alda Benjamen and Sinan Antoon have told me that there were Assyrian *taba'iyya* individuals who were also deported to Iran in the early 1980s. The Boxfiles Database from the Ba'th Regional Command Collection contained a few documents with a list of *taba'iyya*, including the names of two Assyrian Iraqis (batch 3721 0001, box 3721, pages 01_3721_0001_0005 and 01_3721_0001_0006-0031-0034). I'm not focusing on the cases of Assyrian *taba'iyya*, given the dearth of sources and the fact that only certain individuals, rather than a whole community, were deported.

2. Makiya (1998, 136). It is estimated that 40,000–400,000 Iraqis were deported in the early 1980s. See Babakhan (2002, 198–99).

3. Authors on Iraq often cite the underrepresentation of Shi'a in state offices—such as cabinet posts and the premiership—as an indicator of the exclusion of the Shi'a.

4. Tripp (2007, 13).

5. Nakash (2003, 26–27).

6. Ibid., 26.
7. Ibid., 26–27.
8. Ibid., 27–30.
9. Ibid., 31–35. Nakash shows that nomadic tribes remained Sunnis. Only settled tribes converted to Shi'ism.
10. Ibid., 32–33.
11. Ibid., 45.
12. Deringil (2000, 58–59).
13. Kern (2011, 41–45).
14. Ibid., 44–53.
15. Ibid., 48–49.
16. Ibid., 53–59 and 155.
17. Ibid., 96. From subsequent correspondence on the matter among Ottoman officials, it appears that "people of unknown lineage" refers to the Shi'a.
18. Ibid.
19. Ibid., 14–16.
20. See the full law in ibid., 157–58.
21. Ibid., 14–17.
22. Çetinsaya (2006, 5–6).
23. Kern (2011, 16).
24. The Ottoman word used in the title of the law is *teba'a*, which denotes "subject."
25. Kern (2011, 159).
26. Ibid., 88, 114.
27. See the Iraq Constitution of 21 March 1925, CO 327/65.
28. The Iraq Nationality Law, CO 813/1.
29. "Nationality Law," CO 730/141/2.
30. Hooper (1928, 39–41).
31. Ibid., 39.
32. "Iraq Nationality and Passports," T12419/164/378.
33. In addition to the applicant's and his or her parents' places of birth, the form contains questions about the applicant's nationality prior to the enactment of the Iraqi Nationality Law of 1924.
34. Batatu (1978, 326).
35. Al-Wardi (1992, 33–40).
36. Batatu (1978, 326).
37. Quoted in Batatu (1978, 326). Batatu does not mention the Arabic word for "aliens." The document he quotes is part of the Iraqi Police Files. It is part of his private collection and is unavailable for public use.
38. Nakash (2003, 100–105).
39. Ibid., 101.
40. Ibid., 103–5.
41. Dodge (2003, 67–68).
42. Ibid.

43. Ibid., 67–69.
44. Tripp (2007, 30–31).
45. Al-Wardi (1992, 33–40).
46. The Arab-nationalist discourse alienated and demonized different groups, such as the Kurds, Assyrians, and Jews. For the purposes of this chapter, I focus on the Shi'a.
47. Al-Husri (1967–1968).
48. See, for instance, Zubaida (2002, 205–15).
49. The minister of education was the only Shi'i minister in the government, following the pressure exerted by Cox.
50. Al-Husri (1967–1968, 588–602 [Part I]); (1967–1968, 585 [Part II]).
51. Makiya (1998, 154).
52. Haddad (2011, 44).
53. Al-Jawahiri (1999, 147). In his memoir, al-Jawahiri mentions that the job application for the teaching position included questions about the applicant's sect. Al-Jawahiri (1999, 141–42).
54. *Al-Waqa'i' al-'Iraqiyya*, June 19, 1963.
55. Tikrit is a city in the northwest of Iraq. Ahmad Hasan al-Bakr and Saddam Hussein originally hailed from there.
56. Tripp (2007, 194–95); and Wiley (1992, 46).
57. Tripp (2007, 194–95).
58. For a brief discussion on this instance of deportation in the early 1970s, see footnote 39 in the Introduction.
59. Wiley (1992, 48–49).
60. Ibid., 48.
61. Babakhan (2002, 195).
62. Davis (2005, 191); and Rohde (2010, 32).
63. Tripp (2007, 221).
64. Ibid., 221.
65. Abdul-Jabar (2003, 227–34).
66. Tripp (2007, 221).
67. Davis (2005, 185).
68. Ibid., 131.
69. Ibid., 132.
70. Ibid., 185–87.
71. Rohde (2010, 34).
72. *Al-Sharq al-Awsat*, March 8, 1989. Translation by the author.
73. Ibid. At one point, Saddam Hussein speaks of a person who is of Iranian, Pakistani, or Indian origin. Historically, there were communities who hailed from India in Basra and Najaf. The categories of people of Pakistani or Indian origin did not exist legally, however, so Hussein's reference to them seems to be merely rhetorical.
74. *Al-Waqa'i' al-'Iraqiyya*, May 26, 1980.
75. Interim Constitution of the Republic of Iraq (Washington, DC: Embassy of the

Republic of Iraq, 1964). The same criteria of citizenship apply to the positions of premier, deputy premier, and ministers. Article 72 states: "The Premier, the Deputy Premier and the Ministers shall be Iraqi or have Iraqi parents from a family who has lived in Iraq since at least 1900 CE and was of Ottoman citizenship. He should be at least thirty years old, enjoying all his civil and political rights, and not married to a foreign wife. An Arab wife of Arab parents and grandparents is considered Iraqi for this purpose."

76. The Interim Constitution of 1968. See the Republic of Iraq's Supreme Judicial Council's website, Qa'idat al-Tashriyyat al-Iraqiyya (The Foundation of Iraqi Legislation), https://iraqld.e-sjc-services.iq/LoadLawBook.aspx?page=1&SC=&BookID=18856.

77. Ibid.

78. What is striking about the deportation of the *taba'iyya* is that the word *Shi'a* is never mentioned. Joseph Sassoon has noted a similar silence in the memoranda of the Ba'th Party Secretariat on this matter. The only term used is *taba'iyya iraniyya* (Sassoon, *Saddam Hussein's Ba'th Party*, 2011, 44). This silence stands in stark contrast to the common references to Sunnis and Shi'a by British officials and Iraqi statesmen especially during the Iraqi state's early days when the ulema spearheaded opposition to British rule and new ruling elites. This silence, in light of the regime's persecution of Shi'i opposition parties, its anti-Iranian discourse, and its primordialization of religious categories, is tied to the issue of sectarianism in Iraq. The implications of this silence for our understanding of sectarianism's workings under Hussein's rule in the 1980s, which Fanar Haddad rightly asserts need to be approached as a temporal phenomenon rooted in the struggle over power, remain to be studied (Haddad 2011, 3).

Chapter 4

1. See the interview Haidar al-Na'emi conducted with al-Nadawi in *Al-Shabaka* on September 9, 2018, https://magazine.imn.iq/archives/8864 (accessed on April 5, 2023).

2. Ibid.

3. Gordon (2008, 7). Scholars of Black Studies and Indigenous Studies have employed hauntology to a great extent to discuss the haunted origins of modernity, which was based on settler colonialism, the enslavement of Africans, and the colonization of most of the world. For more details, please see Tuck and Ree (2013), Coly (2019), Parham (2008), Sharpe (2003), and Cacho (2021).

4. Gordon (2008, 190).

5. Ibid., xvi.

6. Ibid., 19.

7. Ibid., 183.

8. Saleh (*Return to Ruin*, 2021, chs. 1 and 2).

9. al-Nadawi (2018, 37). This claim is actually inaccurate as Iraqi Jews never buried the dead in their houses.

10. Ibid., 46.

11. Ibid., 149.

148   *Notes to Chapters 4 and 5*

12. Ibid., 149–50.
13. Ibid., 150.
14. Ibid., 138.
15. Ibid., 138.
16. Ibid., 138–39.
17. Ibid., 139.
18. Ibid., 169.
19. Ibid., 170.
20. Ibid., 165.
21. Scott (2014, 6).
22. Ibid., 6.
23. Ibid., 102.
24. al-Nadawi (2018, 172).
25. Ibid., 171.
26. Ibid., 171.
27. Ibid., 177–78.
28. Ibid., 197–98.
29. Ibid., 205–6.
30. Ibid., 189.
31. Ibid., 228.
32. Ibid., 232.
33. Ibid., 232.
34. Ibid., 270–71.
35. Ibid., 272–73.
36. Ibid., 275–76. During breakfast, Louay and Salar briefly talk about Zainab, their niece. Zainab, who serves them breakfast, did not finish middle school due to the violence in Iraq. Louay is "amazed at the simplicity with which this young woman was deprived of education though she came from a family whose members went to university." When he expresses his surprise to Salar, the latter replies, "What did those who have degrees gain? Every generation has its curse, and this chaos you see now is the curse of her generation. Soon, she'll get married, and she and the educated woman will be the same."
37. Ibid., 279.
38. Ibid., 288.
39. Ibid., 289.
40. Ibid., 293.

Chapter 5

1. Sha'ban (2002, 250). This chapter focuses on laws that authorized gender-based violence at a massive scale during a deportation campaign. Given the fact that there no laws under the monarchy that enacted such gender-based violence against Iraqi Jews, I examine the deportation of *taba'iyya* only in this chapter. However, I do not mean to discount the violence Iraqi Jews endured, whether executions, arrests, or sexual

violence. In chapter 1, I discuss executions and detentions of Iraqi Jews in particular in the late 1970s. During the Farhud in 1941, Bashkin writes that there were ten cases of rape (*New Babylonians*, 2012, 117). Regarding sexual violence in transit camps in Israel against Iraqi Jewish women, Bashkin remarks: "Furthermore, young women were among the most vulnerable elements in the transit camps. The press reported that women were subjected to rape, and a few autobiographies also mention cases of sexual harassment and attempted rape. In other cases, Iraqi men protected women who were sexually harassed; they did not bother waiting for the police and handled the criminals themselves" (2020, 58).

2. Puar (2017, xiv); and Mbembe (2003, 12).

3. Mbembe (2003, 12). Recent scholarship on gender and violence in the Middle East approaches gendered bodies through the lens of national and imperial violence and the state's politics of disability and debility. By moving from the individual to the national and imperial, this scholarship specifically focuses on the ways that bodies endure dispossession and precarity and challenge and resist structures of power in order to build different futures and new forms of community. See Kandiyoti (2019), Al-Ali (2007); Hafez (2019); Açiksöz (2020); and Shakhsari (2020).

4. Ali (2018, 97–98). In an email exchange, Ali informed me that she lost contact with this woman.

5. Navaro (2020, 162).

6. Ibid., 162.

7. Ibid., 165.

8. Irving (2016).

9. *Al-Waqa'i' al-'Iraqiyya*, October 21, 1924.

10. Sha'ban (2002, 186 and 196).

11. Ibid., 231. One Iraqi dinar at that time was equal to three dollars.

12. Ibid., 252–253. See also Sassoon (*Saddam Hussein's Ba'th Party*, 2011, 43–44). Having a foreign wife during Saddam Hussein's reign jeopardized family relations. For instance, Directive 180, which was signed by Saddam Hussein as the head of the Iraqi Revolutionary Command Council, dictated that "a foreign woman married to an Iraq man, who has been a resident in Iraq for five years, cannot stay in the country any longer," and "she has to declare her desire to acquire her Iraqi husband's citizenship or leave Iraq six months after the expiration of this law" (Sha'ban 2002, 225–26). As such, foreign women married to Iraqi men had to choose between staying married and living in Iraq with their family or get divorced and go back to their home country without their Iraqi family.

13. When I presented this chapter at conferences, some scholars remarked that my use of the language of honor reproduces stereotypes about women in the Middle East as being victims of honor killing. I would like to clarify a few things about his chapter. First, the gender-based violence that some deported Iraqi women endured had nothing to do with honor killing. Second, my discussion of gender-based violence is informed by my interlocutors' mobilization of the language of honor in their reflections on silences on divorce and sexual assault. In this framework, the language of honor

should not be understood as a seamless cultural illustration of Middle Eastern conservatism, backwardness, or endemic violence. Rather, Saddam Hussein's regime employed gender-based violence as a mechanism to visit as much injury as possible upon denaturalized Iraqi women and their families in particular and to terrorize Iraqi people in general. My interlocutors' invocation of honor speaks to the fact that Hussein's regime purposefully transgressed social and ethical norms during the deportation campaign. The regime's weaponization of patriarchal values speaks to the loss of the right to have rights, which translates as the loss of the right to bodily integrity in this case. Rather than an intrinsic social value, honor is better approached as a cultural construct that is deeply enmeshed in relations of power, lived realities, and perception of the body as a site of discipline, punishment, and debilitation. For reflections on sexual violence, see Talebi (2023); Mookherjee (2006); and Baxi (2014).

14. Boxfiles Database from the Ba'th Regional Command Collection (batch 3809 0002, box 3809, page 3809_0002_0271–0272). The directive specifies other groups that are exempt from deportation: *taba'iyya* military personnel who were recommended to be handed over to the Bureau of Military Discipline in Baghdad; Iranian women married to Iraqi men; Armenian Iranians; Iranian political asylees living in Iraq; "Arabstanis" living in Iraq (that is, Arab inhabitants of Khuzestan in Iran who relocated to Iraq).

15. I elaborate on the deportation of Iraqi merchants in Saleh, *Return to Ruin* (2021, 143–70).

16. Deeb (2006).

17. For more a more detailed discussion of necroviolence, or the denial of the right to perform death rituals for dead people who disappeared or went missing, see De León (2015).

Conclusion

1. *Al-Waqa'i' al-'Iraqiyya*, March 7, 2006.

2. The two articles that exempt Iraqi Jews in the Nationality Law of 2006 violate the Iraqi Constitution of 2005 (*Al-Waqa'i' al-'Iraqiyya*, December 28, 2006). Article 18 of the Constitution focuses on the question of citizenship. Comprising six clauses, this article decrees that Iraqi citizenship is a right of every Iraqi and that anyone born to an Iraqi father or mother is an Iraqi. More importantly, the first part of the third clause reads that "it is prohibited to strip any Iraqi by birth for any reason, and anyone who was stripped of his citizenship has the right to reclaim." In this framework, the discrepancy between the Iraqi Constitution, which calls for the reinstitution of Iraqi citizenship for any denaturalized Iraqi and acknowledges that there could be lawsuits related to citizenship legislation, and Nationality Law of 2006, which deprives Iraqi Jews of the right to regain their Iraqi citizenship, opens the door for Iraqi Jews who were expelled in 1950–1951 and who fled Iraq in the early 1970s and their children to challenge their exemption in the Iraqi Nationality Law of 2006 on the grounds that Iraqi Jews were unjustly stripped of their Iraqi citizenship, that their parents were Iraqis because they acquired Iraqi citizenship after the establishment of the modern

state of Iraq according to the Iraqi Nationality Law of 1924, that they are Iraqis because their parents held Iraqi citizenship, and that the Iraqi Constitution of 2005 itself gives anyone who was stripped of Iraqi citizenship the right to regain it.

3. In *Return to Ruin* (2021), I focus on the silence about class hierarchies and poverty in the nostalgic narratives about the monarchy.

4. The concept of structure has appealed to scholars of slavery, wars, and settler colonialism because it emphasizes the fact these events reshaped the lived realities for those who lived through them at multiple levels and have future reverberations through the institutionalization of policies that perpetuate dispossession and inequalities for the future generation. By contrast, the notion of an event, which is employed extensively by media pundits and politicians, works to make the reverberations of these events invisible and limited to the past through terms like *legacy* and *aftermath* (Wolfe 2006; Hermez 2017; Tuck and Yang 2012; and Khayyat 2022).

5. In their reflections on the Moroccan film on Moroccan Jews *Adieu mères*, Oren Kosansky and Aomar Boum remark that the filmmaker "has noted that the Jewish exodus of the 1960s marks an initial stage of what would become a more general Moroccan social phenomenon. The globalizing pressures and opportunities that have led to the migration of much larger segments of the Moroccan national community were, Ismail suggested, prefigured by the Jewish emigration in the immediate postcolonial period" (2012, 433–34). In the case of Iraq, the mass expulsion of Iraqi Jews heralded state practices that forced a significant number of Iraqis to flee the country to escape persecution and oppression decades later.

6. Al-Ali (2007); Crane (2021); Hanoosh (2019); Campbell (2016); Jones-Gailani (2020); Saleh (2018); and Sassoon (2011).

7. Said (2000, 176).

8. Ibid., 177.

9. Shohat (2017, 4).

BIBLIOGRAPHY

Archival Material
British Library, London
India Office Records: T12419
Hoover Institution, Stanford University, Stanford, CA
The Boxfiles Database of the Ba'th Regional Command Collection
Library of Congress, Washington, DC
Al-Waqa'i' al-'Iraqiyya
National Archives of the United Kingdom, London
Records of the Colonial Office: CO 327 and CO 813

Other Sources
Abdelhady, Dalia, and Ramy M. K. Aly. *Routledge Handbook on Middle Eastern Diasporas*. London: Routledge, 2023.
Abdul-Jabar, Faleh, ed.. *Ayatollahs, Sufis and Ideologues: State, Religion and Social Movements in Iraq*. London: Saqi, 2002.
———. *The Shi'ite Movement in Iraq*. London: Saqi, 2003.
Abdul Khabeer, Su'ad. "Citizens and Suspects: Race, Gender, and the Making of American Muslim Citizenship." *Transforming Anthropology* 25, no. 2 (2017): 103–19. https://doi.org/10.1111/traa.12098.
Abdullah, Thabit. *A Short History of Iraq*. 2nd ed. London: Routledge, 2016.
Abraham, Nabeel, Sally Howell, and Andrew Shryock, eds. *Arab Detroit 9/11: Life in the Terror Decade*. Detroit: Wayne State University Press, 2011.
Abu-Lughod, Lila, Rema Hammami, and Nadera Shalhoub-Kevorkian, eds.. *The Cunning of Gender Violence: Geopolitics and Feminism*. Durham, NC: Duke University Press, 2023.
Abu-Lughod, Lila. *Veiled Sentiments: Honor and Poetry in a Bedouin Society*. Berkeley: University of California Press, 1999.
Açiksöz, Salih Can. *Sacrificial Limbs: Masculinity, Disability, and Political Violence in Turkey*. Oakland: University of California Press, 2020.

Agamben, Giorgio. "Beyond Human Rights." In *Radical Thought in Italy: A Potential Politics*, ed. Paolo Virno and Michael Hardt, 159-66. Minneapolis: University of Minnesota Press, 2006.

Al-Ali, Nadje Sadig. *Iraqi Women: Untold Stories from 1948 to the Present*. London: Zed Books, 2007.

Alexander, M. Jacqui. *Pedagogies of Crossing: Meditations on Feminism, Sexual Politics, Memory, and the Sacred*. Durham, NC: Duke University Press, 2005.

Al-Hasani, Abd al-Razzaq. *Ta'rikh al-Wizarat al-Iraqiyah*. Vol. 8. Beirut: Dar al-Rafidayn lil-Tiba wa al-Nashr wa a-Tawzi, 1955.

Al-Husri, Abu Khaldun Sati'. *Mudhakkirati: Fī al-'Iraq, 1921–1941*. Vols. 1, 2, 3. Beirut: Dar al-Tali'a, 1967.

Al-Jawahiri, Muhammad Mahdi. *Mudhakkiarti*. Bayrut: Dar al-Muntazar, 1999.

Ali, Zahra. *Women and Gender in Iraq: Between Nation-Building and Fragmentation*. Cambridge: Cambridge University Press, 2018.

Allan, Diana. *Refugees of the Revolution: Experiences of Palestinian Exile*. Stanford, CA: Stanford University Press, 2014.

Allawi, Ali A. *The Occupation of Iraq: Winning the War, Losing the Peace*. New Haven, CT: Yale University Press, 2007.

Allen, Danielle. *Talking to Strangers: Anxieties of Citizenship since Brown v. Board of Education*. Chicago: University of Chicago Press, 2006.

Allen, Danielle, and Jennifer S. Light, eds. *From Voice to Influence: Understanding Citizenship in a Digital Age*. Chicago: University of Chicago Press, 2015.

Al-Nadawi, Hawra. *Qismat*. Berlin: Menshurat al-Jamal, 2018.

Al-Saleh, Danya, and Neha Vora. "Contestations of Imperial Citizenship: Student Protest and Organizing in Qatar's Education City." *International Journal of Middle East Studies* 52, no. 4 (2020): 733–39. https://doi.org/10.1017/S0020743820001026.

Al-Shaibi, Wisam H. "Weaponizing Iraq's Archives." *Middle East Report* 291 (Summer 2019).

Alwan, Mohammed Bakir. "Jews in Arabic Literature 1830–1914." *Al-'Arabiyya* 11, no. 1/2 (1978): 46–59.

Al-Wardi, Ali. *Lamahat Ijtima'yya Min Ta'rikh al-Iraq al-Hadith*. Vol. 6. London: Dar al-Kufan, 1992.

Aly, Ramy M. K. *Becoming Arab in London: Performativity and the Undoing of Identity*. London: Pluto Press, 2015.

Ameeriar, Lalaie. *Downwardly Global: Women, Work, and Citizenship in the Pakistani Diaspora*. Durham, NC: Duke University Press Books, 2017.

Amir, Eli. *Scapegoat*. London: Weidenfeld & Nicolson, 1987.

———. *The Dove Flyer*. New York: New York Review Books, 2014.

Anderson, Benedict R. O'G. *Imagined Communities: Reflections on the Origin and Spread of Nationalism*. London: Verso, 1991.

Andersson, Ruben. *Illegality, Inc.: Clandestine Migration and the Business of Bordering Europe*. Oakland: University of California Press, 2014.

Antoon, Sinan. "Difficult Variations: Saadi Youssef's Impossible Returns." *International Journal of Contemporary Iraqi Studies* 12, no. 2 (2018): 199–211. https://doi.org/10.1386/ijcis.12.2.199_1.

Anzaldúa, Gloria. *Borderlands: The New Mestiza = La Frontera*. San Francisco: Spinsters/Aunt Lute, 1987.

Appadurai, Arjun. *Modernity at Large Cultural Dimensions of Globalization*. Minneapolis: University of Minnesota Press, 1996.

Armenta, Amada. *Protect, Serve, and Deport: The Rise of Policing as Immigration Enforcement*. Oakland: University of California Press, 2017.

Atiyya, Ghassan. *Iraq: 1908–1921: A Socio-Political Study*. Beirut: The Arab Institute for Research and Publishing, 1973.

Aziz, Sahar F., and John L. Esposito. *Racial Muslim: When Racism Quashes Religious Freedom*. Oakland: University of California Press, 2021.

Babakhan, Ali. "The Deportation of Shi'is During the Iran-Iraq War: Causes and Consequences." In *Ayatollahs, Sufis and Ideologues: State, Religion and Social Movements in Iraq*, ed. Faleh Abdul-Jabar, 183–210. London: Saqi, 2002.

Babar, Zahra R. "The Vagaries of the In-Between: Labor Citizenship in the Persian Gulf." *International Journal of Middle East Studies* 52, no. 4 (2020): 765–70. https://doi.org/10.1017/S0020743820001075.

Babo, Alfred. "*Ivoirité* and Citizenship in Ivory Coast: The Controversial Policy of Authenticity." In *Citizenship in Question: Evidentiary Birthright and Statelessness*, ed. Benjamin N. Lawrance, 200–16. Durham, NC: Duke University Press, 2017.

Bald, Vivek. *Bengali Harlem and the Lost Histories of South Asian America*. Cambridge, MA: Harvard University Press, 2013.

Ballantyne, Tony. *Between Colonialism and Diaspora: Sikh Cultural Formations in an Imperial World*. Durham, NC: Duke University Press, 2006.

Banerjee, Sukanya. *Becoming Imperial Citizens: Indians in the Late-Victorian Empire*. Durham, NC: Duke University Press, 2010.

Baram, Amatzia. "A Case of Imported Identity: The Modernizing Secular Ruling Elites of Iraq and the Concept of Mesopotamian-Inspired Territorial Nationalism, 1922–1992." *Poetics Today* 15, no. 2 (1994): 279–319. https://doi.org/10.2307/1773167.

Barbieri, William A., Jr. *Ethics of Citizenship: Immigration and Group Rights in Germany*. Durham, NC: Duke University Press, 1998.

Bargu, Banu, ed. *Turkey's Necropolitical Laboratory: Democracy, Violence and Resistance*. Edinburgh: Edinburgh University Press, 2019.

Barnhart, Edward N. "Citizenship and Political Tests in Latin American Republics in World War II." *The Hispanic American Historical Review* 42, no. 3 (1962): 297–332. https://doi.org/10.2307/2510467.

Barrak, Fadhil. *Al-Madaris al-Yahudiyah Wa al-Iraniyah Fi al-Iraq*. Baghdad: Matbaat Dar al-Rashid, 1984.

Bashir, Bashir, and Leila Farsakh, eds. *The Arab and Jewish Questions: Geographies of Engagement in Palestine and Beyond*. New York: Columbia University Press, 2020.

Bashkin, Orit. "The Barbarism from Within—Discourses about Fascism amongst Iraqi and Iraqi-Jewish Communists, 1942–1955." *Welt Des Islams* 52, no. 3-4 (2012): 400–29. https://doi.org/10.1163/15700607-201200A7.

———. "The Colonized Semites and the Infectious Disease: Theorizing and Narrativizing Anti-Semitism in the Levant, 1870–1914." *Critical Inquiry* 47, no. 2 (2021): 189–217. https://doi.org/10.1086/712116.

———. *Impossible Exodus: Iraqi Jews in Israel*. Stanford, CA: Stanford University Press, 2017.

———. "Multilingual Journeys: Jewish Travel Narratives and Multicultural Identities in Interwar Iraq." *Journal of Contemporary Iraq and the Arab World* 14, no. 1–2 (June 2020): 69–87. https://doi.org/10.1386/jciaw_00019_1.

———. *New Babylonians a History of Jews in Modern Iraq*. Stanford, CA: Stanford University Press, 2012.

———. "On Noble and Inherited Virtues: Discussions of the Semitic Race in the Levant and Egypt, 1876–1918." *Humanities (Basel)* 10, no. 3 (2021): 88–108. https://doi.org/10.3390/h10030088.

———. *The Other Iraq: Pluralism and Culture in Hashemite Iraq*. Stanford, CA: Stanford University Press, 2009.

———. "Subjugated Homeland, Unhappy People—Jewish Communist Women in Iraq and Israel, 1941–1966." Unpublished paper, n.d.

Batatu, Hanna. *The Old Social Classes and the Revolutionary Movements of Iraq: A Study of Iraq's Old Landed and Commercial Classes and of Its Communists, Ba'thists, and Free Officers*. Princeton, NJ: Princeton University Press, 1978.

Baxi, Pratiksha. "Sexual Violence and Its Discontents." *Annual Review of Anthropology* 43, no. 1 (2014): 139–54. https://doi.org/10.1146/annurev-anthro-102313-030247.

Beaman, Jean. *Citizen Outsider: Children of North African Immigrants in France*. Oakland: University of California Press, 2017.

Beaugrand, Claire. "The Absurd Injunction to Not Belong and the Bidūn in Kuwait." *International Journal of Middle East Studies* 52, no. 4 (2020): 726–32. https://doi.org/10.1017/S0020743820001014.

Behar, Ruth. *Translated Woman: Crossing the Border with Esperanza's Story*. Boston: Beacon Press, 1993.

Behrouzan, Orkideh. "Ruptures and Their Afterlife: A Cultural Critique of Trauma." *Middle East—Topics & Arguments* 11 (2018): 131–44. https://doi.org/10.17192/meta.2018.11.7798.

Beinin, Joel. Introduction to *The Last Jews in Baghdad: Remembering a Lost Homeland*, by Nissim Rejwan. Austin: University of Texas Press, 2004.

Bell, Gertrude Lowthian. *The Letters of Gertrude Bell*. New York: H. Liveright, 1928.

Ben-Ari, Eyal, and Yoram Bilu, eds. *Grasping Land: Space and Place in Contemporary Israeli Discourse and Experience*. Albany: State University of New York Press, 1997.

Benjamen, Alda. *Assyrians in Modern Iraq: Negotiating Political and Cultural Space*. Cambridge: Cambridge University Press, 2022.

———. "Narratives of Coexistence and Pluralism in Northern Iraq." *Journal of Contemporary Iraq and the Arab World* 14, no. 1–2 (June 2020): 7–11. https://doi.org/10.1386/jciaw_00015_2.

———. "Village Nostalgia: Assyrians, Folklore and the Hybrid Intellectual Sphere in Modern Iraq." *Journal of Contemporary Iraq and the Arab World* 14, no. 1–2 (June 2020): 89–104. https://doi.org/10.1386/jciaw_00020_1.

Benjamin, Marina. *Last Days in Babylon: The Exile of Iraq's Jews, the Story of My Family*. New York: Free Press, 2008.

Berg, Nancy E. *Exile from Exile: Israeli Writers from Iraq*. Albany: State University of New York Press, 1996.

Berlant, Lauren. "The Subject of True Feeling: Pain, Privacy, and Politics." In *Feminist Consequences: Theory for the New Century*, ed. Elisabeth Bronfen and Misha Kavka, 126–60. New York: Columbia University Press, 2015. https://doi.org/10.7312/bron11704-006.

Bernal, Victoria. *Nation as Network: Diaspora, Cyberspace, and Citizenship*. Chicago: University of Chicago Press, 2014.

Bet-Shlimon, Arbella. *City of Black Gold: Oil, Ethnicity, and the Making of Modern Kirkuk*. Stanford, CA: Stanford University Press, 2020. https://doi.org/10.1515/9781503609143.

———. "Kirkuk as a Crucible: Sargon Boulus and the Question of Pluralism in Northern Iraq." *Journal of Contemporary Iraq and the Arab World* 14, no. 1–2 (June 2020): 127–33. https://doi.org/10.1386/jciaw_00022_1.

Bhabha, Jacqueline. "Embodied Rights: Gender Persecution, State Sovereignty, and Refugees." *Public Culture* 9, no. 1 (1996): 3–32. https://doi.org/10.1215/08992363-9-1-3.

Biehl, João Guilherme, Byron Good, and Arthur Kleinman, eds. *Subjectivity: Ethnographic Investigations*. Berkeley: University of California Press, 2007.

Bloemraad, Irene. *Becoming a Citizen: Incorporating Immigrants and Refugees in the United States and Canada*. Berkeley: University of California Press, 2006.

Bocco, Riccardo, Hamit Bozarslan, Peter Sluglett, and Jordi Tejel, eds. *Writing the Modern History of Iraq Historiographical and Political Challenges*. Hackensack, NJ: World Scientific, 2012.

Boum, Aomar, and Nadjib Berber. *Undesirables: A Holocaust Journey to North Africa*. Stanford, CA: Stanford University Press, 2023.

Boum, Aomar, and Sarah Abrevaya Stein, eds. *The Holocaust and North Africa*. Stanford, CA: Stanford University Press, 2018.

Brooks, Kinitra D. *Searching for Sycorax: Black Women's Hauntings of Contemporary Horror*. New Brunswick, NJ: Rutgers University Press, 2017.

Brubaker, Rogers. *Nationalism Reframed: Nationhood and the National Question in the New Europe*. Cambridge: Cambridge University Press, 1996.

Brubaker, William Rogers. "Immigration, Citizenship, and the Nation-State in France and Germany: A Comparative Historical Analysis." *International Sociology* 5, no. 4 (1990): 379–407. https://doi.org/10.1177/026858090005004003.

Bryant, Rebecca, and Madeleine Reeves, eds. *The Everyday Lives of Sovereignty: Political Imagination beyond the State.* Ithaca, NY: Cornell University Press, 2021.

Bsheer, Rosie. "The Limits of Belonging in Saudi Arabia." *International Journal of Middle East Studies* 52, no. 4 (2020): 748–53. https://doi.org/10.1017/S002074382000104X.

Burgoyne, Elizabeth. *Gertrude Bell: From Her Personal Papers 1914–1916.* London: Ernest Benn, 1961.

Butler, Judith. *Precarious Life: The Powers of Mourning and Violence.* London: Verso, 2004.

Cacho, Lisa Marie. "Racialized Hauntings of the Devalued Dead." In *Critical Dialogues in Latinx Studies: A Reader*, ed. Ana Y. Ramos-Zayas and Mérida M. Rúa, 307–19. New York: New York University Press, 2021.

Calavita, Kitty. *Invitation to Law and Society: An Introduction to the Study of Real Law.* 2nd ed. Chicago: University of Chicago Press, 2016.

Caldeira, Teresa P. R. *City of Walls: Crime, Segregation, and Citizenship in São Paulo.* Oakland: University of California Press, 2020.

Çaliskan, Gül. *Forging Diasporic Citizenship: Narratives from German-Born Turkish Ausländer.* Vancouver: University of British Columbia Press, 2023.

Campbell, Madeline Otis. *Interpreters of Occupation Gender and the Politics of Belonging in an Iraqi Refugee Network.* Syracuse, NY: Syracuse University Press, 2016.

Campos, Michelle. *Ottoman Brothers: Muslims, Christians, and Jews in Early Twentieth-Century Palestine.* Stanford, CA: Stanford University Press, 2010.

Campos, Michelle U. "Imperial Citizenship at the End of Empire: The Ottomans in Comparative Perspective." *Comparative Studies of South Asia, Africa, and the Middle East* 37, no. 3 (2017): 588–607. https://doi.org/10.1215/1089201x-4279272.

Campos, Michelle, Orit Bashkin, and Lior Sternfeld. "MENA Jewry after 'the Middle Eastern Turn': Modernity and Its Shadows." *Jewish Social Studies* 28, no. 2 (2023): 3–40. https://doi.org/10.2979/jewisocistud.28.2.01.

Cantres, James G. *Blackening Britain: Caribbean Radicalism from Windrush to Decolonization.* Lanham, MD: Rowman & Littlefield, 2020.

Cárdenas, Roosbelinda. *Raising Two Fists: Struggles for Black Citizenship in Multicultural Colombia.* Stanford, CA: Stanford University Press, 2024.

Castor, N. Fadeke. *Spiritual Citizenship: Transnational Pathways from Black Power to Ifá in Trinidad.* Durham, NC: Duke University Press, 2017.

Castronovo, Russ. *Necro Citizenship: Death, Eroticism, and the Public Sphere in the Nineteenth-Century United States.* Durham, NC: Duke University Press, 2001.

Çetinsaya, Gökhan. *The Ottoman Administration of Iraq, 1890–1908.* London: Routledge, 2006.

Chandler, Hannah, Neil Boothby, Zahirah McNatt, Margaret Berrigan, Laura Zebib, Patricia Elaine Freels, Hamza Alshannaq, Noor Majdalani, Ahmed Mahmoud, and Esraa Majd. "Causes of Family Separation and Barriers to Reunification:

Syrian Refugees in Jordan." *Journal of Refugee Studies* 33, no. 2 (2020): 371–89. https://doi.org/10.1093/jrs/feaa033.

Chatterjee, Partha. *The Nation and Its Fragments: Colonial and Postcolonial Histories.* Princeton, NJ: Princeton University Press, 1993.

Chatty, Dawn. *Displacement and Dispossession in the Modern Middle East.* New York: Cambridge University Press, 2010.

Chavez, Leo R. *Anchor Babies and the Challenge of Birthright Citizenship.* Stanford, CA: Stanford University Press, 2017.

Chen, Ming Hsu. *Pursuing Citizenship in the Enforcement Era.* Stanford, CA: Stanford University Press, 2020.

Cho, Grace M. *Haunting the Korean Diaspora: Shame, Secrecy, and the Forgotten War.* Minneapolis: University of Minnesota Press, 2008.

Choo, Hae Yeon. *Decentering Citizenship: Gender, Labor, and Migrant Rights in South Korea.* Stanford, CA: Stanford University Press, 2016.

Clifford, James. *Returns: Becoming Indigenous in the Twenty-First Century.* Cambridge, MA: Harvard University Press, 2013.

———. *Routes: Travel and Translation in the Late Twentieth Century.* Cambridge, MA: Harvard University Press, 1997.

Coll, Kathleen. *Remaking Citizenship: Latina Immigrants and New American Politics.* Stanford, CA: Stanford University Press, 2010.

Coly, Ayo A. *Postcolonial Hauntologies: African Women's Discourses of the Female Body.* Lincoln: University of Nebraska Press, 2019.

Corboz, Elvire. *Guardians of Shi'ism: Sacred Authority and Transnational Family Networks.* Edinburgh: Edinburgh University Press, 2015.

Cott, Nancy F. "Marriage and Women's Citizenship in the United States, 1830–1934." *The American Historical Review* 103, no. 5 (1998): 1440–74. https://doi.org/10.1086/ahr/103.5.1440.

Coutin, Susan Bibler. *Exiled Home: Salvadoran Transnational Youth in the Aftermath of Violence.* Durham, NC: Duke University Press, 2016. https://doi.org/10.2307/j.ctv11g96sk.

———. "In the Breach: Citizenship and Its Approximations." *Indiana Journal of Global Legal Studies* 20, no. 1 (2013): 109–40. https://doi.org/10.2979/indjglolegstu.20.1.109.

Crane, Ken R. *Iraqi Refugees in the United States: The Enduring Effects of the War on Terror..* New York: New York University Press, 2021. https://doi.org/10.18574/97814 79812448.

Crapanzano, Vincent. *The Harkis: The Wound That Never Heals.* Chicago: University of Chicago Press, 2011.

Das, Veena. *Violence and Subjectivity.* Berkeley: University of California Press, 2000.

———. "Violence, Gender, and Subjectivity." *Annual Review of Anthropology* 37, no. 1 (2008): 283–99. https://doi.org/10.1146/annurev.anthro.36.081406.094430.

Davis, Eric. *Memories of State: Politics, History, and Collective Identity in Modern Iraq.* Berkeley: University of California Press, 2005.

De Genova, Nicholas P. "Migrant 'Illegality' and Deportability in Everyday Life." *Annual Review of Anthropology* 31, no. 1 (2002): 419–47. https://doi.org/10.1146/annurev.anthro.31.040402.085432.

———. *Working the Boundaries: Race, Space, and "Illegality" in Mexican Chicago.* Durham, NC: Duke University Press, 2005.

De León, Jason. *The Land of Open Graves: Living and Dying on the Migrant Trail.* Oakland: University of California Press, 2015.

Deeb, Lara. *An Enchanted Modern: Gender and Public Piety in Shi'i Lebanon.* Princeton, NJ: Princeton University Press, 2006. https://doi.org/10.1515/9781400840786.

DeGooyer, Stephanie, Alastair Hunt, Lida Maxwell, Samuel Moyn, and Astra Taylor. *The Right to Have Rights.* London: Verso, 2019.

Delnore, Allyson Jaye. "Empire by Example?: Deportees in France and Algeria and the Re-Making of a Modern Empire, 1846–1854." *French Politics, Culture and Society* 33, no. 1 (2015): 33–54. https://doi.org/10.3167/fpcs.2015.330103.

Deringil, Selim. "Legitimacy Structures in the Ottoman State: The Reign of Abdülhamid II (1876–1909)." *International Journal of Middle East Studies* 23, no. 3 (1991): 345–59. https://doi.org/10.1017/S0020743800056336.

———. *The Ottomans, The Turks, and World Power Politics.* Istanbul: Isis Press, 2000.

———, ed. *The Ottoman Twilight in the Arab Lands: Turkish Memoirs and Testimonies of the Great War.* Brighton: Academic Studies Press, 2019.

Dodge, Toby. *Inventing Iraq: The Failure of Nation-Building and a History Denied.* New York: Columbia University Press, 2003.

Domínguez, Virginia R. *People as Subject, People as Object: Selfhood and Peoplehood in Contemporary Israel.* Madison: University of Wisconsin Press, 1989.

Donabed, Sargon. *Reforging a Forgotten History: Iraq and the Assyrians in the Twentieth Century.* Edinburgh: Edinburgh University Press, 2015.

Donati, Sabina. *A Political History of National Citizenship and Identity in Italy, 1861–1950.* Stanford, CA: Stanford University Press, 2013.

Dunbar-Ortiz, Roxanne. *Not "A Nation of Immigrants": Settler Colonialism, White Supremacy, and a History of Erasure and Exclusion.* Boston: Beacon Press, 2021.

Efrati, Noga. *Women in Iraq: Past Meets Present.* New York: Columbia University Press, 2012.

Erakat, Noura. *Justice for Some: Law and the Question of Palestine.* Stanford, CA: Stanford University Press, 2020.

Fadlalla, Amal Hassan. *Branding Humanity: Competing Narratives of Rights, Violence, and Global Citizenship.* Stanford, CA: Stanford University Press, 2018.

Fassin, Didier. "Policing Borders, Producing Boundaries. The Governmentality of Immigration in Dark Times." *Annual Review of Anthropology* 40, no. 1 (October 21, 2011): 213–26. https://doi.org/10.1146/annurev-anthro-081309-145847.

Faulk, Karen Ann. *In the Wake of Neoliberalism: Citizenship and Human Rights in Argentina.* Stanford, CA: Stanford University Press, 2012.

Feldman, Ilana. *Life Lived in Relief: Humanitarian Predicaments and Palestinian Refugee Politics.* Oakland: University of California Press, 2018.

Ferguson, James G. "Of Mimicry and Membership: Africans and the 'New World Society.'" *Cultural Anthropology* 17, no. 4 (2002): 551–69. https://doi.org/10.1525/can.2002.17.4.551.

Fernea, Robert A., and William Roger Louis, eds. *The Iraqi Revolution of 1958: The Old Social Classes Revisited*. London: Tauris, 1991.

Finkelstein, Maura. *The Archive of Loss: Lively Ruination in Mill Land Mumbai*. Durham, NC: Duke University Press Books, 2019.

Fischer, Brodwyn. *A Poverty of Rights: Citizenship and Inequality in Twentieth-Century Rio de Janeiro*. Stanford, CA: Stanford University Press, 2008.

Fong, Vanessa. *Paradise Redefined: Transnational Chinese Students and the Quest for Flexible Citizenship in the Developed World*. Stanford, CA: Stanford University Press, 2011.

Forget Baghdad. Seattle: Arab Film Distribution, 2002. https://www.arabfilm.com/item/265/.

Franke, Katherine. *Repair: Redeeming the Promise of Abolition*. Chicago: Haymarket Books, 2019.

Franzén, Johan. *Red Star over Iraq: Iraqi Communism before Saddam*. New York: Columbia University Press, 2011.

Fraser, Nancy, and Linda Gordon. "Civil Citizenship Against Social Citizenship? On the Ideology of Contract-Versus-Charity." In *The Condition of Citizenship*, ed. Bart van Steenbergen, 90–107. London: SAGE Publications, 1994. https://doi.org/10.4135/9781446250600.n8.

Fredericks, Rosalind. *Garbage Citizenship: Vital Infrastructures of Labor in Dakar, Senegal*. Durham, NC: Duke University Press, 2018.

Friedman, Sara L. *Exceptional States: Chinese Immigrants and Taiwanese Sovereignty*. Oakland: University of California Press, 2015.

García-Colón, Ismael. *Colonial Migrants at the Heart of Empire: Puerto Rican Workers on U.S. Farms*. Oakland: University of California Press, 2020.

Gat, Moshe. *The Jewish Exodus from Iraq, 1948–1951*. London: Frank Cass, 1997.

Gaucher, Megan. *A Family Matter: Citizenship, Conjugal Relationships, and Canadian Immigration Policy*. Vancouver: University of British Columbia Press, 2018. Distributed by University of Chicago Press.

Ginat, Rami. *A History of Egyptian Communism: Jews and Their Compatriots in Quest of Revolution*. Boulder: University of Colorado Press, 2011.

Goodale, Mark. *Anthropology and Law: A Critical Introduction*. New York: New York University Press, 2017.

Gordon, Avery. *Ghostly Matters: Haunting and the Sociological Imagination*. 2nd ed. Minneapolis: University of Minnesota Press, 2008.

Gowayed, Heba. *Refuge: How the State Shapes Human Potential*. Princeton, NJ: Princeton University Press, 2022.

Gravois, John. "Disputed Iraqi Archives Find a Home at the Hoover Institution." *The Chronicle of Higher Education*, January 23, 2008. https://www.chronicle.com/article/disputed-iraqi-archives-find-a-home-at-the-hoover-institution-426/.

Greene, Annie. "The Pioneers of Print in the Ottoman Province of Mosul." *Journal of Contemporary Iraq and the Arab World* 14, no. 1–2 (June 2020): 51–68. https://doi.org/10.1386/jciaw_00018_1.

Gregory, Derek. *The Colonial Present: Afghanistan, Palestine, Iraq.* Malden, MA: Wiley-Blackwell, 2004.

G'sell, Brady. *Reworking Citizenship: Race, Gender, and Kinship in South Africa.* Stanford, CA: Stanford University Press, 2024.

Guirguis, Laure, ed. *The Arab Lefts: Histories and Legacies, 1950s–1970s.* Edinburgh: Edinburgh University Press, 2022.

Gupta, Akhil, and James Ferguson. *Culture, Power, Place Explorations in Critical Anthropology.* Durham, NC: Duke University Press, 1997.

Hack, Karl. "Detention, Deportation and Resettlement: British Counterinsurgency and Malaya's Rural Chinese, 1948–60." *Journal of Imperial and Commonwealth History* 43, no. 4 (2015): 611–40.

Haddad, Fanar. *Sectarianism in Iraq: Antagonistic Visions of Unity.* New York: Columbia University Press, 2011.

Hafez, Sherine. "Gender and Citizenship Center Stage: Sondra Hale's Legacy and Egypt's Ongoing Revolution." *Journal of Middle East Women's Studies* 10, no. 1 (2014): 82–104. https://doi.org/10.2979/jmiddeastwomstud.10.1.82.

———. *Women of the Midan: The Untold Stories of Egypt's Revolutionaries.* Bloomington: Indiana University Press, 2019.

Haim, Sylvia G. "Arabic Antisemitic Literature: Some Preliminary Notes." *Jewish Social Studies* 17, no. 4 (1955): 307–12.

Haj, Samira. *The Making of Iraq, 1900–1963: Capital, Power, and Ideology.* Albany: State University of New York Press, 1997.

Hajj, Nadya. *Networked Refugees: Palestinian Reciprocity and Remittances in the Digital Age.* Oakland: University of California Press, 2021.

Hale, Charles R. "Neoliberal Multiculturalism: The Remaking of Cultural Rights and Racial Dominance in Central America." *Political and Legal Anthropology Review* 28, no. 1 (2005): 10–28.

Hall, Stuart. "Cultural Identity and Diaspora." In *Identity: Community, Culture, Difference*, ed. Jonathan Rutherford, 222–237. London: Lawrence & Wishart, 1990.

Hanley, Will. *Identifying with Nationality: Europeans, Ottomans, and Egyptians in Alexandria.* Illus. ed. New York: Columbia University Press, 2017.

Hannoum, Abdelmajid. *Living Tangier: Migration, Race, and Illegality in a Moroccan City.* Philadelphia: University of Pennsylvania Press, 2020.

Hanoosh, Yasmeen. *The Chaldeans: Politics and Identity in Iraq and the American Diaspora.* London: I. B. Tauris, 2019.

Hansen, Thomas Blom, and Finn Stepputat, eds. *Sovereign Bodies: Citizens, Migrants, and States in the Postcolonial World.* Princeton, NJ: Princeton University Press, 2005.

Harris, Cheryl I. "Whiteness as Property." *Harvard Law Review* 106, no. 8 (1993): 1707–91. https://doi.org/10.2307/1341787.

Harrison, Olivia C. *Transcolonial Maghreb: Imagining Palestine in the Era of Decolonization*. Stanford, CA: Stanford University Press, 2016.
Hartman, Saidiya. *Wayward Lives, Beautiful Experiments: Intimate Histories of Social Upheaval*. New York: W. W. Norton, 2019.
Heckman, Alma Rachel. *The Sultan's Communists: Moroccan Jews and the Politics of Belonging*. Stanford, CA: Stanford University Press, 2021.
Hermez, Sami. *War Is Coming: Between Past and Future Violence in Lebanon*. Philadelphia: University of Pennsylvania Press, 2017.
Hirsch, Dafna. "Zionist Eugenics, Mixed Marriage, and the Creation of a 'New Jewish Type.'" *The Journal of the Royal Anthropological Institute* 15, no. 3 (2009): 592–609. https://doi.org/10.1111/j.1467-9655.2009.01575.x.
Holston, James, ed. *Cities and Citizenship*. Durham, NC: Duke University Press, 1998.
Hooper, Charles A. *The Constitutional Law of Iraq*. Baghdad: Mackenzie & Mackenzie, 1928.
Hopwood, Derek, Habib Ishow, Thomas Koszinowski, and St. Antony's College. *Iraq: Power and Society*. Middle East Monographs Series, vol. 29. Reading, UK: published for St. Antony's College, Oxford, by Ithaca Press, 1993.
Horton, Sarah B., and Josiah Heyman, eds. *Paper Trails: Migrants, Documents, and Legal Insecurity*. Durham, NC: Duke University Press, 2020.
Howard-Hassmann, Rhoda, and Margaret Walton-Roberts, eds. *The Human Right to Citizenship: A Slippery Concept*. Philadelphia: University of Pennsylvania Press, 2015.
Hunter, Wendy, and Francesca Reece. "Denationalization in the Dominican Republic: Trapping Victims in the State's Administrative Maze." *Latin American Research Review* 57, no. 3 (2022): 590–607. https://doi.org/10.1017/lar.2022.48.
Iğsız, Aslı. *Humanism in Ruins: Entangled Legacies of the Greek-Turkish Population Exchange*. Stanford, CA: Stanford University Press, 2018.
Inhorn, Marcia C., and Lucia Volk, eds. *Un-Settling Middle Eastern Refugees: Regimes of Exclusion and Inclusion in the Middle East, Europe, and North America*. New York: Berghahn, 2021.
Ireland, Philip. *Iraq: A Study in Political Development*. New York: Macmillan, 1938.
Irving, Helen. *Citizenship, Alienage, and the Modern Constitutional State: A Gendered History*. Cambridge: Cambridge University Press, 2016.
Isaacs, Carol. *Wolf of Baghdad*. Oxford: Myriad Editions, 2020.
Isakhan, Benjamin, Shamiran Mako, and Fadi Dawood, eds. *State and Society in Iraq: Citizenship Under Occupation, Dictatorship and Democratisation*. London: I. B. Tauris, 2017.
Ismael, Tareq Y. *The Rise and Fall of the Communist Party of Iraq*. Cambridge: Cambridge University Press, 2007.
Ismael, Tareq Y., and Jacqueline S. Ismael. *Iraq in the Twenty-First Century: Regime Change and the Making of a Failed State*. London; New York: Routledge, 2017.
Jaimes Guerrero, Marie Anna. "Civil Rights versus Sovereignty: Native American Women in Life and Land Struggles." In *Feminist Genealogies, Colonial Legacies,*

Democratic Futures, ed. M. Jacqui Alexander and Chandra Talpade Mohanty, 143–64. London: Routledge, 1996.

Jamal, Amaney, and Nadine Naber, eds. *Race and Arab Americans Before and After 9/11: From Invisible Citizens to Visible Subjects*. Illus. ed. Syracuse, NY: Syracuse University Press, 2008.

Jankowski, James P., and I. Gershoni, eds. *Rethinking Nationalism in the Arab Middle East*. New York: Columbia University Press, 1997.

Jarrín, Alvaro. *The Biopolitics of Beauty: Cosmetic Citizenship and Affective Capital in Brazil*. Oakland: University of California Press, 2017.

Jayal, Niraja Gopal. *Citizenship and Its Discontents an Indian History*. Cambridge, MA: Harvard University Press, 2013.

Jeevendrampillai, David. *Citizenship, Democracy and Belonging in Suburban Britain: Making the Local*. London: University College London Press, 2022. Distributed by University of Chicago Press.

Jones, Marc Owen. "Digital De-Citizenship: The Rise of the Digital Denizen in Bahrain." *International Journal of Middle East Studies* 52, no. 4 (2020): 740–47. https://doi.org/10.1017/S0020743820001038.

Jones-Gailani, Nadia. *Transnational Identity and Memory Making in the Lives of Iraqi Women in Diaspora*. Toronto: University of Toronto Press, 2020.

Kamens, David H. *A New American Creed: The Eclipse of Citizenship and Rise of Populism*. Stanford, CA: Stanford University Press, 2019.

Kandiyoti, Deniz, Nadje al-Ali, and Kathryn Spellman-Poots, eds. *Gender, Governance and Islam*. Edinburgh: Edinburgh University Press, 2019.

Kattan, Naim. *Farewell, Babylon: Coming of Age in Jewish Baghdad*. Translated by Sheila Fischman. Boston: David R. Godine, 2007.

Kedourie, Elie. "Anti-Shiism in Iraq under the Monarchy." *Middle Eastern Studies* 24, no. 2 (1988): 249–53. https://doi.org/10.1080/00263208808700740.

———. "The Shiite Issue in Iraqi Politics, 1941." *Middle Eastern Studies* 24, no. 4 (1988): 495–500. https://doi.org/10.1080/00263208808700760.

Kelidar, Abbas. "States without Foundations: The Political Evolution of State and Society in the Arab East." *Journal of Contemporary History* 28, no. 2 (1993): 315–39. https://doi.org/10.1177/002200949302800206.

———. "The Shii Imami Community and Politics in the Arab East." *Middle Eastern Studies* 19, no. 1 (1983): 3–16. https://doi.org/10.1080/00263208308700530.

Kern, Karen M. *Imperial Citizen: Marriage and Citizenship in the Ottoman Frontier Provinces of Iraq*. Syracuse, NY: Syracuse University Press, 2011.

Khadduri, Majid. *Independent Iraq, 1932–1958: A Study in Iraqi Politics*. New York: Oxford University Press, 1960.

Khayyat, Munira. *A Landscape of War: Ecologies of Resistance and Survival in South Lebanon*. Oakland: University of California Press, 2022.

Khazzoom, Aziza. "Orientalism at the Gates: Immigration, the East/West Divide, and Elite Iraqi Jewish Women in Israel in the 1950s." *Signs: Journal of Women in Culture and Society* 32, no. 1 (2006): 197–220. https://doi.org/10.1086/505889.

———. *Shifting Ethnic Boundaries and Inequality in Israel: Or, How the Polish Peddler Became a German Intellectual*. Stanford, CA: Stanford University Press, 2008.
Klein, Janet. "The Kurds and the Territorialization of Minorityhood." *Journal of Contemporary Iraq and the Arab World* 14, no. 1–2 (June 2020): 13–30. https://doi.org/10.1386/jciaw_00016_1.
Klein, Menachem. "Arab Jew in Palestine." *Israel Studies* (Bloomington, IN) 19, no. 3 (2014): 134–153. https://doi.org/10.2979/israelstudies.19.3.134.
Kosansky, Oren, and Aomar Boum. "The 'Jewish Question' in Postcolonial Moroccan Cinema." *International Journal of Middle East Studies* 44, no. 3 (2012): 433–434.
Kymlicka, Will. *Multicultural Citizenship: A Liberal Theory of Minority Rights*. Oxford: Clarendon Press, 1995.
Lavie, Smadar. *Wrapped in the Flag of Israel: Mizrahi Single Mothers and Bureaucratic Torture*. Rev. ed. Lincoln: University of Nebraska Press, 2018.
Lawrance, Benjamin N., and Jacqueline Stevens, eds. *Citizenship in Question: Evidentiary Birthright and Statelessness*. Durham, NC: Duke University Press, 2017.
Lea, Tess. "Desiring Bureaucracy." *Annual Review of Anthropology* 50, no. 1 (2021): 59–74. https://doi.org/10.1146/annurev-anthro-101819-110147.
Lee, Stephen. "Family Separation as Slow Death." *Columbia Law Review* 119, no. 8 (2019): 2319–84.
LeVine, Mark. *Struggle and Survival in Palestine/Israel*. Berkeley: University of California Press, 2012.
Levy, Lital. "Historicizing the Concept of Arab Jews in the 'Mashriq.'" *The Jewish Quarterly Review* 98, no. 4 (2008): 452–69. https://doi.org/10.1353/jqr.0.0024.
———. *Poetic Trespass: Writing between Hebrew and Arabic in Israel/Palestine*. Princeton, NJ: Princeton University Press, 2014.
Lewin, Ellen. *Gay Fatherhood: Narratives of Family and Citizenship in America*. Chicago: University of Chicago Press, 2009.
Lie, Siv B. *Django Generations: Hearing Ethnorace, Citizenship, and Jazz Manouche in France*. Chicago: University of Chicago Press, 2021.
Lipsitz, George. *The Possessive Investment in Whiteness: How White People Profit from Identity Politics*. Twentieth anniv. ed. Philadelphia: Temple University Press, 2018.
Lockman, Zachary. *Comrades and Enemies: Arab and Jewish Workers in Palestine, 1906–1948*. Berkeley: University of California Press, 1996.
Longrigg, Stephen Hemsley, and Frank Stoakes. *Iraq*. New York: Frederick A. Praeger, 1958.
López, Jane Lilly. *Unauthorized Love: Mixed-Citizenship Couples Negotiating Intimacy, Immigration, and the State*. Stanford, CA: Stanford University Press, 2021.
Lori, Noora. "Citizens-in-Waiting: Strategic Naturalization Delays in the USA and UAE." *Ethnic and Racial Studies* 45, no. 6 (2022): 1075–95. https://doi.org/10.1080/01419870.2021.1962937.
———. *Offshore Citizens: Permanent Temporary Status in the Gulf*. Cambridge: Cambridge University Press, 2019.
———. "Time and Its Miscounting: Methodological Challenges in the Study of

Citizenship Boundaries." *International Journal of Middle East Studies* 52, no. 4 (2020): 721–25. https://doi.org/10.1017/S0020743820001002.

Louro, Michele. "The Johnstone Affair and Anti-Communism in Interwar India." *Journal of Contemporary History* 53, no. 1 (2018): 38–60. https://doi.org/10.1177/002 2009416688257.

Lücking, Mirjam. *Indonesians and Their Arab World: Guided Mobility among Labor Migrants and Mecca Pilgrims*. Ithaca, NY: Southeast Asia Program Publications, 2021.

Lybarger, Loren D. *Palestinian Chicago: Identity in Exile*. Oakland: University of California Press, 2020.

Maas, Willem, ed. *Multilevel Citizenship*. Philadelphia: University of Pennsylvania Press, 2013.

Mackey, Sandra. *The Reckoning: Iraq and the Legacy of Saddam Hussein*. New York: Norton, 2002.

Makdisi, Ussama. *Age of Coexistence: The Ecumenical Frame and the Making of the Modern Arab World*. Oakland: University of California Press, 2019.

Makiya, Kanan. *Republic of Fear: The Politics of Modern Iraq*. Berkeley: University of California Press, 1998.

Maktabi, Rania. "Female Citizenship in Syria: Framing the 2009 Controversy over Personal Status Law." In *Syria from Reform to Revolt*, ed. Raymond A. Hinnebusch and Tina Zintl, 176–98. Syracuse, NY: Syracuse University Press, 2015.

Malkki, Liisa H. *Purity and Exile: Violence, Memory, and National Cosmology among Hutu Refugees in Tanzania*. Chicago: University of Chicago Press, 1995.

Mamdani, Mahmood. *Citizen and Subject: Contemporary Africa and the Legacy of Late Colonialism*. Princeton, NJ: Princeton University Press, 1996.

———. *Neither Settler nor Native: The Making and Unmaking of Permanent Minorities*. Cambridge, MA: Belknap Press, an imprint of Harvard University Press, 2022.

Markowitz, Fran. *Toward an Anthropology of Nation Building and Unbuilding in Israel*. Lincoln: University of Nebraska Press, 2015.

Marr, Phebe. *The Modern History of Iraq*. 3rd ed. Boulder, CO: Westview Press, 2012.

Marshall, T. H. *Citizenship and Social Class*. London: Pluto Press, 1992.

Mathews, Nathaniel. *Zanzibar Was a Country: Exile and Citizenship between East Africa and the Gulf*. Oakland: University of California Press, 2024.

Mavelli, Luca. *Neoliberal Citizenship: Sacred Markets, Sacrificial Lives*. Oxford: Oxford University Press, 2022.

May, Chelsie. "'Not a Figure in the Past': Zionist Imperial Whiteness, the Iraqi Communist Party, and Their Reverberating Histories of Race and Gender, 1941–1951." *Journal of Middle East Women's Studies* 16, no. 1 (2020): 41–61. https://doi.org/10.1215/15525864-8016491.

Mbembe, Achille. "Necropolitics." *Public Culture* 15, no. 1 (2003): 11–40.

Meijer, Roel, James N. Sater, and Zahra R. Babar, eds. *Routledge Handbook of Citizenship in the Middle East and North Africa*. London; New York: Routledge, 2020.

Meir-Glitzenstein, Esther. "Our Dowry: Identity and Memory among Iraqi Immigrants in Israel." *Middle Eastern Studies* 38, no. 2 (2002): 165–86. https://doi.org/10.1080/714004453.

———. *Zionism in an Arab Country: Jews in Iraq in the 1940s*. London: Routledge, 2004.

Meiu, George Paul. *Queer Objects to the Rescue: Intimacy and Citizenship in Kenya*. Chicago: University of Chicago Press, 2023.

Menjívar, Cecilia, and Leisy J. Abrego. "Legal Violence: Immigration Law and the Lives of Central American Immigrants." *American Journal of Sociology* 117, no. 5 (March 2012): 1380–1421. https://doi.org/10.1086/663575.

Mikdashi, Maya. *Sextarianism: Sovereignty, Secularism, and the State in Lebanon*. Stanford, CA: Stanford University Press, 2022.

Miraftab, Faranak. *Global Heartland: Displaced Labor, Transnational Lives, and Local Placemaking*. Bloomington: Indiana University Press, 2016.

Molina, Natalia. *How Race Is Made in America: Immigration, Citizenship, and the Historical Power of Racial Scripts*. Berkeley: University of California Press, 2014.

Mookherjee, Nayanika. "'Remembering to Forget': Public Secrecy and Memory of Violence in the Bangladesh War of 1971." *The Journal of the Royal Anthropological Institute* 12, no. 2 (June 2006): 433–450.

Morawetz, Nancy. "Citizenship and the Courts." *University of Chicago Legal Forum* 1, no. 4 (2007): 447–69.

Moreh, Shmuel, and Zvi Yehuda. *Al-Farhud: The 1941 Pogrom in Iraq*. Jerusalem: The Hebrew University Magnes Press, 2010.

Naar, Devin E. *Jewish Salonica: Between the Ottoman Empire and Modern Greece*. Stanford, CA: Stanford University Press, 2016.

Naber, Nadine Christine. *Arab America: Gender, Cultural Politics, and Activism*. New York: New York University Press, 2012.

Naguib, Rim. "The Ideological Deportation of Foreigners and 'Local Subjects of Foreign Extraction' in Interwar Egypt." *Arab Studies Journal* 28, no. 2 (2020): 6–43.

Nakash, Yitzhak. *The Shi'is of Iraq*. Princeton, NJ: Princeton University Press, 2003.

Navaro, Yael. "The Aftermath of Mass Violence: A Negative Methodology." *Annual Review of Anthropology* 49, no. 1 (2020): 161–73. https://doi.org/10.1146/annurev-anthro-010220-075549.

Newendorp, Nicole. *Uneasy Reunions: Immigration, Citizenship, and Family Life in Post-1997 Hong Kong*. Stanford, CA: Stanford University Press, 2008.

Nicholls, Walter J. *The Immigrant Rights Movement: The Battle over National Citizenship*. Stanford, CA: Stanford University Press, 2019.

Nikhil, Anand. *Hydraulic City: Water and the Infrastructures of Citizenship in Mumbai*. Durham, NC: Duke University Press, 2017.

Nobles, Melissa. *Shades of Citizenship: Race and the Census in Modern Politics*. Stanford, CA: Stanford University Press, 2000.

Okruhlik, Gwenn. "Citizenship and Belonging in the Arabian Peninsula." *International Journal of Middle East Studies* 52, no. 4 (2020): 719–20. https://doi.org/10.1017/S0020743820001087.

Ong, Aihwa. *Buddha Is Hiding: Refugees, Citizenship, the New America*. Berkeley: University of California Press, 2003.

———. *Flexible Citizenship: The Cultural Logics of Transnationality*. Durham, NC: Duke University Press, 1999.

Panourgiá, Neni. *Dangerous Citizens: The Greek Left and the Terror of the State*. Illus. ed. New York: Fordham University Press, 2009.

Parham, Marisa. *Haunting and Displacement in African American Literature and Culture*. New York: Routledge, 2008.

Park, Lisa Sun-Hee. *Consuming Citizenship: Children of Asian Immigrant Entrepreneurs*. Stanford, CA: Stanford University Press, 2005.

Parla, Ayşe. *Precarious Hope: Migration and the Limits of Belonging in Turkey*. Stanford, CA: Stanford University Press, 2019.

Parrenas, Rhacel Salazar. "Transgressing the Nation-State: The Partial Citizenship and 'Imagined (Global) Community' of Migrant Filipina Domestic Workers." *Signs* 26, no. 4 (2001): 1129–54. https://doi.org/10.1086/495650.

———. *Unfree: Migrant Domestic Work in Arab States*. Stanford, CA: Stanford University Press, 2021.

Pašeta, Senia. *Suffrage and Citizenship in Ireland, 1912–18*. Institute of Historical Research. London: University of London Press, 2019. Distributed by University of Chicago Press.

Paz, Alejandro I. "Communicating Citizenship." *Annual Review of Anthropology* 48, no. 1 (2019): 77–93. https://doi.org/10.1146/annurev-anthro-102317-050031.

Perez, Elizabeth. "Spiritist Mediumship as Historical Mediation: African-American Pasts, Black Ancestral Presence, and Afro-Cuban Religions." *Journal of Religion in Africa* 41, no. 4 (2011): 330–65. https://doi.org/10.1163/157006611X604760.

Pérez, Miguel. *The Right to Dignity: Housing Struggles, City Making, and Citizenship in Urban Chile*. Stanford, CA: Stanford University Press, 2022.

Petryna, Adriana, and Karolina Follis. "Risks of Citizenship and Fault Lines of Survival." *Annual Review of Anthropology* 44, no. 1 (2015): 401–17. https://doi.org/10.1146/annurev-anthro-102313-030329.

Phillips, Sarah D. *Disability and Mobile Citizenship in Postsocialist Ukraine*. Bloomington: Indiana University Press, 2010.

Povinelli, Elizabeth A. *Economies of Abandonment: Social Belonging and Endurance in Late Liberalism*. Durham, NC: Duke University Press, 2011.

———. *The Cunning of Recognition: Indigenous Alterities and the Making of Australian Multiculturalism*. Durham, NC: Duke University Press, 2002.

Price, Polly J. "Jus Soli and Statelessness: A Comparative Perspective from the Americas." In *Citizenship in Question: Evidentiary Birthright and Statelessness*, ed. Benjamin N. Lawrance and Jacqueline Stevens, 27–42. Durham, NC: Duke University Press, 2017.

Puar, Jasbir K. *The Right to Maim: Debility, Capacity, Disability*. Durham, NC: Duke University Press, 2017.

Pursley, Sara. *Familiar Futures: Time, Selfhood, and Sovereignty in Iraq*. Stanford, CA: Stanford University Press, 2019.

Qasmi, Ali Usman. *Qaum, Mulk, Sultanat: Citizenship and National Belonging in Pakistan*. Stanford, CA: Stanford University Press, 2023.

Qazaz, Nassim, ed. *Watha'q Wa Mutqtafat Min al-Sahafa and al-Masadir al-Iraqiyya 'an Yhood al-Iraq Fi al-Asr al-Hadith*. Haifa: Maktabat Kul Shee, 2013.

Quayson, Ato, and Girish Daswani, eds. *A Companion to Diaspora and Transnationalism*. Hoboken, NJ: Wiley-Blackwell, 2013.

Raffety, Matthew Taylor. *The Republic Afloat: Law, Honor, and Citizenship in Maritime America*. Chicago: University of Chicago Press, 2013.

Raheja, Natasha. "Fuzzy Borders: Media, Migration Brokerage, and State Bureaucracy." *American Ethnologist* 51, no. 2 (2024): 270–284. https://doi.org/10.1111/amet.13224.

Raheja, Natasha, Karen Strassler, and Zeynep Devrim Gürsel. "Bureaucratic Portraiture and Practices of Citizenship." *Visual Anthropology Review* 39, no. 1 (2023): 168–76. https://doi.org/10.1111/var.12293.

Rejwan, Nissim. *The Last Jews in Baghdad: Remembering a Lost Homeland*. Austin: University of Texas Press, 2004.

Richard, Analiese. *The Unsettled Sector: NGOs and the Cultivation of Democratic Citizenship in Rural Mexico*. Stanford, CA: Stanford University Press, 2016.

Roby, Bryan K. *The Mizrahi Era of Rebellion: Israel's Forgotten Civil Rights Struggle 1948–1966*. Syracuse, NY: Syracuse University Press, 2015.

Rohde, Achim. *State-Society Relations in Ba'thist Iraq: Facing Dictatorship*. London: Routledge, 2010.

Rosaldo, Renato. "Cultural Citizenship, Inequality, and Multiculturalism." In *Latino Cultural Anthropology: Claiming Identity, Space, and Rights*, ed. William Vincent and Rina Benmayor, 27–38. Boston: Beacon Press, 1997.

———, ed. *Cultural Citizenship in Island Southeast Asia: Nation and Belonging in the Hinterlands*. Berkeley: University of California Press, 2003.

Roseneil, Sasha, Isabel Crowhurst, Tone Hellesund, Ana Cristina Santos, and Mariya Stoilava. *The Tenacity of the Couple-Norm: Intimate Citizenship Regimes in a Changing Europe*. London: University College London Press, 2021. Distributed by University of Chicago Press.

Ryburn, Megan. *Uncertain Citizenship: Everyday Practices of Bolivian Migrants in Chile*. Oakland: University of California Press, 2018.

Saada, Emmanuelle. *Empire's Children: Race, Filiation, and Citizenship in the French Colonies*. Translated by Arthur Goldhammer. Chicago: University of Chicago Press, 2012.

Sa'ar, Amalia. "Economic Citizenship at the Intersection of Nation, Class, and Gender: The Case of Palestinian Women in Israel." *Current Anthropology* 64, no. 1 (2023): 104–22. https://doi.org/10.1086/723299.

Sabar, Ariel. *My Father's Paradise: A Son's Search for His Family's Past*. Chapel Hill, NC: Algonquin Books, 2009.

Sahlins, Peter. *Boundaries: The Making of France and Spain in the Pyrenees*. Berkeley: University of California Press, 1989.

———. *Unnaturally French: Foreign Citizens in the Old Regime and After*. Ithaca, NY: Cornell University Press, 2003.

Said, Edward W. *Orientalism*. 25th anniv. ed. New York: Vintage Books, 1994.
———. *Reflections on Exile and Other Essays*. Cambridge, MA: Harvard University Press, 2000.
Saleh, Zainab. "Ethnographic Narratives as Living Archives among the Iraqi Diaspora." *Journal of Contemporary Iraq and the Arab World* 16, no. 2 (2022): 89–102.
———. "On Iraqi Nationality: Law, Citizenship, and Exclusion." *Arab Studies Journal* 21, no. 1 (2013): 48–78.
———. "Precarious Citizens: Iraqi Jews and the Politics of Belonging." *Political and Legal Anthropology Review* 44, no. 1 (2021): 107–22. https://doi.org/10.1111/plar.12420.
———. *Return to Ruin: Iraqi Narratives of Exile and Nostalgia*. Stanford: Stanford University Press, 2021.
———. "'Toppling' Saddam Hussein in London: Media, Meaning, and the Construction of an Iraqi Diasporic Community." *American Anthropologist* 120, no. 3 (2018): 512–22. https://doi.org/10.1111/aman.13007.
———. "Uprooted Memories: Iraqi Jewish Narratives of Displacement and Longing in Documentary Films." *Comparative Studies of South Asia, Africa, and the Middle East* 43, no. 1 (2023): 110–21. https://doi.org/10.1215/1089201X-10375396.
Salem, Sara. *Anticolonial Afterlives in Egypt: The Politics of Hegemony*. Cambridge: Cambridge University Press, 2020.
Sandifer, Durward V. "A Comparative Study of Laws Relating to Nationality at Birth and to Loss of Nationality." *The American Journal of International Law* 29, no. 2 (1935): 248–79. https://doi.org/10.2307/2190490.
Sassoon, Joseph. *The Iraqi Refugees: The New Crisis in the Middle East*. London: I. B. Tauris, 2011.
———. *Saddam Hussein's Ba'th Party: Inside an Authoritarian Regime*. Cambridge: Cambridge University Press, 2011.
———. *The Sassoons: The Great Global Merchants and the Making of an Empire*. New York: Pantheon, 2022.
Sassoon, Joseph, and Michael Brill. "The North Iraq Dataset (NIDS) Files: Northern Iraq under Ba'thist Rule, 1968–91." *Journal of Contemporary Iraq and the Arab World* 14, no. 1–2 (2020): 105–126. https://doi.org/10.1386/jciaw_00021_1.
Schiller, Nina Glick, and Georges Eugene Fouron. *Georges Woke Up Laughing: Long-Distance Nationalism and the Search for Home*. Durham, NC: Duke University Press, 2001.
Scott, David. *Omens of Adversity: Tragedy, Time, Memory, Justice*. Durham, NC: Duke University Press, 2014.
Sha'ban, Abud-Hussein. *Men Hwa Al-Iraqi? Ishaliat al-Jinsiya Wa La-Jinsiya Fi al-Qanun al-Iraqi Wa al-Duwali*. London: Center for Oriental Studies, 2002.
Shafir, Gershon, ed. *The Citizenship Debates: A Reader*. Minneapolis: University of Minnesota Press, 1998.
Shafir, Gershon, and Yoav Peled. *Being Israeli: The Dynamics of Multiple Citizenship*. Cambridge: Cambridge University Press, 2002.
Shakhsari, Sima. *Politics of Rightful Killing: Civil Society, Gender, and Sexuality in Weblogistan*. Durham, NC: Duke University Press, 2020.

Shamash, Cynthia Kaplan. *The Strangers We Became: Lessons in Exile from One of Iraq's Last Jews*. Waltham, MA: Brandeis University Press, 2015.

Shamash, Violette, and Shmuel Moreh. *Memories of Eden: A Journey Through Jewish Baghdad*. Edited by Tony Rocca and Mira Rocca. London: Forum Books, 2008.

Sharkey, Heather J. *A History of Muslims, Christians, and Jews in the Middle East*. Cambridge: Cambridge University Press, 2017.

Sharma, Aradhana, ed. *The Anthropology of the State*. Malden, MA: Wiley-Blackwell, 2006.

Sharpe, Jenny. *Ghosts of Slavery: A Literary Archaeology of Black Women's Lives*. Minneapolis: University of Minnesota Press, 2003.

Sheller, Mimi. *Citizenship from Below: Erotic Agency and Caribbean Freedom*. Durham, NC: Duke University Press, 2012.

Shenhav, Yehouda. "Ethnicity and National Memory: The World Organization of Jews from Arab Countries (WOJAC) in the Context of the Palestinian National Struggle." *British Journal of Middle Eastern Studies* 29, no. 1 (2002): 27–56.

Shiblak, Abbas. *Iraqi Jews, A History of the Mass Exodus*. London: Saqi, 2005.

Shlaim, Avi. *Three Worlds: Memoirs of an Arab-Jew*. London: Oneworld Publications, 2023.

Shohat, Ella. *Israeli Cinema: East/West and the Politics of Representation*. Rev. ed. London: I. B. Tauris, 2010.

———. *On the Arab-Jew, Palestine, and Other Displacements: Selected Writings*. London: Pluto Press, 2017.

———. "On Orientalist Genealogies: The Split Arab/Jew Figure Revisited." In *The Edinburgh Companion to the Postcolonial Middle East*, ed. Anna Ball and Karim Matter, 118-159. Edinburgh: Edinburgh University Press, 2019.

———. "Dislocated Identities: Reflections of an Arab Jew." *Movement Research: Performance Journal*, no. 5 (Fall 1991–Winter 1992): 8.

———. "Remembering a Baghdad Elsewhere: An Emotional Cartography." *Biography* 37, no. 3 (2014): 784–90. https://doi.org/10.1353/bio.2014.0034.

———. "Sephardim in Israel: Zionism from the Standpoint of Its Jewish Victims." *Social Text* 19/20 (1988): 1–35.

———. *Taboo Memories, Diasporic Voices*. Durham, NC: Duke University Press, 2006.

Shohat, Ella, and Robert Stam. "Genealogies of Orientalism and Occidentalism: Sephardi Jews, Muslims, and the Americas." *Studies in American Jewish Literature (1981)* 35, no. 1 (2016): 13–32. https://doi.org/10.5325/studamerjewilite.35.1.0013.

Simon, Reeva S., and Eleanor Tejirian, eds. *The Creation of Iraq, 1914–1921*. New York: Columbia University Press, 2004.

Simon, Reeva S. *Iraq between the Two World Wars: The Creation and Implementation of a Nationalist Ideology*. New York: Columbia University Press, 1986.

Simpson, Audra. *Mohawk Interruptus: Political Life Across the Borders of Settler States*. Illus. ed. Durham, NC: Duke University Press Books, 2014.

Sims, Michael B. "Claiming the Ezidis (Yezidis): Nineteenth- and Twentieth-Century Assyrian, Kurdish and Arab Sources on Ezidi Religious and Ethnic Identity." *Journal of Contemporary Iraq and the Arab World* 14, no. 1–2 (June 2020): 31–49. https://doi.org/10.1386/jciaw_00017_1.

Slack, Jeremy, Daniel E. Martinez, Scott Whiteford, and Emily Peiffer. "In Harm's Way: Family Separation, Immigration Enforcement Programs and Security on the US-Mexico Border." *Journal on Migration and Human Security* 3, no. 2 (2015): 109–28. https://doi.org/10.1177/233150241500300201.

Sluglett, Peter. *Britain in Iraq: Contriving King and Country*. 2nd rev. ed. New York: Columbia University Press, 2007.

Smiley, Calvin John. *Purgatory Citizenship: Reentry, Race, and Abolition*. Oakland: University of California Press, 2023.

Snir, Reuven. *Arab-Jewish Literature*. Leiden: Brill Publishers, 2019.

———. "'Arabs of the Mosaic Faith': Chronicle of a Cultural Extinction Foretold." *Welt Des Islams* 46, no. 1 (2006): 43–60. https://doi.org/10.1163/157006006776562183.

Solinger, Dorothy J. *Contesting Citizenship in Urban China: Peasant Migrants, the State, and the Logic of the Market*. Berkeley: University of California Press, 1999.

Somekh, Sasson. *Baghdad, Yesterday: The Making of an Arab Jew*. Jerusalem: Ibis Editions, 2007.

Stein, Sarah Abrevaya. *Extraterritorial Dreams: European Citizenship, Sephardi Jews, and the Ottoman Twentieth Century*. Chicago: University of Chicago Press, 2016.

———. *Saharan Jews and the Fate of French Algeria*. Illus. ed. Chicago: University of Chicago Press, 2014.

Sternfeld, Lior B. *Between Iran and Zion: Jewish Histories of Twentieth-Century Iran*. Stanford, CA: Stanford University Press, 2020.

———. "Combating the Double Erasure: Can a Jew (Kalimi) Be an Iranian in the Islamic Republic?" *International Journal of Middle East Studies* 55, no. 2 (2023): 299–320. https://doi.org/10.1017/S0020743823000697.

St-Georges, Charles. *Haunted Families and Temporal Normativity in Hispanic Horror Films: Troubling Timelines*. Lanham, MD: Lexington Books, 2018.

Stock, Margaret D. "American Birthright Citizenship Rules and the Exclusion of 'Outsiders' from the Political Community." In *Citizenship in Question: Evidentiary Birthright and Statelessness*, ed. Benjamin N. Lawrance and Jacqueline Stevens, 179–99. Durham, NC: Duke University Press, 2017.

Subramanian, Narendra. *Nation and Family: Personal Law, Cultural Pluralism, and Gendered Citizenship in India*. Stanford, CA: Stanford University Press, 2014.

Sunder Rajan, Rajeswari. *The Scandal of the State Women, Law, Citizenship in Postcolonial India*. Next Wave. Durham, NC: Duke University Press, 2003.

Surkis, Judith. *Sex, Law, and Sovereignty in French Algeria, 1830–1930*. Ithaca, NY: Cornell University Press, 2019.

Tabili, Laura. "Outsiders in the Land of Their Birth: Exogamy, Citizenship, and Identity in War and Peace." *The Journal of British Studies* 44, no. 4 (2005): 796–815. https://doi.org/10.1086/431942.

Talebi, Shahla. "Power, Subjectivity, and Sexuality in Iranian Political Prisons." In *The Cunning of Gender Violence: Geopolitics & Feminism*, ed. Lila Abu-Lughod, Rema Hammami, and Nadera Shalhoub-Kevorkian, 259–290. Durham, NC: Duke University Press, 2023.

Tauber, Eliezer. "Sayyid Talib and the Young Turks in Basra." *Middle Eastern Studies* 25, no. 1 (1989): 3–22. https://doi.org/10.1080/00263208908700764.

Tejel, Jordi, and Ramazan Hakkı Öztan, eds. *Regimes of Mobility: Borders and State Formation in the Middle East, 1918–1946*. Edinburgh: Edinburgh University Press, 2022.

Thomas, Deborah A. *Exceptional Violence: Embodied Citizenship in Transnational Jamaica*. Durham, NC: Duke University Press, 2011.

Tripp, Charles. *A History of Iraq*. Cambridge: Cambridge University Press, 2007.

Tsoffar, Ruth. "Forget Baghdad: Roundtrip to the Promised Land." *Anthropological Quarterly* 79, no. 1 (2006): 133–43. https://doi.org/10.1353/anq.2006.0013.

Tuck, Eve, and C. Ree. "A Glossary of Haunting." In *Handbook of Autoethnography*, ed. Stacey Holman Jones, Tony E. Adams, and Carolyn Ellis, 639–58. Walnut Creek, CA: Left Coast Press, 2013.

Tuck, Eve, and K. Wayne Yang. "Decolonization Is Not a Metaphor." *Decolonization: Indigeneity, Education and Society* 1, no. 1 (2012): 1–40.

Volk, Lucia. "'Being German, Becoming Muslim: Race, Religion, and Conversion in the New Europe' by Esra Özyürek." Review. *American Anthropologist* 117, no. 4 (2015): 861–62. https://doi.org/10.1111/aman.12423.

Vora, Neha. *Impossible Citizens: Dubai's Indian Diaspora*. Durham, NC: Duke University Press, 2013. https://doi.org/10.2307/j.ctv1134f8d.

Vortherms, Samantha A. *Manipulating Authoritarian Citizenship: Security, Development, and Local Membership in China*. Stanford, CA: Stanford University Press, 2024.

Walter, Alissa. "The Repatriation of Iraqi Ba'th Party Archives: Ethical and Practical Considerations." *Journal of Contemporary Iraq and the Arab World* 16, no. 1–2 (June 2022): 117–36. https://doi.org/10.1386/jciaw_00076_1.

Weil, Patrick. *The Sovereign Citizen: Denaturalization and the Origins of the American Republic*. Philadelphia: University of Pennsylvania Press, 2013.

Werbner, Pnina, and Nira Yuval-Davis, eds. *Women, Citizenship and Difference*. London: Zed, 1999.

Weston, Kath. "Families in Queer States: The Rule of Law and the Politics of Recognition." *Radical History Review* 2005, no. 93 (2005): 122–41. https://doi.org/10.1215/01636545-2005-93-122.

Whewell, Emily. "Deporting Indian Political Suspects: Treaty Port China's Legal Connection to India, 1914–30." *Journal of Colonialism & Colonial History* 20, no. 3 (2019). https://doi.org/10.1353/cch.2019.0040.

Whiting, Rebecca Abby. "Living and Dying on Record: 'Atrocity Archives' as Sacred Remains." *Journal of Contemporary Iraq and the Arab World* 16, no. 1–2 (June 2022): 137–50. https://doi.org/10.1386/jciaw_00077_1.

Whitlock, Craig, and *The Washington Post*. *The Afghanistan Papers: A Secret History of the War*. New York: Simon & Schuster, 2021.

Wiley, Joyce N. *The Islamic Movement of Iraqi Shi'as*. Boulder, CO: Lynne Rienner, 1992.

Wilson, Elana. "Gender, Nationalism, Citizenship, and Nunavut's Territorial 'House':

A Case Study of the Gender Parity Proposal Debate." *Arctic Anthropology* 42, no. 2 (2005): 82–94. https://doi.org/10.1353/arc.2011.0071.

Wolfe, Patrick. "Settler Colonialism and the Elimination of the Native." *Journal of Genocide Research* 8, no. 4 (2006): 387–409. https://doi.org/10.1080/14623520601056240.

Wolfe-Hunnicutt, Brandon. "Oil Sovereignty, American Foreign Policy, and the 1968 Coups in Iraq." *Diplomacy & Statecraft* 28, no. 2 (April 3, 2017): 235–53. https://doi.org/10.1080/09592296.2017.1309882.

———. "U.S.-Iraq Relations, 1920–2003." Oxford Research Encyclopedia of American History. Oxford: Oxford University Press, 2018. https://doi.org/10.1093/acrefore/9780199329175.013.463.

Wuest, Joanna. *Born This Way: Science, Citizenship, and Inequality in the American LGBTQ+ Movement*. Chicago: University of Chicago Press, 2023.

Yadav, Stacey Philbrick. "Effective Citizenship, Civil Action, and Prospects for Post-Conflict Justice in Yemen." *International Journal of Middle East Studies* 52, no. 4 (2020): 754–58. https://doi.org/10.1017/S0020743820001051.

Yehuda, Zvi. *The Babylonian Diaspora, The Rise and Fall of the Jewish Community in Iraq, 16th-20th Centuries C.E.* Leiden: Brill Publishers, 2017.

Young, Gabriel. "Archives after State Unmaking: Researching Provincial Urban Histories in Iraq." *Journal of Contemporary Iraq and the Arab World* 16, no. 1–2 (June 2022): 71–87. https://doi.org/10.1386/jciaw_00073_1.

Young, Iris Marion. "Polity and Group Difference: A Critique of the Ideal of Universal Citizenship." *Ethics* 99, no. 2 (1989): 250–74. https://doi.org/10.1086/293065.

Yue, Audrey, and Jun Zubillaga-Pow, eds. *Queer Singapore: Illiberal Citizenship and Mediated Cultures*. Hong Kong: Hong Kong University Press, 2012. Distributed by University of Chicago Press.

Yuval-Davis, Nira. "Women, Citizenship and Difference." *Feminist Review* 57, no. 1 (1997): 4–27. https://doi.org/10.1080/014177897339632.

Zamkanei, Shayna. "The Politics of Defining Jews from Arab Countries." *Israel Studies* 21, no. 2 (2016): 1–26. https://doi.org/10.2979/israelstudies.21.2.01.

Zentgraf, Kristine M., and Norma Stoltz Chinchilla. "Transnational Family Separation: A Framework for Analysis." *Journal of Ethnic and Migration Studies* 38, no. 2 (2012): 345–66. https://doi.org/10.1080/1369183X.2011.646431.

Zimudzi, Tapiwa B. "Spies and Informers on Campus: Vetting, Surveillance and Deportation of Expatriate University Lecturers in Colonial Zimbabwe, 1954–1963." *Journal of Southern African Studies* 33, no. 1 (2007): 193–208. https://doi.org/10.1080/03057070601136715.

Zubaida, Sami. "Community, Class and Minorities in Iraqi Politics." In *The Iraqi Revolution of 1958: The Old Social Classes Revisited*, ed. Robert A Fernea and William Roger Louis, 197–210. London: I. B. Tauris, 1991.

———. "The Fragments Imagine the Nation: The Case of Iraq." *International Journal of Middle East Studies* 32, no. 2 (2002): 205–15.

———. *Islam, the People and the State: Political Ideas and Movements in the Middle East*. 3rd ed. London: I. B. Tauris, 2009.

INDEX

al-Bakr, Ahmad Hasan, 77
al-Da'wa Party, 78
al-Duri, 'Abd al-'Aziz, 78–79
al-Hasani, Abd al-Razzaq, 23, 31–32
al-Hassani, Jihad, 36–37
al-Husayni, Hajj Amin, 20
al-Husri, Sati', 74–75
Ali, Zahra, 106
al-Jawahiri, Muhammad Mahdi, 48–49, 74–75
al-Jimhuriyya, 35–37
al-Kaylani, Rashid 'Ali, 20, 45
al-Khalisi, Shaykh Mahdi, 9, 72–73
Alliance Israélite Universelle, 16–17, 29, 42, 47
al-Nadawi, Hawra, 18, 84–86, 101. See also *Qismat*
al-Nahda, 23, 25–26, 140n11
al-Naquib, Sayyid Talib, 9
al-Rabita Bookshop, 45–46
al-Safwani, Salman, 23
al-Said, Nuri, 30–31
al-Sha'b, 25
al-'Umayri, 'Uthman, 79
al-Yaqdha, 23–26, 140n11
Anglo-Iraqi Treaty of 1922, 9, 72
Anglo-Iraqi Treaty of 1948 (Portsmouth Treaty), 46, 140n11
anti-Semitic/anti-Jewish rhetoric, 11, 18, 20–27, 32, 35–38, 44

Arab Jewish identity, 40–42, 47, 50, 54–59, 62. *See also* Jews, Iraqi
Arab nationalism, 40–41, 46, 59–60, 65, 72, 74
Arabness, 22, 39–41, 56, 59, 72, 75, 82, 112. *See also* Persianness
Arendt, Hannah, 6–7
Arif, Abdul Rahman, 35
Assyrians, persecution of, 10, 28, 76, 123, 129, 144n1

Babakhan, Ali, 81
Bashkin, Orit, 20, 30–31, 61
Ba'th regime, 65, 76–77, 139n39; anti-Jewish campaigns of, 22, 34, 56; archives of, 109–12; coups d'état of, 13, 34, 37, 56, 77, 90
Begum, Shamima, 3–4
Behrouzan, Orkideh, 19
belonging, sense of, 6, 14–15, 21–22, 39, 50, 52, 54, 56, 84, 87, 92, 102, 130–32; to Iraq in exile, 4, 57; for Iraqi Jews, 142n4
British colonial rule (Mandatory Iraq), 20, 22, 32, 65, 68–69, 73–74; deportations under, 8–9, 19, 22, 72, 125, 129; opposition to, 2, 8–9, 17, 41, 50–52, 65, 87–88

Certificate of Citizenship, Iraqi, 57, 69, 71–73, 76, 78–82

citizenship rights, 1–5, 21, 57–58, 64–68, 81, 125–28. *See also* denaturalization; right to reclaim; right to uproot

colonialism, opposition to, 40, 50, 53, 55–56, 58. *See also* British colonial rule (Mandatory Iraq)

communists, 16, 31, 40, 45, 50–53; suppression of in Iraq, 5, 8, 10–13, 25–26, 29, 54, 76, 124, 129. *See also* Iraqi Community Party

Coutin, Susan Bibler, 6

Cox, Percy, 74

Davis, Eric, 78–79

Dawoud, Nour al-Din, 25–26

DeGooyer, Stephanie, 7

denaturalization, 1–8, 125–30. *See also* Assyrians, persecutions of; communists, suppression of in Iraq; foreignness as pretext for denaturalization or deportation; Jews, Iraqi, denaturalization and deportation of; Ottoman Iraq, citizenship and denaturalization in; *taba'iyya*, denaturalization of

deportation, 1–9, 125, 127–30. *See also* British colonial rule (Mandatory Iraq), deportations under; foreignness as pretext for denaturalization or deportation; Jews, Iraqi, denaturalization and deportation of; Shi'as, deportation of; *taba'iyya*, deportation of

disappearance (of men aged 18–28), 6, 8, 13, 105–6, 112–13, 126. *See also* right to disappear; *taba'iyya*, disappearance/detention of

Dodge, Toby, 74

DuBois, W. E. B., 137n7

exclusion (political), 14–15, 29, 33, 39, 41, 58, 69, 72, 82, 126–27, 131–32

exile, 130–31; experiences of Iraqis in, 84–85, 91–97, 113–15. *See also* uprootedness

families, separation of, 6, 8, 82, 85, 90–92, 96, 105, 110, 113–14, 117–22. *See also taba'iyya*, incentives to divorce

Farhud (pogrom, 1941), 20, 22, 45, 148–49n1

Faysal I (king of Iraq), 9, 31, 65, 69–70, 72. *See also* monarchical regime (1921–1958)

Firhad, Adnan, 24–25

Follis, Karolina, 21

foreignness as pretext for denaturalization or deportation, 1–2, 4–7, 9–14, 21–22, 28–29, 40, 67–68, 80, 82, 112, 125, 129

gender-based violence. *See taba'iyya*, sexual violence against

gender equality, 11, 14, 87, 89–90. *See also* patriarchy; women's rights

Gordon, Avery, 85–86

Hamadi, Sa'adoun Shakir, 116

haunting, 81, 84–88, 90–93, 98, 100–103, 122, 147n3

Hecht, Ben, 35

Hindiyya canal, construction of, 66

honor (*sharaf*), 89, 106–8, 114, 116, 122, 149–50n13. *See also* patriarchy; suicide

Hooper, Charles, A., 70

Hoover Institution, 109–110

Hunt, Alastair, 7

Hussein regime: aftermath of, 18, 57, 85, 98–99, 105, 120, 125; atrocities of, 13, 64, 76–78, 84, 104–24, 127–30, 133–34; citizenship laws under, 13, 80–82, 65, 76–83

Ibrahim, Abdel Fattah, 45–46
Interim Constitutions (of 1964, 1968, and 1970), 81
Iran: deportations to (see *taba'iyya*, deportation of); migration to Israel via, 37, 54; reception of Iraqi deportees in, 84, 114
Iran-Iraq War, 13, 64, 78–80, 84, 86, 92, 97, 104, 107, 113–14, 116
Iraqi Communist Party, 11, 22, 25–26, 50–53, 56–58, 77. *See also* communists
Israel: discrimination against Iraqi Jews in, 21–22, 40, 54–56, 60; effects of the establishment of in Iraq, 11–12, 20, 23–24, 26–27, 49, 54, 60, 62; migration of Iraqi Jews to, 21, 27, 30, 32, 34, 40, 51, 59, 61. *See also* Palestine; Zionism
Israeli Communist Party, 51, 55–56, 58

Jabr, Salih, 27
Jewish institutions in Baghdad, bombings of (1950–1951), 29–30, 32, 59, 61
Jews, Iraqi: confiscation of property of, 6, 11, 14, 23, 26, 29–31, 33–34, 37–38, 54; denaturalization and deportation of, 11–13, 21–22, 26–34, 58, 87–89, 123–24, 126, 141n47; denial of Arab/Iraqi identity of, 21, 23–26, 29, 32, 34–37, 39–40, 54; discrimination against in Israel, 21–22, 40, 54–56, 60; executions of, 37–38, 54; prohibition of against reclamation of Iraqi citizenship and property, 14, 58, 126–28, 150–51n2; sexual violence against, 148–49n1

Kern, Karen, 67–68
Kurds, persecution of, 13, 64, 77–78, 84, 123, 139n39

League to Combat Zionism, 50–51, 53
legislation for citizenship and denaturalization, 1–4. *See also specific laws in Index of Legislation*
literature, Arabic, 42–45, 47–50

Mahmud II (sultan), 66–67
Maxwell, Lida, 7
monarchical regime (1921–1958): deportations under (*see* Jews, Iraqi, denaturalization and deportation of); idealization of, 8, 123–24, 128–29, 134; Iraqi citizenship under, 12–13, 22, 73, 76 (*see also* 1924, Law 42 of (Iraqi Nationality Law) *in Index of Legislation*)
Moreh, Shmuel, 23
Moyn, Samuel, 7
Munazzamat al-'Amal al-Islami, 78
Muwafaq, 35

Nakash, Yitzhak, 66, 73
Nationality Act (United States, 1940), 2
Nationality and Borders Bill (United Kingdom), 3
Navaro, Yael, 108
Nowaihd, Ajaj, 36

Orientalism, 21, 40, 55, 60, 73–74, 131–33
Ottoman Iraq: citizenship and denaturalization in, 9, 67–68; conflict with Persia, 67–68, 139n49; Persian nationality under, 13, 17, 64–65, 68, 71–73, 76, 80, 116, 139n39 (see also *taba'iyya*)

pan-Arabism, 35, 46, 59, 79. *See also* Arab nationalism
Palestine, 20, 22–24, 38, 46, 53, 56, 60, 62–63
patriarchy, 87, 89, 102, 106–8, 112, 115–16, 123. *See also* gender equality; women's rights

Persianness, 81–82. *See also* Arabness
Petryna, Adriana, 21
property, confiscation of, 8, 30–31; of Jews, 6, 11, 14, 23, 26, 29–31, 33–34, 37–38, 54; of *taba'iyya*, 6, 14, 64, 82, 84–86
Protocols of the Elders of Zion, The, 36

Qasim, Abdul al-Karim, 12–13, 33–34
Qazaz, Nassim, 23, 140n11
Qismat (novel by Hawra al-Nadawi), 84–103

reclamation. *See* Jews, Iraqi, prohibition of against reclamation of Iraqi citizenship and property; right to reclaim; *taba'iyya*, reclamation of Iraqi citizenship and property by
Rejwan, Nissim, 18, 42–47
right to disappear, 106, 116–23
right to have rights, 6–7, 125, 150n13
right to reclaim, 14–19, 41, 58–59, 62, 85, 91, 103, 126–27, 130–31, 150n2
right to uproot, 5–8, 14–15, 17–18, 65–66. *See also* uprootedness
right to violate, 111–16

Said, Edward, 130–31
Scott, David, 95
Sha'ban, Abud-Hussein, 81, 139n39
Shalim, Avi, 18, 27, 29, 31, 41, 58–62
Sharara, Muhammad, 48–49
Shi'as, 139n49, 147n78; deportation of, 72–73, 76; opposition to British colonial rule, 17, 65, 69, 73–74; persecutions of, 17, 64, 67, 74–78, 84, 124; spread of in Ottoman Iraq, 66–68. *See also taba'iyya*
Shimun, Eshai (Assyrian patriarch), 10
Shohat, Ella, 39, 60, 131
shu'ubiyya, 75, 78–80
Simele massacre, 10, 123, 129
Somekh, Sasson 18, 42–43, 47–50

suicide, 85–90, 98, 100–102, 107, 114
Suwaydi, Tawfiq, 27, 29–31

taba'iyya: confiscation of property of, 6, 14, 64, 82, 84–86; denaturalization of, 76–77, 85, 104; deportation of, 64, 77–78, 82, 84–86, 91–96, 112–14, 116, 118, 122, 139n39; disappearance/detention of, 6, 13, 64, 104–6, 108, 110, 112–13, 116–22; execution of, 105, 112–13, 120–21; incentives to divorce, 13, 64, 82, 104–6, 109–16, 122; Iraqi identity of, 93–97, 112; prejudice against in Iran, 84, 114; reclamation of Iraqi citizenship and property by, 14, 85, 99–100, 126–28; sexual violence against, 6, 64, 82, 104–8, 110, 112–14, 116, 122–23; torture of, 105, 116, 121
Talmud, 35–36, 39, 60
Tanzimat reforms, 68
Taylor, Astra, 7
Thomas, Deborah, 15
Treaty of Lausanne, 69–71

uprootedness, 38, 40, 49, 56, 62, 91, 94–95, 97, 131, 133. *See also* right to uproot
US invasion of Iraq, aftermath of, 51, 102, 109, 124–25, 128, 130, 134

Vasili, Pyotr, 138–39n32

Wahabis, 66
Wathba (1948 protests), 54
Weil, Patrick, 2
Williams, Zoe, 4
women's rights, 16, 42, 45, 51, 56. *See also* gender equality; patriarchy

Zainab, Sayyida, 119
Zionism, 18, 40, 53–55, 59–63; conflation of Judaism with, 20–21, 23–27, 32, 38, 40–41. *See also* Jews, Iraqi

INDEX OF LEGISLATION

1869, Ottoman Nationality Law of, 67–71
1924, Law 42 of (Iraqi Nationality Law),
    9, 12–13, 64–66, 69–74, 76, 111, 126, 129
1933, Law 62 of, 9–11, 28, 138–39n32
1938, Law 51 of (Baghdad Penal Code of),
    10–12
1950, Decree 1 of, 11, 27–28
1950, Law 1 of, 14, 126
1951, denaturalization law of, 13
1951, Law 5 of, 30–31, 33–34
1951, Law 12 of, 14, 30, 34, 126
1954, Law 17 of, 11–12
1963, Iraqi Nationality Law of, 76
1968, Law 10 of, 37
1980, Directive 3884, 116
1980, Law 666 of, 13, 80
1980, Resolution 474, 111
2006, Law 26 of (Iraqi Nationality Law
    of), 14, 58, 125–28, 150n2

www.ingramcontent.com/pod-product-compliance
Lightning Source LLC
Jackson TN
JSHW020002121025
92422JS00003B/4